HANDBOOK

FOR

READERS AND STUDENTS,

INTENDED AS A HELP TO INDIVIDUALS, ASSOCIATIONS, SCHOOL-DISTRICTS, AND SEMINARIES OF LEARNING, IN THE SELECTION OF WORKS FOR READING, INVESTIGATION, OR PROFESSIONAL STUDY.

BY A. POTTER, D.D.

IN THREE PARTS.

"He that will inquire out the best books in every science, and inform himself of the most material authors of the several sects of philosophy and religion, will not find it an infinite work to acquaint himself with the sentiments of mankind concerning the most weighty and comprehensive subjects."—LOCKE.

"Under our present enormous accumulation of books, I do affirm that a most miserable distraction of choice must be very generally incident to the times ; that the symptoms of it are in fact very prevalent, and that one of the chief symptoms is an enormous 'gluttonism' for books."—DE QUINCEY

FOURTH EDITION.

NEW YORK:
HARPER & BROTHERS, PUBLISHERS,
329 & 331 PEARL STREET,
FRANKLIN SQUARE.
1855.

CONTENTS.

Page
INTRODUCTION vii

PART I.

COURSES OF STUDY 15

CAUTIONS AND COUNSELS 16
I. *General Course* 22
II. *Particular Courses* 31
1. History 31
Ancient History 32
Modern " 35
American " 38
2. Speculative Philosophy 40
3. Political Philosophy 41
4. Polite Literature 43
5. Mathematical and Physical Science . . . 44
6. Chemistry and Natural History 45
7. Theology 46
" (Elementary Course) 48
8. Medicine 50
" (Elementary Course) 50
9. Law 53
" (Elementary Course) 53

PART II.

STANDARD AUTHORS 61

PRINCIPLES 63
I. *Poets:*
" Greek 65
" Latin 67

Page
Poets (Mediæval) 70
" Modern 72
" " English and American 72
" " French 87
" " German 91
" " Italian 94
" " Spanish, &c. 95
II. *Philosophers:*
" Greek 97
" Roman 99
" Christian 99
" Mediæval 101
" Modern 103
" " English and American . . 103
" " German 106
" " French 108
III. *Natural Sciences:*
Ancient 111
Modern 112
IV. *Historians:*
" Greek 119
" Roman 120
" Mediæval 124
" Modern (English and American) . . 126
" " French 129
" " Italian and Spanish . . . 133
" " German 136
V. *Historical Memoirs* 139
VI. *Biography* 143
VII. *Geography, Travels, &c.* 150
VIII. *Polite Literature* 159
IX. *Theology* 181

PART III.

BOOKS FOR POPULAR AND MISCELLANEOUS LIBRARIES 193
PRINCIPLES 195
I. *History* (Universal) 197
" Ancient 198

		Page
	History (Modern)	208
	" American	220
II.	*Biography*	225
III.	*Voyages, Travels, &c.*	239
IV.	*Politics, Law, &c.*	251
V.	*Ethics, Mental Philosophy, &c.*	256
VI.	*Criticism and Belles-Lettres*	266
VII.	*Poetry*	274
VIII.	*Physical Science and Natural History*	281
IX.	*The Useful and Ornamental Arts, Engineering, &c.* .	287
X.	*Theology*	291
XI.	*Periodicals*	296
XII.	*Encyclopædias*	298

INTRODUCTION.

THIS work was first undertaken at the request of the Young Men's Association of the State of New-York.* It was mainly intended, at the outset, as a help to Associations, Lyceums, School Districts, &c., &c., in selecting useful and interesting works for their libraries. In proportion as such libraries are multiplied, and spread out their stores before the whole people, in the same proportion it is important that they should be composed of useful and improving books, to the exclusion of all that are noxious, or merely worthless. In this great object the compiler

* Extract from the Proceedings of the Second Annual Meeting of the Young Men's State Association, held at Auburn, August 4th, 1842:

Whereas libraries for young men's associations, school districts, &c., are most important instruments for the education and improvement of our people; and whereas the persons immediately charged with the duty of selecting books often find it extremely difficult to make judicious selections, which will be satisfactory to their employers; therefore,

Resolved, that, in the estimation of this Association, it is highly desirable that a small volume, of the size of one of the volumes of the School District Library, be prepared under the supervision of the Association, to contain a course of reading, bibliographical notices of books in different departments of learning, and catalogues of libraries, both large and small, for the use of young men's associations, school district libraries, private persons, &c., &c.

On motion of Mr. French, of Albany,

Resolved, that Messrs. Alonzo Potter, Amos Dean, and Francis Dwight, be requested to see whether arrangements can be made for the publication of such a volume, and be a committee to prepare the same.

has felt so deep an interest, that he has considered it a privilege to rescue from other, and engrossing cares, an occasional hour for this labour of love.

It occurred to him, in the progress of the work, that it might be advantageously extended, so as to meet the wants of *scholars* in the earlier stages of their researches, and of *young persons*, who may desire some aid in tracing out a judicious course of reading or study. This volume is accordingly composed of *three* parts:

PART FIRST

embraces various *courses of reading or study* for general readers, professional students, and for those who are engaged in investigating particular branches of literature.

PART SECOND

contains a series of authors in philosophy, literature, and science, who have gained the rank of classics in their respective departments. They are arranged in chronological order, with brief notices, so that this part of the work may be found useful, not only as a compendium of Bibliography, but also as a very brief sketch of literary history. It is intended especially for the use of those who are engaged in original researches, or who are anxious to collect around them the great teachers of wisdom who belong to history. It should be understood, however, that its pretensions are humble. It does not profess to supersede the larger works on Bibliography, nor to give a complete catalogue of classic or standard works, but merely to guide the student in the earliest stages of investigation.

PART THIRD

contains a list of about 1500 works (with critical notices, prices, &c., &c.), adapted to general reading. It will be found useful in collecting miscellaneous libraries, and in finding books which treat on the various branches of literature.

In one or two respects, this manual will be found more convenient than the ordinary works on Bibliography. It assigns the first, and most prominent place, to *intellectual*, as distinguished from *material* Bibliography. The latter is occupied mainly with *titles, editions, prices, scarcity*, &c., &c., and is arranged alphabetically; the former, treating of the *subject* and literary and historic value of works, is arranged on the principles of the "Catalogue Raisonné," *i. e.*, by subjects. Most of the great works which are used by scholars are constructed on the alphabetical plan, and are much more rich in information respecting the *material* character of books than respecting their object, scope, or critical value. Most of the later works, too, have been published on the Continent of Europe, and are therefore incomplete in English and American literature. Perhaps none of them is superior, for general use, to Brunet's "*Manual de Libraire*," an admirable French work, in 6 vols. 8vo; and yet this work, costing, in this country, about $16 00, rather presupposes than communicates information in regard to the literary character of works, and the general scope of their contents. It is also incomplete in regard to recent literature in our own language. Such a work may be valuable to the practised and erudite scholar, but can afford little aid to that great mass of readers who are chiefly anxious about the moral and intellectual character of books, and who would learn from what sources they can obtain information on particular subjects. It is for such readers that this manual has been compiled. The undertaking is in a considerable degree novel, but it is believed that, in the present state of the world, and especially of our own country, it will not be regarded as untimely or unimportant. Indeed, the want of some such hand-book as the present, combining comprehensiveness and cheapness, is generally recognised; and the compiler will feel abundantly satisfied if he shall seem to have succeeded, even partially, in supplying the want. No one can be more sensible than he is that the work will be found imperfect, and that, in the estimation of many, it will seem to have omitted some of the most important contributors to literature. To say nothing of the difficulty of making selections from the immense mass of works that invite attention, it should be remembered that a great part of the work is intended for a specific purpose; that this purpose requires regard primarily to the moral spirit and tendency of books; and that this manual does not profess to exhibit a complete enumeration even of the best works in our own language. On professional subjects it touches but incidentally, and enters with no great fulness into those of a scientific, ecclesiastical, or technical nature. Though not designed entirely for general readers, it must be considered that this is its main object.

I add the names of some of the principal works in *general* and *special* Bibliography, to which the student should have recourse :

1. Brunet's Manuel de Libraire.
2. Gesner's Bibliotheca Universalis, published about A.D. 1550.
3. Peignot's Dictionnaire raisonné de Bibliologie.
4. Lownde's Bibliographer's Manual of Books published in, or relating to Great Britain and Ireland.
5. Watt's Bibliotheca Britannica.
6. Orme's Bibliotheca Biblica and Theologica.
7. Walchius' Bibliotheca Theologica.
8. " " Patristica.
9. Le Long's " Theologica.
10. Muesel's Bibliotheca Historica.
11. Haller's Bibliotheca Botanica, Anatomica, &c.
12. Murhard's " Mathematica and Physica.
13. Horne's (Thos. H.) Introduction to the Study of Bibliography.
14. A good, though brief medical Bibliography will be found in Dr. Dunglisson's "*Medical Student.*"
15. Bibliotheca Americana.
16. " " (continued by O. Rich.)
17. Reed's Bibliotheca Nova Legum Anglica.

To these may be added, Dupin's History of Ecclesiastical Writers, Marsh and Campbell's Lectures on the Study of Divinity, Hoffman's Course of Legal Study, Moss's Classical Bibliography, Dr. Adam Clarke's Bibliography (principally of Oriental and Sacred Literature), the several Bibliothecæ of Fabricius, and Eschenburg's Classical Manual, translated and edited by Professor Fisk.

It is proper to state, in closing this introduction, that most of the critical notices of books in this volume have been selected, under the compiler's general superintendence, by Mr. Victor G. Benne, a graduate of the Military School, Hanover (Germany), and a gentleman of much intelligence and worth. This labour would have been so irksome, and would have interfered so seriously with other engagements, that it probably would never have been performed but for Mr. B.'s aid; and to him, therefore, the reader will be indebted for any assistance or gratification that this part of the work may afford. Considerable reluctance has been felt at admitting so many selected notices,* some of which, of course, are not sufficiently discriminating, while others may appear too laudatory. In regard, however, to many works which the compiler had never carefully examined, it was necessary that he should avail himself of the assistance of others; while, in regard to others, it was desirable that his own opinions should be enforced by what the reader would be apt to regard as higher authority. In some instances he has found it necessary to modify these selected notices, and in such cases the name of the original critic has been withheld; nor is it to be supposed that in every case those which have been retained express accurately or fully the opinion of the compiler.

The *synchronistic* tables, at the end of the volume, have been prepared by Mr. Benne, and will be found useful and interesting.

* Notices not credited are, with a few exceptions, from the hand of the compiler.

PART I.

COURSES

OF

READING AND STUDY.

"I here present thee with a hive of bees, laden, some with wax, and some with honey. Fear not to approach! There are no wasps, there are no hornets here. If some wanton bee should chance to buzz about thine ears, stand thy ground, and hold thy hands; there's none will sting thee if thou strike not first. If any do, she hath honey in her bag will cure thee too."—QUARLES.

HANDBOOK.

COURSES OF READING, &c.

"Of those who were so civil as to assist a novice with their advice what method to take, few agreed in the same; some saying one thing, some another, and among them rarely any one that was tolerably just."—ROGER NORTH.

SOME prejudice against what are called "courses of study" has been justly provoked by the great number and variety of those which have been proposed from time to time. When any particular course is recommended to the exclusion of all others, it may well be suspected, since no method of study can be devised which is equally adapted to all minds, or to the diversities of situation in which men will find themselves. Instead of inferring, therefore, from the variety of these courses, that none of them are "tolerably just," it would be more reasonable to conclude that each one may have its value. They are generally suggested by the experience of their authors, and are published because they have been found useful in practice. Inasmuch, however, as every mind has its peculiarities of character and condition, and since these peculiarities will be likely to modify any methods of study it may adopt, and thus impair their value for general use, it would seem desirable to construct a system on broader principles, and with an enlightened reference, as well to the more fundamental laws of the human mind as to the existing state of literature. "To pretend to advise," says North, speaking of law studies, "is a matter of great judgment, which requires a true skill in books and men's capacities." To such skill the compiler of the following outline can make no pretensions. The utmost that he can claim for himself is, that he has felt the difficulty as well as importance of the undertaking, and has endeavoured to keep steadily in view the wants of different classes of minds. For the methods recommended, he can only hope that they will prove useful and seasonable *helps* to the young and inexperienced. At the outset, almost any *course* of reading is better than the desultory and irregular habits which prevail so extensively. When once the student has acquired a taste for good books, and some just ideas of the object and uses of reading, he may be safely left to glean for himself, from the counsels of others, such hints and directions as are best adapted to his own case.

I put down the following, as cautions and suggestions, to which every reader or student ought to have constant reference if he would have books prove benefactors indeed.

CAUTIONS AND COUNSELS.

1. Always have some useful and pleasant book ready to take up in "odd ends" of time. A good part of life will otherwise be wasted. "There is," says Wyttenbach, "no business, no avocation whatever, which will not permit a man who has *an inclination* to give a little time every day to the studies of his youth."

2. Be not alarmed because *so many* books are recommended. They are not all to be read at once, nor in a short time. "*Some travellers*," says Bishop Hall, "*have more shrunk at the map than at the way;* between both, how many stand still with their arms folded."

3. Do not attempt to *read much or fast.* "To call him *well read* who reads *many authors*," says Shaftesbury, "is improper." "*Non refert quam multos libros*," says Seneca, "*sed quam bonos habeas.*" Says Locke, "This is that which I think great readers are apt to be mistaken in: those who have read of everything, are thought to understand everything too; but it is not always so. Reading furnishes the mind only with *materials* of knowledge; it is thinking that makes what we

read ours. *We are of the ruminating kind*, and it is not enough to cram ourselves with a great load of collections; unless we chew them over again, they will not give us strength and nourishment."

A mistake here is so common and so pernicious, that I add one more authority. Says Dugald Stewart, "*Nothing, in truth, has such a tendency to weaken, not only the powers of invention, but the intellectual powers in general, as a habit of extensive and various reading* WITHOUT REFLECTION. The activity and force of mind are gradually impaired, in consequence of disuse; and not unfrequently all our principles and opinions come to be lost in the infinite multiplicity and discordancy of our acquired ideas. It requires courage, indeed (as Helvetius has remarked), to remain ignorant of those useless subjects which are generally valued; but it is a courage necessary to men who either love the truth, or who aspire to establish a permanent reputation."

4. Do not become so far enslaved by any system or course of study as to think it may not be altered when alteration would contribute to the healthy and improving action of the mind. These systems begin by being our servants; they sometimes end by becoming masters, and tyrannical masters they are.

5. Beware, on the other hand, of frequent *changes* in your plan of study. This is the besetting sin of young persons. "The man who resolves," says Wirt, "but suffers his resolution to be changed by the first counter-suggestion of a friend; who fluctuates from opinion to opinion, from plan to plan, and veers like a weathercock to every point of the compass with every breath of caprice that blows, can never accomplish anything great or useful. Instead of being progressive in anything, he will be at best stationary, and more probably retrograde in all. It is only the man who carries into his pursuits that great quality which Lucan ascribes to Cæsar, *nescia virtus stare loco*, who first consults wisely, then resolves firmly, and then executes his purpose with inflexible

perseverance, undismayed by those petty difficulties which daunt a weaker spirit, that can advance to eminence in any line. Let us take, by way of illustration, the case of a student. He commences the study of the dead languages; presently comes a friend, who tells him he is wasting his time, and that, instead of obsolete words, he had much better employ himself in acquiring new ideas. He changes his plan, and sets to work at the mathematics. Then comes another friend, who asks him, with a grave and sapient face, whether he intends to become a professor in a college; because, if he does not, he is misemploying his time; and that, for the business of life, common mathematics is quite enough of the mathematics. He throws up his Euclid, and addresses himself to some other study, which, in its turn, is again relinquished on some equally wise suggestion; and thus life is spent in changing his plans. You cannot but perceive the folly of this course; and the worst effect of it is, the fixing on your mind a habit of indecision, sufficient in itself to blast the fairest prospects. No, take your course wisely, but firmly; and, having taken it, hold upon it with heroic resolution, and the Alps and Pyrenees will sink before you. The whole empire of learning will be at your feet, while those who set out with you, but stopped to change their plans, are yet employed in the very profitable business of changing their plans. Let your motto be, *Perseverando vinces.* Practice upon it, and you will be convinced of its value by the distinguished eminence to which it will conduct you."

6. Read always the *best* and most recent book on the subject which you wish to investigate. "You are to remember," says Pliny the younger, "that the most approved authors of each sort are to be carefully chosen, for, as it has been well observed, though we should read much, we should not read many authors."

7. Study *subjects* rather than books: therefore, compare different authors on the same subjects; the statements of authors, with information collected from other sources; and the

conclusions drawn by a writer with the rules of sound logic. "Learning," says Feltham, "falls far short of wisdom; nay, so far, that you scarcely find a greater fool than is sometimes a mere scholar."

8. Seek opportunities to *write* and *converse* on subjects about which you read. "Reading," says Bacon, "maketh a *full* man, conference a *ready* man, and writing an *exact* man." Another benefit of conversation is touched upon by Feltham: "Men commonly write more formally than they practice. From conversing only with books, they fall into affectation and pedantry," and he might have added into many mistakes. "He who is made up of the press and the pen shall be sure to be ridiculous. Company and conversation are the best instructers for a noble nature." "An engagement and combating of wits," says Erasmus, "does in an extraordinary manner both show the strength of geniuses, rouses them and augments them. If you are in doubt of any thing, do not be ashamed to ask, or if you have committed an error, be corrected."

9. Accustom yourself to refer whatever you read to the general head to which it belongs, and trace it, if a fact, to the principle it involves or illustrates; if a principle, to the facts which it produces or explains. "I may venture to assert," says Mr. Starkie, speaking of the study of the law, and the remark is equally applicable to other studies, "that there is nothing which more effectually facilitates the study of the law than the constant habit on the part of the student of attempting to trace and reduce what he learns by reading or by practice to its appropriate *principle*. Cases apparently remote, by this means are made to illustrate and explain each other. Every additional acquisition adds strength to the principle which it supports and illustrates; and *thus* the student becomes armed with principles and conclusions of important and constant use in forensic warfare, and possesses a power, from the united support of a principle, fortified by a number of dependant cases and illustrations; while the des-

ultory, non-digesting reader, the man of indices and abridgments, is unable to bear in his mind a multiplicity of, to him, unconnected cases; and could he recollect them, would be unable to make use of them if he failed to find one exactly suited to his purpose."

10. Endeavour to find opportunities to *use* your knowledge, and to apply it in practice. "They proceed right well in all knowledge," says Bacon, "which do couple study with their practice, and do not first study altogether, and then practice altogether."

11. Strive, by frequent reviews, to keep your knowledge *always at command.* "What booteth," says an old writer, "to read much, which is a weariness to the flesh; to meditate often, which is a burden to the mind; to learn daily, with increase of knowledge, when he is to seek for what he hath learned, and perhaps, then, especially when he hath most need thereof? Without this, our studies are but lost labour." "One of the profoundest and most versatile scholars in England," says Mr. Warren, in his Law Studies, "has a prodigious memory, which the author once told him was a magazine stored with wealth from every department of knowledge. 'I am not surprised at it,' he added, 'nor would you be, or any one that knew the pains I have taken in *selecting* and *depositing* what you call my "wealth." I take care always to ascertain the *value* of what I look at, and if satisfied on that score, I most carefully stow it away. I pay, besides, frequent visits to my "magazine," and keep an inventory of at least everything important, which I frequently compare with my stores. It is, however, *the systematic disposition and arrangement* I adopt, which lightens the labours of memory. I was by no means remarkable for memory when young; on the contrary, I was considered rather defective on that score.'"

12. *Dare to be ignorant of many things.* "In a celebrated satire (*the Pursuits of Literature*), much read in my youth," says De Quincy, "and which I myself read about twenty-five

years ago, I remember one counsel there addressed to young men, but, in fact, of universal application. 'I call upon them,' said the author, 'to *dare* to be ignorant of many things;' a wise counsel, and justly expressed; for it requires much courage to forsake popular paths of knowledge, merely upon a conviction that they are not favourable to the ultimate ends of knowledge. In you, however, *that* sort of courage may be presumed; but how will you 'dare to be ignorant' of many things, in opposition to the cravings of your own mind? Simply thus: destroy these false cravings by introducing a healthier state of the organ. *A good scheme of study will soon show itself to be such by this one test*, that it will exclude as powerfully as it will appropriate; it will be a system of repulsion no less than of attraction; once thoroughly possessed and occupied by the deep and genial pleasures of one truly intellectual pursuit, you will be easy and indifferent to all others that had previously teased you with transient excitement."

To show that these counsels are neither novel nor frivolous, the author has enforced each one of them by the authority of some honoured name.

The courses will be arranged as follows:

I. A General Course.

II. Particular Courses, viz.,

1. *History.* 2. *Speculative Philosophy.* 3. *Political Philosophy.* 4. *Poetry, Belles-Lettres, and Oratory.* 5. *Mathematical and Physical Science.* 6. *Chemistry and Natural History.* 7. *Theological Studies.* 8. *Legal Studies.* 9. *Medical Studies.*

I. A GENERAL COURSE OF READING.

Letters, "the sciences, and philosophy, are all conducive to any profession whatsoever. I take a taste of all, that I be not ignorant of any; and the rather that, having tasted of all, I may the better choose that I am fittest for."—ERASMUS.

THIS course is designed especially for those who are engaged *in academical and professional study*, or in *active pursuits.* It is intended to occupy the intervals of regular occupation for the space of four or six years,* and, with some modifications, will be found adapted to the wants of under-graduates, students of law, medicine, &c., &c., and also to those of clerks, apprentices, and other persons not well acquainted with books.

It is supposed that the first and great object of such a course should be to develop and cultivate a healthy taste for books, and to form good mental habits. Hence, but a small number are set down under each head; and these are selected rather with reference to the awakening of intellectual activity, and the formation of studious habits and correct tastes, than to the amount or completeness of the knowledge which they impart.

As to the *order* in which these books should be read, much must be left to the discretion of the student. It is not intended, of course, that all the books under each head should be perused, in the order set down, before passing to the next. As a general rule, it may be well to have more than one work on hand at the same time; one for very short intervals of leisure, mere fragments of time; one for seasons, more protracted, of serious application; and a third, perhaps, calling for less intellectual effort, but putting in requisition a different set of faculties, and to be taken up occasionally. Or it may

* The number of books which can be read profitably during this period will depend, of course, on the amount of leisure enjoyed, the nature of the books, and the habits and capacity of the reader.

be still better, having finished the perusal of a work in one department, to pass to something kindred in another department. Advantageous transitions may be made, for instance, from *Biography* to *History*, and from *History* to *Voyages and Travels*, or from either to *Polite Literature* and *Science*.

The *subjects* are arranged with special reference to the case of those who have not yet acquired a taste for reading.

I. Biography.—Works of this kind are especially useful to the young, and those not accustomed to read, because they come home to our sympathies, to "the business and bosoms of men," thus inspiring interest and quickening curiosity. They also furnish the readiest means of exciting an enthusiasm for different pursuits and studies. The higher object of making us acquainted with remarkable individuals, and through them with human nature, and with the times in which the individuals lived, must be kept steadily in view, but the objects first named are most urgent and important at the outset. It is with special reference to them that the following books are recommended:

1. If it be our object to *inspire a reverence for Christianity* and *interest in its duties*, the Life of Schwartz, of William Wilberforce, of John Howard, of Harlan Page, of Hannah More, of Bishop Heber, of Richard Baxter, of Henry Martyn, and the collection of lives by Bishop Burnett and Izaak Walton, will be found adapted to this purpose.

2. If we wish to excite and cultivate *a taste for letters* and *to form a scholar to right views and habits*, Teignmouth's Life of Sir William Jones, Boswell's Life of Dr. Johnson, Wakefield's Memoirs of his own Life, Prior's Life of Goldsmith, or Washington Irving's sketch of the same, Prior's Life of Burke, Life of Sir James Mackintosh, Roscoe's Lorenzo di Medici, Lockhart's Life of Scott, may be read with great advantage.

3. If a taste for *scientific* knowledge and inquiry is to be awakened, Sir David Brewster's Life of Newton and his Martyrs of Science, the Life of Sir H. Davy by his brother, the

Life of Baron Cuvier, Arago's Eloge on James Watt, Colden's Life of Fulton, &c., would be adapted to the purpose.

4. If our object is to *acquire right views and principles* in regard to *political* life, we should use the Life of Washington by Sparks or Marshall, Jay's Life by his son, Sparks's Life of Franklin, Memoirs of the Duke of Sully, Life of Cecil (Lord Burleigh), British Statesmen by Mackintosh, do. by Lord Brougham, &c., &c. If the reader is destined for a *military* or *naval* career, he should read the Life of Washington, Sketches of the American Generals of the Revolutionary War in Sparks's American Biography, Memoirs of Napoleon, Southey's Life of Nelson, and the Public and Private Correspondence of Vice-admiral Collingwood, with Memoirs of his Life. In some of these works, the reader should guard carefully against the pernicious effect of brilliant exploits in blinding the author to the moral turpitude of his hero. Southey's Life of Nelson is an instance in which a very pure and entertaining writer has not escaped this seductive influence. If the reader is looking forward to the *medical* profession, let him read the Life of Boerhaave, the Memoirs of Dr. John Mason Good by Olinthus Gregory, the Life of Dr. Samuel Bard by Rev. J. M'Vickar, D.D., &c., &c. If he is to enter the legal profession, the Life of Lord Hale, Memoirs of Sir Samuel Romily, Wheaton's Life of William Pinkney, Wirt's Memoirs of Patrick Henry, and the Life of Alexander Hamilton by his son, &c., &c. These works are selected in some instances more with reference to the formation of right principle in the reader than to the eminence of the person commemorated.

5. If we propose to acquire general views of remarkable men at different periods as a preparation for the study of History, Plutarch's Lives, Sketches of Eminent Men in the British Library of Entertaining Knowledge, Cunningham's Lives of the Painters, and other similar works, should be read.

II. History.—This records the biography of nations and the great movements and revolutions of humanity. At first, authors should be selected who are best calculated to inspire interest and awaken curiosity. Such interest depends partly upon the eloquence and skill of the author, and partly upon the connexion of the events described with ourselves, our own country and time. As a general rule, the student should, in commencing, prefer *particular* to *general* histories. Universal histories, so called, have very little value to the beginner, except as books of reference. When reading any particular history, allusions to the past and to other countries will occur, which ought to be explained, and reference to a universal history for the purpose, and also for getting a general view of the state of the world at the period under examination, is to be earnestly recommended. The student should remember that some knowledge of geography is indispensable in reading history to advantage, and that he ought to have by him when reading maps and chronological tables. Geography and chronology have been justly called the *eyes* of history. Synchronistic *tables* have recently been introduced, especially by the French and German historians, which are a great improvement upon those formerly in use. Parallel columns are assigned to the leading countries of the world, and contemporaneous events happening in these different countries appear side by side on the same horizontal line, and opposite to the proper date. (See Œuvres de Michelet, tome i., for a good specimen of modern tables, called "Tableaux Synchroniques de l'Histoire Moderne.")

1. Selecting historical works upon the principles suggested above, the student might begin advantageously with Botta's History of the War of American Independence, proceeding thence to one or more volumes of Bancroft's Colonial History of the United States; thence to Prescott's Reign of Ferdinand and Isabella, or Robertson's Charles V., Miss Aikin's Court of Elizabeth, Lord Herbert's Life of Henry VIII., Bacon's Henry VII., Hume's Account of the Reign of Edward III., Irving's Conquest of Grenada, Ranke's History of the Popes, D'Aubigné's Reformation, &c. The author would mention here

one of the very few useful purposes to which some works in prose fiction may be applied. He refers to historical romances, especially to those of Sir W. Scott, G. P. R. James, and J. F. Cooper. They furnish accounts, always graphic, and often correct, of the spirit, manners, and personages of the most remarkable eras commemorated in history. For instance, after reading the Courts of Elizabeth or James I., by Miss Aikin, it might materially assist both the memory and understanding of the student, if he should read Scott's Kenilworth, and Fortunes of Nigel, for the purpose, especially, of comparing the historian with the novelist. Shakspeare's historical dramas might be read in like manner, in connexion with the corresponding parts of history. The historian and dramatist could not but reflect mutual light and interest upon each other.

The subscriber would recommend here, as a useful compilation, " Great Events by Great Historians," prepared by Dr. Lieber; also " Historical Parallels," published by the British Society for the Diffusion of Useful Knowledge.

Having thus introduced himself to history, the student might profitably read Hume's History of England, Hallam's Middle Ages, and the more popular work of Sir F. Palgrave on the same subject, Sismondi's Roman Empire, Ferguson's Roman Republic, or the compilation from Wachsmuth and Schlosser in the Cabinet Cyclopædia, portions of Livy and Tacitus in the original, or in a translation; also, Herodotus and Thucydides, Mitford's Grecian History, &c., &c., Sharon Turner's Sacred History of the Bible, and Prideaux's Connexions.

This course might be modified advantageously, perhaps, by taking up ancient history at an earlier period. On this and many other questions the student must judge for himself. He should remember that the grand object of history is *to make him acquainted with man*, by making him acquainted with the causes of events, and the motives which have influenced human actions, and that these lessons can never be duly learned by a torpid or listless mind, or by one that reads merely for amusement or excitement.

III. Travels, Voyages, &c.—The object of these works is to enlarge our acquaintance with the world, and especially with civil and physical geography. They are cheap and convenient substitutes for travelling, with the advantage of enabling us, in many cases, to see through another more than we should have been likely to discover ourselves. To awaken an interest in this kind of reading, the student should begin with books remarkable for a spirited and graphic, as well as truthful delineation of character, incidents, and natural objects; such, for example, as Barrow's Bible in Spain, Dana's Two Years before the Mast, Stephens's Travels in Central America and Yucatan, and the different works of the same author, recounting his visits to different parts of the Old World, Miss Sedgwick's Letters from Abroad, Kohl's Russia and the Russians, Sir John Malcolm's Travels in the East, with many others belonging to the same class.

It would then be well to return to some of the travellers and voyagers of the last century, among whom More, author of Views of Society in Italy in 1776, and in France in 1771, and Lady Montagu, are excellent. The student will then be prepared for the voyages of discovery, the scientific travels, and the political and statistical tours which have been given to the world in such abundance of late. To this head belong Humboldt's Travels, the Voyages of Parry, Franklin, and Ross, in our own time, of Cook, Anson, &c., &c., in earlier periods, the visit of Reaumer and Prince Puckler-Muskau to England, of Prince Saxe-Weimar, Buckingham, Chevalier, &c., to the United States, &c., &c., &c. The missionary tours and journals are especially rich in information and in materials for philosophical reflection.

IV. Polite Literature, including prose and poetry. Its principal object is to cultivate taste and imagination in connexion with the other powers and susceptibilities of the soul, and hence special importance is attached to form or style of composition. The following books are deserving of particular notice, and should be read in the order most congenial with the tastes and capacities of the student, viz.: 1. The Spectator and other British Essays, the Essays of Charles Lamb, Sketch-book of Washington Irving, and the best papers of the Quarterly, Edinburgh, and other Reviews (to be read occasionally). 2. Shakspeare, to be read in connexion with Schlegel's Critical Lectures, or Hazlitt's Essays, and Mrs. Jameson's Female Characters of Shakspeare. 3. Milton's poetry and prose writings. 4. Sermons of Jeremy Taylor and Dr. Barrow. 5. Ancient and modern orators, viz., Demosthenes, Cicero, Pitt, Fox, Burke, Canning, Webster, &c., &c. 6. British poets: Spenser, Dryden, Goldsmith, Akenside, Cowper, Wordsworth, Scott, Coleridge, Southey, Mrs. Hemans, Tennyson, &c., &c. 7. American poets: Bryant, Halleck, Dana, &c., &c.

V. Speculative and Political Philosophy.—Books in this department, if well selected and thoroughly read, are calculated to develop habits of thought and discrimination, while they accustom us to trace back moral and political facts to fundamental principles, and to consider practical questions in the light of those principles. Selecting books with reference to the wants of beginners, I know of none better than the following: 1. Abercrombie's Inquiry into the Intellectual Powers. 2. Dugald Stewart's Elements of the Philosophy of the Mind, and also his Active and Moral Powers, with frequent reference to the essays of his master, Dr. Reid, a delightful thinker. 3. Locke's Essay on the Understanding, to be read in connexion with Cousin's Review of the same, in his Psychology, translated by Professor Henry. 4. Berkeley's philosophical works, the model, so far as style is concerned, of metaphysical writing. 5. Smith's Moral Sentiments, rich in illustrations and examples, as well as in materials for thought, though unsound in theory. 6. Wayland's Moral Science, with parallel chapters in Paley.

7. Mackintosh's Progress of Ethical Philosophy, a masterly sketch. 8. Paley's Natural Theology.

In Political Philosophy.—1. Kent's Commentaries, 1st volume, or Story on the Constitution of the United States. 2. Montesquieu's Spirit of Laws. 3. De Tocqueville on American Democracy. 4. Smith's Wealth of Nations, in connexion with the Political Economy of Willard Phillips. 5. Hooker's Ecclesiastical Polity, 1st and 8th books. 6. Burke's works, a treasure-house of wisdom and eloquence. 7. Wheaton's Law of Nations.

VI. Physical Science and Natural History.—The student who wishes to review the great principles of *mechanical philosophy*, or to learn them for the first time, should take up some popular treatise by a master. Of this kind are Arnott's Physics, Euler's Letters, Haüy's or Fisher's Physics, Ferguson's Lectures. He may also read with advantage Sir J. W. Herschel's Discourse on the Study of Natural Philosophy. One elementary work is sufficient for a general reader, if properly studied. It should be his great object to make himself perfectly master of a few fundamental and prolific laws; such, for example, as the law of inertia, the doctrine of compound forces, or, as it is usually called, the parallelogram of forces, and the laws of falling bodies. These, combined with a clear understanding of the difference between solid, liquid, and aëriform bodies, and the effects which their peculiar properties must have in modifying the action of mechanical forces, will place the student on such a vantage-ground that he will find little trouble in the subsequent parts, or in dealing with any ordinary question which may present itself. The great secret of acquiring knowledge easily and rapidly, is to master the elementary and central truths of any branch so thoroughly that they are always present to the mind, and seem perfectly familiar, though seen under the most dissimilar phases.

In order to gain a knowledge of the laws of *light*, *electricity*, *magnetism*, &c., &c., the Introduction of Mr. Daniell to the

Study of Chemical Philosophy, and the various treatises on these subjects in the British Library of Useful Knowledge, may be used with advantage. The first has been republished by Professor Renwick, in the School District Library. Kane's Elements of Chemistry, as edited by Professor Draper, contains the most recent, and, therefore, the most complete elementary view of chemistry now extant. Turner's, Beck's, Gray's, &c., &c., will also suffice for ordinary purposes.

For *Astronomy*, the treatise of Herschel, or the translation, by Haskins, of Arago's admirable Sketch, or the late work of Professor Olmstead, will be amply sufficient for general readers.

In the department of Natural History, Gray's Botanical Text-Book, Lindley's Botany, M'Murtrie's edition of Cuvier's Zoology, Smellie's Philosophy of Natural History, Sheppard's or Dana's Mineralogy, Lyell's Elements and Principles of Geology, and De la Beche's How to Observe in Geology. As a treatise preliminary to the study of Natural History, and calculated to interest the student deeply in its wonders, no book is more admirable than White's Natural History of Selborne. Smellie's Philosophy of Natural History is also a very useful and interesting introduction to the study.

VII. Suggestive Works.—I throw together here a few works which have a surpassing value as guides, and provocatives to thought: 1. Bacon's Essays. 2. Coleridge's Aids to Reflection. 3. Pascal's Thoughts. 4. Selden's Table-Talk. 5. Cecil's Remains. 6. Montague's Selections from Old English Writers. 7. Especially Butler's Analogy and Sermons on Human Nature. 8. Chillingworth. 9. Herder's Ideas on the Study of Mankind, translated.

II. PARTICULAR COURSES OF STUDY.

These are intended as helps to those who contemplate a more thorough and extended investigation of subjects than is provided for in the *general* course.*

1. HISTORY.

"What is the true sense of History? I will answer you by quoting what I have read somewhere or other in Dionysius Halicarnassensis, I think, that *History is Philosophy 'teaching by examples.'*"—LORD BOLINGBROKE.

THE study of History as a science should be preceded by a careful examination of the leading principles of chronology and geography. More recent and popular treatises will generally be sufficient; but a thorough investigation will render it necessary to have recourse to the original authorities.

In *Chronology*, these are the Chronicon of Eusebius Pamphilus, published in the fourth century, the "De Emendatione Temporum" of Joseph Scaliger (sixteenth century), the Chronology of Ancient Kingdoms, amended by Sir I. Newton (1728), and Kennedy's "Complete System of Astronomical Chronology, unfolding the Scriptures." So far as Grecian Chronology is concerned, the most comprehensive, valuable, and elaborate work is that of Mr. H. F. Clinton, entitled "Fasti Hellenici," the Civil and Literary Chronology of Greece from the Earliest Accounts to the Death of Augustus.

The Chronological Tables of Sir Harris Nicolas (1832), contained in one small volume, are among the most recent and convenient.

In Geography, the original authorities, 1, *among the an-*

* Books are not arranged in these *courses* in the order in which they should be read. In many instances reference has been had only to *chronological* order.

cients, are Herodotus (the geographical descriptions contained in his History), Polybius (the same), Ptolemy, Pausanias's admirable description of Greece, and especially the great work of Strabo on Physical Geography and Topography. 2. Of the *modern* authorities, some of the best are Malte-Brun, Murray, Balbi, Ritter (a German work), our countrymen Dr. Robertson, Worcester, &c., &c. The student will find no difficulty in procuring good atlases. The great work of Lavoisne, or Le Sage (properly Las Casps), may be recommended as combining the advantages of both ancient and modern chronological and genealogical tables, historical charts, &c., &c.

(A.) ANCIENT HISTORY.*

This may be subdivided into (*a*) Oriental; (*b*.) Grecian; (*c*.) Roman.

(*a*.) ORIENTAL HISTORY.

In this department of history the distinction between ancient and modern is not so clear and definite as in the others, and, therefore, will not be adhered to rigidly in the following list. Books generally, which throw light on the history and state of civilization of the East, will be recommended.

1. *Assyria and Egypt.*—The most valuable original authorities among the *ancients* are, the Old Testament, Herodotus, Diodorus Siculus, Arrian, and Strabo. Among the *moderns*, Shuckford and Prideaux's Connexions, Caylus, Young, Wilkinson, Lane, Rossalini, Champollion, &c., on the Antiquities, Monumental History, &c., &c., of the Egyptians.

2. *Persia.*—The Zendavesta, translated by Anquetil du Perron, and now regarded as authentic. De Sacy's Memoires sur diverses Antiquitées de la Perse, Malcolm's His-

* On the *Philosophy of History* the student may consult Bossuet, Voltaire, Turgot (second volume of his complete works), Guizot, Cousin, Vico (Nuova Scienza), Herder (Ideas), Lessing (Education of the Human Race), Miller (History Philosophically considered).

tory of Persia, Frazer's ditto, Ouseley's Oriental Collections, Travels of Morier, Frazer, Ker Porter, &c., &c.

3. *India.*—Maffei's History of India, Robertson's Historical Disquisition on India, Malcolm's Memoir on Central India, Asiatic Researches, especially Papers by Sir William Jones, Colebrook, and Professor Wilson, Travels in India by Bishop Heber and others.

4. *China.*—Mendoza's History of China, written in the sixteenth century, Davis's late and interesting work, entitled "The Chinese," De Guigney's Voyage to Pekin, Du Halde's great work, entitled "Description Geographique, Historique, &c., &c., de l'Empire de la Chine, et de la Tartarie Chinoise," published in 1735; the Embassies of Staunton, Macartney, &c., &c., the more recent travellers, and the publications of Remusat, Klaproth, Morrison, Marshman, Gutzlaff, and others, on the Literature and Antiquities of the Chinese.

On the subject of the East generally, the student is referred particularly to the great work of Heeren, "Reflections on the Politics, Intercourse, and Commerce of the Chief Nations of Antiquity." With respect to the Asiatic and African nations, the subject is fully discussed, and with an ingenuity and freedom before unknown. The same author's "Manual of the History of the Ancient States" will also be found useful, not only for the general outline which it gives, but especially for its references to original authorities, in which it is very rich. See, too, Herder's second volume of "Ideas towards the Philosophy of the History of Mankind."

The publications of the Oriental Translation Fund are also valuable, for the light they cast upon the literary and social history of the East.

(*b*.) GRECIAN HISTORY.

Ancient Authors.—*Herodotus* on the Persian Wars, with many digressions on the history of other countries and of earlier ages; *Thucydides* on the Peloponnesian War, with a general survey of Grecian History, in his first book, down to that war; *Xenophon's* Hellenica, from the close of the Peloponnesian war to the battle of Mantinea, B.C. 362; *Diodorus Siculus* (sixteenth book) and the Attic Orators on the period intervening between B.C. 362 and the accession of Alexander; *Arrian*, *Quintus Curtius*, *Diodorus*, and *Plutarch* on the history of Alexander; *Justin*, *Polybius*, *Plutarch*, and *Diodorus* for the remaining periods.

Modern Authors.—*Gillies* and *Mitford*, from the earliest times to the death of Alexander; *Gast*, for the succeeding periods; *Thirlwall's* General History of Greece; *Keightley's* abridged Survey; *Heeren's* Researches on Ancient Greece; *Böckh's* Economy of Athens, and the German works of O. Von Müller and Wachsmuth, which have not been translated into English.

(*c.*) ROMAN HISTORY.

Ancient Authors.—*Aurelius Victor* on the Origin of the Roman People; *Livy* on the general History of Rome, from the earliest times down to 745 A.U.C.; *Cæsar's* Commentaries on the Wars in Gaul, &c.; *Sallust* on the Conspiracy of Catiline and the War against Jugurtha; *Tacitus* on Rome under the Emperors to the time of Vespasian, and on the Life of Agricola; *Scriptores Historiæ Augustæ*, or writers of Imperial History; Dion Cassius, Herodian, &c., &c., may also be consulted.

Modern Authors.—*Niebuhr* and *Wachsmuth* on the earliest periods; *Ferguson's* Roman Republic; *Michelet's* Republique Romaine; *Gibbon*, *Crevier*, *Tillemont*, and *Heubler*, and the *Byzantine Historians*, on the History of the Empire; *Vertot's* Revolutions in Roman History, and the able compilation from the later German historians, published as one of the numbers in Lardner's Cabinet Cyclopædia. It was republished by Carey and Lea in one volume 8vo (1837), under the title "The History of Rome," and is very valuable as imbodying the researches of Niebuhr, Schlosser, Wachsmuth, Heeren, &c., &c.

(B.) MEDIÆVAL HISTORY.

See on this subject the first seven Lectures of Smyth on the Study of Modern History.

Earlier Authors.—Gregory of Tours on the Ecclesiastical History of the Franks; Venerable *Bede* on Church History, translated into Saxon by Alfred the Great; *Eginhard's* Annals of the Franks, and Life of Charlemagne, to whom he was private secretary; *Gulielmus Tyrius,* one of the best historians of the Crusades, of which he was an eyewitness; *Geoffrey of Monmouth,* &c., &c.: see 2d part;* *Sale's* translation of the Koran; Philip de Comines, Froissart, Brantome, later Byzantine historians.

Later Authors.—Hallam on the Middle Ages; *Koch* on do.; *Sir F. Palgrave's* History of the Anglo-Saxons; *Turner's* History of the Anglo-Saxons; *Churton's* History of the early English Church; *Prideaux's* Life of Mohammed; *Adam Smith* on the Progress of Cities in the Middle Ages (in the 3d book of Wealth of Nations); *Gibbon's* Decline and Fall of the Roman Empire; *Montesquieu's* Spirit of Laws; *Robertson's* Charles V. (vol. i.); *Guizot's* Lectures on European Civilization (2d to 9th); *Michaud's* History of the Crusades and *Barante's* History of the Dukes of Burgundy.

(C.) MODERN HISTORY.

General History of Europe.

Earlier Authors.—Froissart's Chronicles down to 1400, Monstrelet from 1400–1467; *Comines* from 1464–1498; *De Thou* from 1545–1607; *Burnet,* History of his own Times from 1660–1689, with an introductory sketch, reaching back to 1603; *Puffendorf's* Introduction to the History of the principal Kingdoms and States of Europe.

Later Authors.—Modern Universal History; *Millot's* Elements of General History; *Von Müller's* do.; *Tytler's* do.; *Rotteck's* do.; *Schlosser's* History of Europe in the 18th century; *Russell's* Modern Europe; *Michelet's* Elements of Modern History; *Heeren's* Manual; *Raumer's* History of the 16th

* Of Handbook.

and 17th centuries; *Lord John Russell's* Memoirs on affairs of Europe since the peace of Utrecht.

L'terary History.—Eichhorn's General History of Modern Literature in Europe; *Bouterweck's* History of Modern Poetry and Eloquence; *Sismondi's* History of the Literature of the South of Europe; *Hallam's* History of Literature; *Mager's* History and Character of the French National Literature; *Ginguene's* Histoire de la Litérature d'Italie; also *Villemain's* Cours, &c.

PARTICULAR COUNTRIES.

1. *England.*

Earlier Authors are, *Matthew Paris; Bacon's* Life of Henry VII.; *Lord Herbert's* Life of Henry VIII.; *Camden's* Britannia and Elizabeth; *Baker's* Chronicle; *Clarendon's* Rebellion; *Rapin's* History of England from Julius Cæsar to the Revolution of 1688.

Later Authors.—Hume, with the continuation of Smollett, Bissett, &c., &c.; *Henry's* History (for progress of the Arts, Learning, &c., &c.); *Belsham's* History; *Adolphus's* do.; *Guizot's* Reign of Charles I.; *Villemain's* History of Cromwell; *Thierry's* Norman Conquest; *Lingard* (an able historical champion of the Roman Catholics); *Sir James Mackintosh's* Fragment of English History.

For a more extended course, see "Smyth's Lectures on Modern History," a work which cannot be too often recommended to the student.

2. *Scotland and Ireland.*

Buchanan's History of Scotland; *Robertson's* do.; Stuart's do.; *Plowden's* History of Ireland; *O'Connell's* do.; *Madden's* History of the United Irishmen, and *Thomas Moore's* History of Ireland.

3. *France.*

Earlier Authors.—Duchesne, Montfaucon, Davila, Voltaire, Mably, Sully's Memoirs, *De Retz's* do.

Later Authors.—Henault, D'Anquetil, La Cretelle, Michelet

Capefigue, *Sismondi*, *Mignet*, *Augustin Thierry*, *Amadée Thierry*, *Thiers*, *Barante*, *Guizot*, *Villemain*.

4. *Spain, Portugal, and Low Countries.*

Earlier Authors.—*Mendoza*, *Ferreras*, and *Mariana* for Spain; *Grotius*, *Bentivoglio*, and *Strada* for the Low Countries.

Later Authors.—*Gibbon* in part, *Robertson* (Charles V.), *Watson* (Philip II., Philip III.), *Prescott* (Ferdinand and Isabella), *Mrs. Calcott*, *Schiller*, *Southey's* Peninsular War, Napier's do., *Florian's* History of the Moors, *Laclede's* History of Portugal.

5. *Italy.*

Earlier Authors.—*Platina*, *Politianus*, *Machiavelli*, *Guicciardini*, *Muratori*.

Later Authors.—*Tiraboschi*, *Giannone*, *Daru*, *Botta*, *Sismondi*, *Bossi*, *Leo*, *Roscoe*.

6. *Germany.**

Earlier Authors.—*Tacitus* (De Germania), *Cæsar's* Commentaries, Chronicles of Bishop Otho.

Later Authors.—*Pfeffel*, *Johannes Von Müller*, *Schmidt*, *Schiller*, *Raumer*, *Ranke*, *Coxe's* House of Austria, *Thiebauld* (Frederic), *Kohlrausch*, *Pertz's* Fundamenta Historiæ Germaniæ, *Grimm's* German Antiquities.

7. *North of Europe.*

Puffendorf's History of Sweden; *Harte's* Gustavus Adolphus; *Voltaire's* Charles XII.; *Connor's* History of Poland; *Fletcher's* do.; *Palmer's* Life of Sobieski; *Castelnau's* History of Russia; *Barrow's* Peter the Great; *Tooke's* View of Russia and Life of Catharine; Napoleon's Expedition to Russia (*Ségur*); *Wraxall's* Tour in Denmark; *Andrews's* History of the Danish Revolution; *Crichton's* and *Wheaton's* History of

* The best history of Switzerland is Von Müller's.

Denmark; *Williams's* Rise, Progress, &c., &c., of the Northern Government; *Steffen's* History of Sweden; *De Ségur's* History of Russia.

8. *American History.*

1. *General.—Earlier Authors.—Royal Society* of Danish Antiquaries on the Ante-Columbian History of America; *Hackluyt's* Collections of Voyages touching the Discovery of America; *Herrera's* History; *Ulloa's* Voyage, Memoirs, &c.; *Gumilla's* Hist. de l'Orenoque; *Cassani* on Jesuits' Settlements in New Grenada; *Rochefolt's* Hist. d'Antilles; *Dobrizzhoffer's* Travels; *Charlevoix's* Hist. de la Nouvelle France and Travels; Lettres Edifiantes et Curieuses; *Colden's* Five Nations; *Mrs. Grant's* American Lady; *Kalm's* Travels.

Later Authors.—Oldmixon's British Empire; *Burke's* European Settlements in America; *Wynne's* General History of the British Empire in North America; *Robertson's* History of America; *Southey's* History of Brazil; *Murray's* British North America.

2. United States.—*Earlier Authors.—Morton's* Memorial; *Mather's* Magnalia; *Vanderdonck's* Account of the New Netherlands; *Winthrop's* Journal; *Hutchinson's* History of Massachusetts; *Smith's* New-York; *De Vries, De Laet, Acrelius's* New Sweden, &c., &c.

Later Authors.—Holmes's Annals; *Belknap's* New-Hampshire; *Chalmers's* Annals; *Bancroft's* History of the United States; *Hinton's* History and Topography of the United States; *Grahame's* History of do.; *Pitkin's* Political and Civil History; *Marshall's* Life of Washington; *Lyman's* Diplomacy of the United States; *Digest* of the Proceedings of the first four sessions of Congress; *Botta's* American Revolution; *Almon's* Register, Madison Papers, &c., &c., &c.

As it may interest the student, Lord Mansfield's short plan for reading ancient history is added.

"In the wide field of ancient history," says his lordship, "I have skipped over the rugged places, because I mean to lead you on carpet ground; I have passed over the unprofitable, because I would not give you the trouble of one step which does not lead directly to useful knowledge. Commence with Fleury, Du Choix de la Conduite des Etudes (§ 26 Histoire, § 31 Rhetorique); Cicero, De Oratore (lib. ii., § 51–63); De Legibus (lib. i., § 1, 2); De Officiis (lib. i., c. xxii., xxiii.); Dr. Priestley's Chart, and Playfair's Chronological Tables, for the duration and extent of the Assyrian, Persian, Grecian, and Roman Empires, and the Goths and Vandals; various portions of Raleigh's History of the World, Xenophon, Thucydides, Tourreil's History, Preface to Demosthenes (book i., c. i., § 2–8). Over and over the speeches of Demosthenes, in the original, or a translation; Vertot's Roman Revolution (book xi., xii., xiii., xiv., throughout); Sallust; Montesquieu's De la Grand. et de la Decad. des Romains (c. ii., and xi.); Cicero's fourteen speeches against Marc Antony (the second, which cost him his life, is the only speech of length). When you have finished the above course in the manner proposed, go over the whole a second time, which, if you make yourself master of it the first time, need not cost you many days. The next thing in order is, that you have some notion of the history of the Roman Empire, from Julius Cæsar to the end of the 5th century. Read ch. xii. to xviii. of De la Grandeur des Romains et de leur Décadence, 'adding the chronology, and throwing on paper enlargements in particular parts; especially the grand epochas;' "Bishop Meavie's Disc. on Univ. Hist. Lit. de l'Empire Romain, 'to the end.'

"This," he concludes, "will give you a small map, sufficient at present. Reflect on the Roman imperial government, military and tyrannical, like the Turkish and Russian."

On the study of modern history, "the best and most profitable manner," his lordship adds, "appears to me to be this: first, to take a succinct view of the whole, and get a general idea of the several states of Europe, with their rise, progress, principal revolutions, connexions, and interests; and when you have once got this general knowledge, *then to descend to particulars*, and study the periods which most deserve closer examination. The best way of getting this general knowledge is by reading the history of one or two of the principal states of Europe, and taking that of the smaller states, occasionally, as you go along, so far as it happens to be connected with the history of those leading powers, which you will naturally make your principal objects, and consider the others only as accessories."

2. SPECULATIVE PHILOSOPHY.

"Whether an early habit of reflection, although obtained by speculative sciences, may not have its use in practical affairs."—BERKELEY'S QUERIST.

"If a man's wit be not apt to distinguish or find differences (*i. e.*, be not subtile), let him study the schoolmen, for they are the *Cymini Sectores*."—BACON.

Ancient Authors.—Xenophon's Memorabilia, being an exposition of the philosophy of Socrates; the *Dialogues of Plato*, imbodying his Ideal or Spiritual Philosophy, especially his Phædo, Banquet, Cratylus, and the Republic; the *Metaphysics, Ethics, &c., of Aristotle*, imbodying his Sensuous Philosophy; *Cicero's* Academical Questions, being an exposition of the doctrines of the New Academy or Later Platonism; also his treatises, *De Legibus* and *De Finibus*, the one on the Philosophy of Jurisprudence, the other on the Chief Good and Ill of Man; his *De Officiis*, which has justly been called the heathen *Whole Duty of Man;* his *Tusculan Questions* on some branches of practical ethics; his *De Amicitia* and De Senectute; *Seneca's* Philosophical Writings; *Diogenes Laertius* on the Lives of the Philosophers. The works of *Plotinus, Porphyry*, &c., on the New Platonism of the Alexandrian School.

Mediæval Writers.—John Scotus Erigena, Berengarius of

Tours, and the great *Anselm* of *Canterbury*, representatives of the first period of the Scholastic Philosophy (the period of Realism); *Roscelinus*, *Abelard*, *Peter Lombard*, *John* of *Salisbury*, representing the second period of Scholastic Philosophy (separation of Nominalism and Realism); *Vincent* of *Beauvais*, *Bonaventura*, *Thomas Aquinas*, *Duns Scotus*, belonging to the third period of the same Philosophy (Absolute Realism, and the union of the Church with Aristotelian Philosophy); *Occam*, &c., &c., belonging to the fourth and last period of Scholastic Philosophy (triumph of Nominalism, and separation of Theology and Philosophy).

Modern Writers.—*Melancthon's* Moral Philosophy, &c., &c.; *Ramus's* Logic; *Gassendi's* works, reviving and modifying the Epicurean Philosophy; *Bacon's* Novum Organum, &c., &c.; *Des Cartes's* Discourse upon Method, Meditations, and Principia; also his Logic, lately published by Cousin; *Hobbes's* Leviathan; *Gale's* Court of the Gentiles; *Cudworth's* Intellectual System; *Malebranche's* Search of Truth; *Arnauld's* Art of Thinking, and True and False Ideas; *Pascal's* Thoughts; *Spinoza's* Ethics; *Locke* on the Understanding; *Stillingfleet's* Criticism of Locke; *Butler's* Analogy, &c.; *Berkeley's* Minute Philosopher, &c.; *Leibnitz's* Tracts; *Edwards* on the Will; *Reid's* Essays; *Smith's* Moral Sentiments; *Stewart's* Elements, Essays, &c.; *Brown's* Philosophy; *Mackintosh's* History of Ethical Philosophy; *Cousin's* Psychology; *Jouffroy's* Essays; *Kant's* Criticism of Pure Reason, with Fichte, Hegel, and Schelling; *Tenneman's* History of Philosophy; *Brucker's* or Enfield's do.; Epitome of the History of Philosophy, translated from the French by *C. S. Henry;* and *Whewell's* Philosophy of the Inductive Sciences.

3. POLITICAL PHILOSOPHY.

"And for matter of policy or government, that learning should rather hurt than enable thereunto is a thing very improbable. We see it is accounted an error to commit a natural body to empiric physicians, which commonly have a few pleasing receipts, whereupon they are confident and adventurous, but know neither the causes of diseases, nor the complexions of patients, nor peril of accidents, nor the true method of cures. We see it is a like error to rely upon advocates or lawyers, which are only men of practice, and not grounded in their books; who are many times easily surprised when matter falleth out besides their experience, to the prejudice of the cause they handle: so, by like reason, it cannot be but a matter of doubtful consequence if states be managed by empiric statesmen, not well mingled with men grounded in learning. But contrariwise, it is almost without instance contradictory, that ever any government was disastrous that was in the hands of learned governors."—BACON.

1. *Theoretical Politics.*—*Plato's* Republic; *Xenophon's* Cyropædia; *Aristotle's* Politics; *Machiavelli's* Prince and Discourses on Livy; Anti-Machiavelli of *Frederic the Great*; *Languest's* Vindiciæ contra Tyrannos; *Mariana's* De Rege et Regis Institutione; *Hobbes's* De Cive and Leviathan; *Buchanan's* De Jure Regni; *Bodin's* Republic; *More's* Utopia; *Grotius's* De Jure Belli et Pacis; *Puffendorf's* Elements; *Locke's* two Treatises on Government; *Harrington's* Oceana; *Sidney* on Government; *Rousseau's* Contrat Social; *Salmasius's* Defensio pro Carolo I.; Answer by *Milton*; *Milton's* ready and easy way to establish a free Commonwealth; *Wolf's* Jus Naturæ; *Ferguson* on Civil Society; *Hume's* Essays; *Montesquieu's* Spirit of Laws; *Chas. Compte* on Legislation; *Bentham* on Morals and Legislation; *Dahlman's* Politics (German); *Livingston's* Introduction to the Louisiana Code; *Lucas* on Common Law; and *Beccaria* on Criminal Law.

2. *International Law and Relations.*—*Rutherford's* Institutes (as well as *Grotius*, *Puffendorf*, &c., &c.); *Vattel's* Le Droit des Gens; *G. F. Von Marten's* Precis du Droit des Gens Moderns de l'Europe, and Diplomatic History; *Charles Marten's* Causes Célébres du Droit des Gens; *Koch's* Abrégé de l'Histoire des Traités de Paix, &c., &c., in Europe; Cours de Style Diplomatique; *Wheaton's* Law of Nations.

3. *Constitutional Law.*—*Sismondi's* Etudes sur les Constitutions; *R. Constant* on Constitutions; *La Croix's* Constitutions of the Principal States of Europe and of the United States; *Von Marten's* Collection of the most important Fundamental Laws (German); *Dumont* on Legislation; *Fritot's*

Science of the Publicist (French); The Federalist; *Adams* on the American Constitutions; *Story* on the Constitution of the United States; *Madison* Papers, &c., &c., &c.

Political Economy.—*Stuart's* Inquiry (an exposition of the Mercantile System); *Quesnay's* Tableau Economique, &c., &c. (an exposition of the Agricultural System); *Turgot's* Recherchées sur les richesses, &c., &c.; *Smith's* Wealth of Nations; *Say's* Political Economy; *Storch's* Cours d'Economie Politique; *Sismondi's* Nouveaux Principes; and *Franklin, Hamilton, Ricardo, Malthus, Senior, Whateley, M'Culloch*, &c., &c., &c.

4. POLITE LITERATURE.

"No doubt the philosopher, with his learned definitions, be it of virtues or vices, matters of public or private government, replenisheth the memory with many infallible grounds of wisdom, which, notwithstanding, lie dark before the imagination and judging power, if they be not illuminated or figured forth by the speaking picture of poesy."—SIR P. SIDNEY.

Our limits will permit us to notice only some of the leading English writers.

Earlier Poets.—Chaucer, Gower, Wyatt, Surrey, Spenser, Daniel, Shakspeare, Ben Jonson, Drayton, Beaumont and Fletcher, Waller, Milton, Cowley, Dryden, Otway.

Later Poets.—Prior, Swift, Congreve, Addison, Young, Pope, Gay, Thomson, Johnson, Shenstone, Collins, Akenside, Goldsmith, Cowper, Crabbe, Burns, Rogers, Wordsworth, Scott, Coleridge, Southey, Lamb, Campbell, Byron, Shelley, Mrs. Hemans, Milman, Joanna Baillie, Tennyson.

Earlier Prose Writers.—Sir Thomas More, George Herbert, Sir P. Sidney, Selden's Table-Talk, Burton's Anatomy of Melancholy, Bacon's Essays, Hooker, Evelyn, Sir W. Raleigh, Jeremy Taylor, Hall, Barrow, South, Howe, Baxter, Dryden's Prefaces, Sir William Temple, Lady Russell's Letters, Cowley, Howell's Letters.

Later Prose Writers.—Addison, Steele, Swift, Gay, Pope, Bolingbroke, Richardson, Warburton, Hurd, Gray, Blair,

Walpole, Cumberland, Mackenzie, Burke, Hazlitt, Godwin, Walter Scott, Southey, Coleridge, Dennie, Ames, Wirt, Channing.*

5. MATHEMATICAL AND PHYSICAL SCIENCE.

"If a man's wit be wandering, let him study the mathematics; for in demonstrations, if his wit be called away never so little, he must begin again."—BACON.

"As tennis is a game of no use in itself, but of great use in respect it maketh a quick eye, and a body ready to put itself into all postures; so in the mathematics, *that use which is collateral and intervenient* is no less worthy than that which is principal and intended."—BACON.

A few authorities, who may be considered as classics, are mentioned.

Earlier Writers.—Euclid, Archimedes, Copernicus's *De Orbium Cœlestium revolutionibus*, Kepler's *Astronomia nova*, Pascal, Halley, Wallis, Huygens, Newton, Leibnitz, Des Cartes.

Later Writers.—Euler, D'Alembert, Lalande, Maclaurin, La Grange, La Place, Young, Gauss, Le Gendre, Herschel, Playfair, Simpson, Leslie.

Good Elementary Works for the Beginner.—In *Arithmetic*, Davies, Perkins, and Colburn. In *Algebra*, Davies, Perkins, and Bourdon. In *Geometry*, Brewster's Le Gendre and Trigonometry, or Playfair's Euclid. In *Conic Sections*, Jackson. In *Analytical Geometry*, Davies and Le Gendre. In *Descriptive Geometry*, Monge or Davies, Davies's Shades and Shadows. In *Differential and Integral Calculus*, Davies. In *Pure Mechanics*, Boucharlat. In *Physical Mechanics*, Whewell, Moseley's Illustrations, Lardner's Hydrostatics. In *Physics*, Bache's edition of Brewster's Optics, Bartlett's Optics, Fisher's Physics, Daniell's Introduction. In *Astronomy*, Biot, Norton, Herschel, Arago or Olmstead. Whewell's History of the Inductive Sciences.

* In this, the next, and several other departments, we omit *living* writers

6. CHEMISTRY AND NATURAL HISTORY.

"Nature never did betray
The heart that loved her; 'tis her privilege,
Through all the years of this our life, to lead
From joy to joy: for she can so inform
The mind that is within us, so impress
With quietness and beauty, and so feed
With lofty thoughts, that neither evil tongues,
Rash judgments, nor the sneers of selfish men,
Nor greetings where no kindness is, nor all
The dreary intercourse of daily life,
Shall e'er prevail against us, or disturb
Our cheerful faith, that all which we behold
Is full of blessing." . . . .

WORDSWORTH

(A.) CHEMISTRY.

Earlier Authors.—Roger Bacon, Boyle, Hooke, Stahl, Boerhaave, Black, Cavendish, Priestley, Bergman, Scheele, Lavoisier.

Later Authors.—Berthollet, Fourcroy, Klaproth, Vauquelin, Gay Lussac, Thenard, Wollaston, Davy, Dalton, Thompson, Berzelius, Faraday, Oken.

(B.) MINERALOGY AND GEOLOGY.

Mineralogy.—Agricola, Von Brommel, Linnæus, Pallas, Werner, Haüy, Mohs, Phillips, Jameson, Cleaveland, Brongniart, Leonhard, Dana, Shepard.

Geology.—Hooke, Whiston, Burnett, Hutton, Woodward, Werner, De Luc, Saussure, Playfair, Smith, Cuvier, Brongniart, Von Buch, Buckland, Sedgwick, Hitchcock, Lyell, Humboldt, Hausman, &c., &c., &c.

(C.) BOTANY.

Ancient Authors.—Theophrastus, Dioscorides, Pliny.

Earlier Modern Authors.—Parkinson, Gesner, Fuchs, Matthiolus, Lobelius, Clusius, Cæsalpinus, Bauhin, Ray, Morrison, Tournefort, Vaillant, Dillenius, Haller.

Later Modern Authors.—Linnæus, Jussieu, Wahlenberg, Robert Brown, Humboldt, Willdenow, De Candolle, Hooker, Lindley, Martius, Bentham, Endlicher, Kunth.

American Authors.—Cornutus, Plukenet, Clayton, Cutler, Muhlenberg, Michaux, Bigelow, Pursh, Torrey, Elliott, Nuttall, Eaton, Darlington, Gray, Beck.

(D.) ZOOLOGY.

Ancient Authors.—Aristotle, Pliny.

Modern Authors.—Gesner, Belon, Rondelet, Willoughby, Ray, Redi, Malpighi, Swammerdam, Linnæus, Buffon, Illiger, Blumenbach, Cuvier, Lacepede, Agassiz, Wilson, Bonaparte, Brongniart, Spence and Kirby, Daubenton, Ferussac, Home, Huber, Humboldt, Lacretelle, Selby, Sowerby, Swainson, Say, Audubon, Nuttall, Harlan.

(E.) NATURAL HISTORY OF NORTH AMERICA.

Godman's American Natural History; Richardson's Fauna; Wilson's, Bonaparte's, and Audubon's American Ornithology; Michaux, Colden, Barton, Bigelow, Nuttall, and Torrey on the Botany and Dendrology of North America; Cleaveland, Shepard, and Dana on Mineralogy; Maclure, Hitchcock, and Eaton on Geology; the Reports of Drs. Jackson, the brothers Rogers, Emmons, Mather, Vanuxen, and the Natural History of the State of New-York.

7. THEOLOGY.

"Our minister will not offer to God of that which costs him nothing, but takes pains aforehand with his sermons. Demosthenes never made any oration on the sudden; yea, being called upon, he never rose up to speak except he had well studied the matter; and he was wont to say that he showed how he honoured and reverenced the people of Athens, because he was careful what he spake to them."—Fuller.

(A.) GENERAL.

1. *Latin Fathers.*—Clement of Rome, Irenæus, Tertullian, Justin Martyr, Jerome, Ambrose, Augustine, Lactantius, Cyprian.

2. *Greek Fathers.*—Ignatius, Clement of Alexandria, Origen, Eusebius, Chrysostom, Athanasius, Basil, Gregory Nazianzen.

3. *Mediæval.*—Bede, Alcuin, Averroes, Aquinas, Thomas à Kempis, Duns Scotus, Wickliff, Albertus Magnus, Occam, Raymonde de Sebonde, Ficinus, Grosseteste.

4. *Modern.*—Erasmus, Luther, Cranmer, Melancthon, Hooper, Ridley, Calvin, Beza, Jewell, Chemnitz, Bellarmin, Paul Sarpi, Hooker, Plessis du Mornay, Claud, Laud, Grotius, Usher, Episcopius, Daillé, Chillingworth, Hammond, Jeremy Taylor, Baxter, Owen, Bossuet, Barrow, Tillotson, Bourdaloue, Bull, Stillingfleet, Whitby, Burnet, Turretin, Dupin, Fleury, Gill, Patrick, Secker, Mosheim, Campbell, Lowth, Horseley, Porteus, White, Dwight, &c., &c., &c.

(B.) BIBLICAL.

1. *Patristic.*—Origen's Commentaries and Scholia, preserved in part only; Chrysostom's Homilies on most of the Old and New Testaments; Theophylact's Scholia; Jerome's Commentary; Hilary on the Psalms and St. Matthew; St. Augustine's Commentary, and the various Catenæ.

2. *Rabbinical.*—Aben Ezra, David Kimchi, Abarbanel, Ben Maimon or Maimonides, Carpzovius.

3. *Mediæval.*—Bede's Catenæ; Alcuin's Commentary; Anselm's Glossary; Aquinas's Catenæ; Nicholas de Lyra's Postills.

4. *Modern.—General.*—Luther's Commentaries; Calvin's do.; Critici Sacri; Pool's Synopsis; Cocceius, Calmet, Hammond, Whitby, Patrick, Lowth, Matthew Henry, Gill, Adam Clarke, Bishop Hall, Wesley.

Particular.—Grotius, Schultens, Walton, Lightfoot, Leighton, Simon, Pococke, Lowth, Michaelis, Kennicott, Blayney, Bishop Percy, Vitringa, Newcome, Schleusner, Kuinoel, Jahn, Brettschneider, Jebb, Suicer, Griesbach, Gesenius, M'Knight, Bishop Horne, Rosenmüller, Ernesti, Castell, Lowman, Turretin, Witsius, Tholuc.

(C.) ECCLESIASTICAL HISTORY.

Socrates, Eusebius, Epiphanius, Sozomen, Theodoret, Gregory of Tours, Bede, Baronius, Budæus, Fox, Davanzati, Vossius, Chemnitz, The Centuriators, Usher, Calixtus, Bossuet, Spanheim, Fuller, Daillé, Stillingfleet, Tillemont, Bull, Burnet, Dupin, Witsius, Strype, Henry, Echard, Collier, Lardner, Jortin, Bingham, Fosbrooke, Beausobre, L'Enfant, Gibbon, Wall, Mosheim, Milner, Lingard, Southey, Gieseler, Neander, Ranke.

(D.) ELEMENTARY COURSE FOR CANDIDATES FOR THE MINISTRY.

1. *Biblical Learning.*—Horne's Introduction, a general work, covering the whole ground, vols. ii., iii., and iv.

(*a.*) *Grammatical*, &c., &c.—Stewart's Hebrew Grammar and Chrestomathy, or Nordheimer's Hebrew Grammar; Gesenius's Lexicon of the Old Testament (translated by Gibbs); Stewart's Grammar of the New Testament; Wahl's Lexicon of the New Testament, translated by Robinson, or the Lexicons of Brettschneider and Schleusner; Septuaginta (Boss or Van Ess), and Schleusner's Septuaginta Lexicon.

(*b.*) *Biblical Hermeneutics.*—Marsh's Lectures; Stewart's Ernesti, Morus and Keil's Hermeneutica; Campbell's Dissertations (preliminary to his translation of the Gospels); Planck's Introduction (translated by Professor Turner); Gerard's Institutes; Lowth's Hebrew Poetry; Herder's ditto; Jebb's Sacred Literature.

(*c.*) *Biblical Archæology.*—Jahn's Archæology (translated by Upham); Butler's Classical Geography; Robinson's Calmet; Wells's Sacred Geography; Harris's Natural History of the Bible; Paxton's Illustrations of Scripture; Harmer's Observations; Pococke's Travels; Modern Traveller; Robinson's Travels, &c., &c.

(*d.*) *Interpretation.*—Jahn's Introduction to the Old Testament (translated by Turner); Hug's Introduction to the New

Testament (translated at Andover); Marsh's Michaelis; Carpzov and Walton; Pool's Synopsis and Annotations; Patrick, Lowth, and Whitby; Calvin's Commentaries; Mant and D'Oyley's Bible; Henry's Commentary; Doddridge's Expositor; M'Knight on the Epistles; Stewart on Hebrews and Romans; Leighton on St. Peter; Horne, Horseley, and Good on the Psalms; Wesley's Notes; Adam Clarke's Commentary; Rosenmüller's Scholia; Kuinoel's Commentary; Campbell on the Gospels; Newcome's and Muenscher's Harmony of the Gospels; Michaelis and Warburton on the Laws of Moses, Tholuck, &c., &c.; Horsley, Hurd, Newton, and Keith on the Prophecies.

2. *Sacred and Ecclesiastical History.*—Turner's Sacred History; Josephus, Shuckford, and Prideaux's Connexions; Jahn's Hebrew Commonwealth; Basnage's History of the Jews; Eusebius, Kay, Burton, Neander, Mosheim, Milner, and Burnet's Histories; Wall's History of Infant Baptism, and Gale's Reply; Magdeburg Centuriators and Annals of Baronius; Muenscher's Manual of Dogmatic History.

3. *Systematic Theology.*—Butler's Analogy; Paley's Natural Theology, with the Dissertations of Brougham, Bell, &c., &c. (and reference to D. Stewart, Hume, Dr. Reid, and Dr. S. Clark); Leland's Necessity of Revelation, and Views of Deistical Writers; Paley's Evidences, and Horæ Paulinæ; Campbell and Hume on Miracles; Leslie's Short and Easy Method; Homilies of the Church of England; Pearson on the Creed; Calvin's Institutes; Burnet on the Thirty-nine Articles; White's Comparative View, &c., &c.; Turretin; Magee on the Atonement; Smith's S. S. Testimony to the Messiah; Hengstenberg's Christology; Watson's Institutes; Dwight's Theology; Leucke (German), &c.

4. *Homiletics*, &c., &c.—Claude on the Composition of a Sermon; Maury's Principles of Eloquence; Burnet on the Pastoral Care; Baxter's Reformed Pastor; Wilson's Parochialia.

8. MEDICINE.

"To be a physician, let a man read Galen and Hippocrates; but when he practises he must apply his medicines according to the temper of those men's bodies with whom he lives, and have respect to the heat and cold of climes; otherwise, that which in Pergamus, where Galen lived, was physic, in our cold climate may be poison."—SELDEN'S *Table-Talk.*

Ancient and Mediæval Authors.—Hippocrates, Aristotle, Cælius Aurelianus, Celsus, Galen, Avicenna, Avenzoar, Averroes, Mondino.

Modern Authors.—Plater, Sennert, Paracelsus, Willis, Sydenham, Harvey, Borelli, Mead, Stahl, Hoffman, Boerhaave, Haller, Cullen, Brown, Darwin, Hunter, Bichat, Heberden, Fothergill, Rush, Currie, Bell, Wistar, Gregory, J. M. Good, Astley Cooper, Abernethy, Charles Bell, &c., &c.

ELEMENTARY AUTHORS, FOR THE STUDENT AND YOUNG PRACTITIONER.

Anatomy.—Horner's Special and General Anatomy; Bell's (John and Charles) Anatomy and Physiology; Dublin Dissector, or Manual of Anatomy; Meckel's General, Descriptive, and Pathological Anatomy; Paxton's Introduction to the Study of Human Anatomy; Sarlandier's Anatomical Plates and Tables; Becklard's General Anatomy; Bichat's Anatomy, applied to Physiology and Medicine; Horner's Pathological Anatomy; Andral's ditto; Edwards's Manual of Surgical Anatomy; Parson's Directions for making Anatomical Preparations.

Physiology.—Dunglison's Human Physiology; Jackson's Principles of Medicine, founded on the Organism; Edwards's Anatomy and Physiology; Müller's Physiology; Magendie's Physiology; Roget's Animal and Vegetable Physiology.

Surgery.—Gibson's Institutes and Practice of Surgery; Abernethy's Lectures; Bourgery on Minor Surgical Operations; Sir Astley Cooper's Lectures; Doane's Surgery Illustrated; Cooper's Dictionary of Practical Surgery; Bell's Principles of Surgery; Liston's ditto.

Therapeutics and Pathology.—Dunglison's General Therapeutics; Eberle's Practice of Medicine; Armstrong's Lectures; Good's Study of Medicine.

Obstetrics.—Déwees's Midwifery; Meigs's Practice of Midwifery; Ramsbotham's Practical Observations.

Materia Medica.—Chapman's Elements; Eberle's Materia Medica; Wood's Dispensatory of the United States.

Medical Jurisprudence, &c., &c.—Beck's Medical Jurisprudence; Ryan's Manual of do.; Kane's Elements of Chemistry; Dunglison's New Medical Dictionary; Hooper's Lexicon; Combe's Physiology applied to the Preservation of Health; Gregory's Duties and Qualifications of a Physician; Dunglison's Medical Student.

Note.—In the opinion of an experienced physician, who has kindly furnished the following hints, medical students commit two or three important mistakes in preparing for their profession. 1. In the country, they enter an office and read medical works for one or two years before attending lectures. This is too long. It should not be more than *three* or *six months.* During this time, if the student has access to a skeleton, he can study with profit the *anatomy of the bones.* To read the anatomy of the nerves, muscles, bloodvessels, &c., &c., at this stage of his studies, is almost a waste of time. He should endeavour, also, during the same time, to gain some acquaintance with *Botany* and *Materia Medica.* 2. Students read too much without the aid of ocular demonstration. In materia medica, for example, they should never proceed without a specimen of the article before them; they will thus become familiar, at least, with the sensible properties of medicine. 3. They consider it a drudgery to compound the medical prescriptions of their preceptor. They ought rather to regard it as a privilege; and it would be useful if the preceptor would always write out his prescriptions in Latin, so as to familiarize the pupil with the proper *names* of medicines. Says Dr. Dunglison, "Perhaps the most proper work to be placed in the student's hands (during the first year of office study) would be a treatise on Physiology, which contains sufficient anatomy to enable him to acquire the terms, and to have a general idea of the structure and functions of the different parts of the organism. If he possesses but a slight acquaintance with chemistry, general anatomy, or the anatomy of the textures, can be studied at this period almost as well as at any other."

To Dr. Dunglison's work, entitled "The Medical Student," every one should have recourse who wishes to become a well-read and thoroughly-accomplished physician.

A learned physician of England gives one caution which is equally applicable to all the professions. "They have," says he, "one way of glorifying themselves, which is common to all. It is by setting forth a vast array of preparatory studies, and pretending they are indispensable in order to fit a man for the simple exercise of the practical duties that belong to them. I once saw a list of books recommended by a professor of divinity to the study of those going into holy orders. They were more numerous than the majority even of studious men ever read in their whole lives; yet these were a few prolegomena, introductory to the office of a parish priest. We, too, conceive that it befits our dignity to magnify ourselves at certain seasons. The commencement of a session (of lectures) is usually the time chosen; and then what a crowd of wonderful things are marshalled, by authority, round the entrance of our profession! and through this crowd, it is implied, every man must press his way before he can obtain admission. . . . . . . Now I do protest, in the name of common sense, against all such proceedings as this. . . . . It is a truth, that the whole circle of the sciences is required to comprehend a single particle of matter; but the most solemn truth of all is, that '*the life of man is threescore years and ten.*' You may *recommend* that every man, before he enters the study of physic, shall obtain the best general education within his reach, but you must specify nothing as absolutely necessary but what bears immediately upon his profession."

9. LAW.

"Melancholy and untrue is the picture which they draw of the legal study who represent its prominent features to be those of subtlety and impudence, and of labour dry and barren; rather would I compare it to a mountain, steep and toilsome on its first approaches, but easy and delightful in its superior ascent, and whose top is crowned with a rich and lasting verdure."—RAITHBY, *Study and Practice of the Law.*

CIVIL LAW.

Earlier Authors.—*Pomponius* (Enchiridion), *Tribonian* (Institutes, Pandects, &c.), *Hottoman; Vinius* on the Institutes; *Voet* on the Pandects; *Persius* on the Code; Leibnitz, Godefroy, Cujacius.

Later Authors.—Heineccius, Pothier, Barbeyrac, Eichhorn, Hugo, Savigny, Feurbach, Mittelmayer, Thibaut, Mühlenbruch; *Goëschen's* Institutes of Gaius; *Mackelday's* Institutes; *Livingston's* Introduction to the Code of Louisiana; *Schweppe's* History of Roman Law.

COMMON LAW.

Earlier Authors.—Glanville, Bracton, Fortescue (all on the laws of England); Littleton on Tenures; Lord Bacon, Coke, Shepherd's Touchstone (by Doddridge).

Later Authors.—Hale, Gilbert, Wood, Hawkins, Bacon, Blackstone, Sanders, Cruise, Sugden, Comyn, Viner, &c., &c., &c.

ELEMENTARY COURSE.

Preliminary.—1. *Writers on the Study of Law, viz.:* Blackstone on the Study of the Law; Hoffman's Course; Warren's Law Studies; Wynne's Eunomus. 2. *Historical Writers.*—Hume generally; Kent's 1st volume, from x.–xvth. Lectures, for a history and sketch of the Constitution of the United States; Appendix II. to Hume's History for a sketch of the Feudal System; the introductory chapter to 4th volume of Blackstone's Commentaries on do., and Hallam's Middle Ages (chapter xi., parts i. and ii.). For the Constitutional History of England, read last chapter in Blackstone, Gilbert Stuart's Discourse on the Laws and Government of England, prefixed to Sullivan's Lectures, Hallam's Middle Ages (chapter viii., parts i., ii., iii.), and Hallam's Constitutional History; also Reeve's History of English Law.

I add *three* different courses of law-reading, which seem to be founded on different principles, and each of which is the result of much experience in the profession. The first was published anonymously several years since in New-York, and is understood to have proceeded from the hands of John Anthon, Esq.; the second is compiled from the "Law Studies" of Mr. Warren; for the third I am indebted to the eminent Royall professor of law in Harvard University (Hon. S. Greenleaf).

1.

Vattel's Law of Nations, with Grotius.

Blackstone's Commentaries on the Laws of England, to which ought now to be added Kent's Commentaries on American Law.

Woodeson's Lectures on the Laws of England.

Wood's Institutes, with Hale's History of the Common Law.

Reperusal of Blackstone, with Christian's Notes.

Reeve's History of the English Law, in connexion with a reperusal of Hume.

Coke upon Lyttleton.

Reperusal of Blackstone, with Tucker's Notes on American Law.

Cruise's Digest of the Law of Real Property.

Reperusal of Coke upon Lyttleton, with special attention to Hargrave and Butler's Notes.

Shepherd's Touchstone on Common Assurances.

Saunders on Uses and Trusts.

Espinasse's Digest of the Law of Nisi Prius.
Comyn on Contracts.
Chitty, Baily, and Kyd, on Bills of Exchange.
Abbott on Shipping.
Marshall and Park on Insurance.
Brown's Treatise on the Civil Law.
Appendix to Sellon's Practice.
Gilbert's Common Pleas Practice.
The 3d volume of Blackstone.
Sellon's Practice, Tidd's do., with Anthon's Appendix. (Archbold on Practice has appeared since.)
Chitty on Pleading.
Hale's and Hawkins's Crown Law.
Peake's Compendium of the Law of Evidence.
M'Nally's Rules of Evidence. (The works of Phillips, Greenleaf, and Starkie have since superseded the above.)
Reading of Reports.

Note.—It should be remembered that the above course was drawn up previous to 1810, since which time many valuable works have been published, and the Law itself has undergone some material changes. Mr. Anthon's course seems to be founded upon the idea of making the student acquainted first with the general principles of Law, and leading him afterward to the knowledge of practice.

The next course (Warren's) requires the student to cultivate practical and theoretical knowledge together, beginning, however, with the former. Mr. W. holds that a knowledge of the *machinery* of the Law is indispensable, in order to a proper understanding of its *principles* and *terms*.

2.

1. Elementary Treatise on Pleading (Stephens), with Saunders on Pleading and Practice.
2. Elementary Treatise on Practice (Tidd and Archbold), with reference to the 1st part of Stephens.
3. Chitty's Pleading.

4. After, or at the same time with the above, 2d volume of Blackstone on Real and Personal Property.

5. Selwyn's Nisi Prius.

6. Pothier on Contracts; Chitty do.

7. Phillips or Starkie on Evidence, (the first dwells more on Practice, the second on Principles). Reference must be made during this time to Chitty on Contracts, Selwyn's Nisi Prius, &c., &c.

8. Blackstone's 2d volume, with Watkins on Conveyancing, and Burton's Law of Real Property, and reference to Coke upon Lyttleton.

9. Cruise's Digest, Woodfall on Landlord and Tenant, Adams on Ejectment.

10. Smith's Compendium of Mercantile Law, with reference to Chitty on Bills of Exchange, and Comyn on Contracts. (Savigny's History of Roman Law in the Middle Ages may be added.)

11. Williams on Executors, Shepherd's Touchstone.

12. Saunders's Reports, Harrison's Digest.

13. Chitty, General Practice of the Law.

Note.—The following American works will claim the attention of students in this country, viz., Story on the Constitution of the United States; also on Bailments, on Agency, on the Conflict of Laws, &c., &c.; Greenleaf on Evidence; the copious and valuable notes of Cowen and Hill appended to Phillips on Evidence; Curtis on Conveyances; Phillips on Insurance; Rand's edition of Long on Personal Property (Sales); Barbour on Criminal Law, &c.

GREENLEAF'S COURSE OF LEGAL STUDY ABRIDGED.

3.

PRELIMINARY STUDIES.

Regular Course.	Parallel Course.
Blackstone's Commentaries.	Letters on the Study of the Law.

Regular Course	Parallel Course.
	Eunomus.
	Reeve's History of English Law.
Kent's Commentaries.	Hoffman's Legal Course.

DOMESTIC SOCIAL RELATIONS.

The proper titles in Bacon's Abridgment.	Reeve's Domestic Relations.
Bingham on Infancy.	Bingham on Coverture.
Story on Partnership.	Collinson on Idiots and Lunatics.
Story on Agency.	Shelford on Lunatics, &c., &c.
Story on Bailments.	Livermore on Agents.
Angell and Ames on Corporations.	Collier on Partnership.
	Kyd on Corporations.

TITLE TO THINGS PERSONAL, BY

1. *Occupancy.*

2 Blackstone's Com., ch. xxvi.
2 Kent's Comm., lect. xxxvi.

2. *Succession.*

2 Blackstone's Com., ch. xxix.

3. *Marriage.*

2 Blackstone's Com., ch. xxix.
2 Kent's Comm., lect. xxviii.

4. *Judgment.*

2 Blackstone's Com., ch. xxix.
2 Kent's Comm., lect. xxxvii.

5. *Contract.*

Chitty on Contracts.	Comyn on Contracts, 2d edition.
Story on Bills.	Chitty on Bills.
	Shepherd's Touchstone, title "Obligations."

6. *Testament and Administration.*

Williams on Executors.	Toller on Executors.

7. *Prize of War.*

Wheaton on Captures.

PERSONAL REMEDIES.

Regular Course.	Parallel Course.
Montagu on Lien.	Selwyn's Nisi Prius.
Starkie on Slander.	Kyd on Awards.
1 Maddock's Chancery, ch. 1 to 7 inclusive.	Holt on Libels.
Newland on Contracts.	Encyclopædia Americana, title "Equity."

REAL PROPERTY.

Regular Course.	Parallel Course.
Angell on Watercourses.	Coke upon Lyttleton.
Angell on Adverse Enjoyment.	Woodfall's Landlord and Tenant.
Cruise's Digest (proper titles).	Powell on Devises.
Bacon's Abridgment, title "Leases."	Sugden's Vendors.
Bacon's Abridgment, title "Fines and Recovery."	

PLEADINGS AND PRACTICE AT COMMON LAW

Regular Course.	Parallel Course.
Chitty on Pleading.	Gould on Pleading.
Stephens on Pleading.	Graham's Practice in New York.
Bacon's Abridgment, these titles, viz., Amendment, Nonsuit, Juries, Trial, Verdict, Damages, Costs, Bills of Exceptions, Scire facias, Escape, Rescue, Bail, Summons and Severance, Tender.	Paine's and Duer's Practice in New-York.
	Howe's Practice in Massachusetts.
	Robinson's Practice in Virginia.
	Troubat and Haly's Practice in Pennsylvania.
	Hammond on Parties.

PLEADINGS AND PRACTICE IN EQUITY.

Regular Course.	Parallel Course.
Maddock's Chancery, ch. viii. to the end.	Fonblanque's Treatise of Equity.
Hoffman's Chancery Practice and Master.	
Jeremy on Equity.	
Eden on Injunctions.	
Story on Equity Pleadings.	

MARITIME LAW.

Regular Course.	Parallel Course.
Abbott on Shipping.	Chitty on Commerce and Manufactures.
Marshall on Insurance.	Curtis on Merchant Seamen.
Philips on Insurance.	

LAW OF EVIDENCE.

Regular Course.	Parallel Course.
Greenleaf's Evidence. Phillips's Evidence, with Cowen and Hill's notes.	

CRIMINAL LAW.

Russell on Crimes.	Chitty's Criminal Law. Archbold's Pleading and Ev idence.

CONSTITUTIONAL LAW.

American Constitutions. Story's Commentaries. Kent's Commentaries, 1st vol.	The Federalist. Rawle on the Constitution.

CIVIL LAW.

Justinian's Institutes.	Pothier on Obligations. Domat's Civil Law, select titles.

LAW OF NATIONS.

Wheaton's Law of Nations. Story on the Conflict of Laws.	Vattel's Law of Nations. Kent's Commentaries, 1st vol.

Note.—Finding it impossible to transfer the whole of Professor Greenleaf's valuable *course* to these pages, the compiler has availed himself of the aid of a professional friend in digesting from it an abridgment, and it is proper to add that the abridgment has been made principally from the first edition. A new and amended edition has just been published.

PART II.

STANDARD AUTHORS

IN

ANCIENT AND MODERN LITERATURE.

"Out of the old fieldes, as men saith,
Cometh all this new corn fro' year to year;
And out of old bookes, in good faith,
Cometh all this new science that men lere."

CHAUCER.

PRINCIPLES.

THE following *principles* have been kept in view in selecting the writers noticed in this *part*.

1. To group them together according to the usual method, and without any attempt at refinement in classification.

2. To arrange the groups according to the *chronological* order in which different branches of literature were developed. Hence Poetry is placed first, Philosophy next, then History, and so on. A different order was proper in the *third* part.

3. Generally to assign each author to the time of his birth rather than to the more doubtful one at which he wrote.

4. To select those who have exerted the greatest influence on the progress of the human mind, but without attempting a complete enumeration, especially of those in recent times.

5. To omit, generally, those whose writings are not now extant, at least in part.

6. To make the enumeration more complete in the departments of Literature, History, and Philosophy, than in those of Physical Science, Politics, and Theology.

7. To omit, for the most part, all *living* writers.

8. To encourage *original* research and investigation.

To those who are engaged in collecting original works, the compiler would respectfully suggest (if their means allow) the expediency, 1. Of endeavouring to make some one department or subdivision of a department *complete* in the best works, best editions, &c. 2. Of ultimately depositing such department in some public library, where it can be made extensively useful to scholars. 3. Of binding up and depositing, from time to time, in some public library, copies of pamphlets, files of newspapers, &c., which exhibit the very body and pressure of the time. These will be precious materials for the future historian. Says Lord Somers, "The bent and genius of the age is best known in a free country by the pamphlets which daily come out, as containing the sense of parties, and sometimes the voice of the nation."

"Rules for the formation of a library must be dependant on the taste of the age, and the purpose for which it is designed, whether private or public. Hence few of those laid down by Gabriel Naudé, in his *Avis pour dresser une Bibliothèque*, are now applicable with respect to the selection of works. Nevertheless, there are authors, historians, moralists, and explorers of natural phenomena who will be always prized, because their writings are founded on immutable truth. Some collectors have addicted themselves to the early editions, to certain sciences, to arts and trades; to works whose chief embellishments are engravings, or to those merely printed on a large size of paper. It is by the union of all these peculiarities that a great public library is formed. But its basis ought to rest on original works of truth, for they alone are the source of knowledge; commentators and critics hold a secondary place; and works of fiction may be introduced for amusement. The extent of a library is indefinite. One of the ancients, celebrated for his learning, is said to have possessed only four volumes. Leibnitz declares that his library had no more than the works of Plato, Aristotle, Archimedes, Euclid, Plutarch, Sextus Empiricus, Pliny, Cicero, and Seneca. Leiglet du Fresnoy makes a calculation, whereby it appears that no one can read above 900 folio volumes in his life; from all which is deduced the inutility of extensive libraries. *These remarks will not apply to those collections destined for public use;* but the words of Seneca should never be forgotten: 'Non refert quam multos libros, sed quam bonos habeas,' inferring that the quality of books, not their number, is the primary condition."—DALZELL.

STANDARD AUTHORS.

I. POETS.

(A.) ANCIENT.

GREEK POETS.

Orpheus, 1250 B.C.

Most of the poems ascribed to him are productions of later times, composed at different periods.—*Eschb.*

The best edition is that of Herman, Lips., 1805, 2 vols. 8vo. The best translation is that of Taylor, 1787, 8vo.

Homer, 1000 B.C.

(See third part.) Best edition, Samuel Clarke, London, 1815, 4 vols. 4to.

Hesiod, 950 B.C.

As a poet he is inferior to Homer, but his poems are valuable, as they make known to us so much respecting the conceptions and modes of thinking which prevailed in a high antiquity upon various subjects.—*Eschb.*

Best edition, Chr. Fr. Loesner, Greek and Latin, Lips., 1778, 8vo. Best translation, Ch. Ab. Elton, London, 1812.

Archilochus, 680 B.C.

He wrote lyric poetry, and was ranked among the greatest poets of Greece, and generally supposed the inventor of iambic verse.—*Eschb.*

His remaining fragments were published by Ign. Liebel, Lips., 1819.

Sappho, 612 B.C.

A lyric poetess, from whom the verse termed Sapphic takes its name.—*Eschb.*

F

Best edition, A. Moebius, Hanover, 1815, 8vo. For translation, see Addison's Spectator, Nos. 223, 229.

Anacreon, 536 B.C.

He was a lyric poet, and wrote in that light kind of ode, of which love, social pleasures, and wine form the subjects. —*Eschb.*

Best edition, Jo. Frid. Fischer, Lips., 1793, 8vo. Best translation, Thos. Bourne, Harper & Brothers, New-York, in one volume, with Pindar, 45 cents.

Pindar, 490 B.C.

(See third part.) The best edition, Aug. Böckh, Greek and Latin, Lips., 1811, 12mo, $1 50.

Æschylus, 490 B.C.

(See third part.) Best edition, Scholefield, Cambr., 1828, 8vo. Æschylus, Sophocles, Euripides, translated by R. Potter. 18mo, $1 00.

Euripides, 480 B.C.

(See third part.) Best edition, Greek and Latin, cum notis variorum, 9 vols. 8vo, Glasgow, 1821, $16 50.

Sophocles, 450 B.C.

(See third part.) Best edition, Samuelis Musgravii, 2 vols. 8vo, $4 50.

Aristophanes, 430 B.C.

(See third part.) Best edition, Comœdiæ and perditarum fragmenta, Greek and Latin, cum indicibus, 8vo, $3 50. Paris, 1838 Best translation, R. Potter, London, 1783, 2 vols. 4to.

Theocritus, 275 B.C.

He was the most distinguished ancient author in the department of pastoral poetry.—*Eschb.*

Best edition, Th. Kiessling, 8vo, 1819, Lips., $3 00. Best translation, E. B. Greene, London, 1767–8.

Callimachus, 260 B.C.

Quintilian ranks him as the first elegiac poet of the Greeks.—*Eschb.*

Best edition, Ernesti, Greek and Latin, Lug. Bat., 1761, 2 vols. 8vo. Best translation, H. W. Tytler, Greek and English, London, 1793–4.

Apollonius Rhodius, 125 B.C.

His chief work is an epic poem on the *Expedition of the Argonauts*, which evinces great application, and has some beautiful passages.—*Eschb.*

Best edition, Wellauer, Lips., 1828, 2 vols. 8vo. Best translation, Fr. Fawkes, London, 1780, 2 vols. 8vo.

LATIN POETS.

Livius Andronicus, 230 B.C.

He was the first dramatic writer among the Romans, and introduced the first play on the stage.—*Eschb.*

But few fragments of his works remain.

Quintus Ennius, 232 B.C.

He contributed much to the improvement of the Latin language, and was the first epic poet in it, and highly valued even by later and better writers.—*Eschb.*

M. Accius Plautus, 200 B.C.

He possessed very happy talents for a comic writer, a rich flow of excellent wit, happy invention, and all the force of comic expression.—*Eschb.*

Best edition, J. Naudet, Paris, 4 vols. Best translation, Bonnel Thornton, London, 1769, 5 vols., $4 00.

P. Terentius Afer, 200 B.C.

His six comedies, still extant, are in every respect excellent, both in regard to the characters, the consistency, and refinement of the dialogue, and the judicious management of the plot.—*Eschb.*

Best edition, Frid. Lindenbrogii, Lond., 1820, 2 vols. 8vo. Best translation, George Colman, Lond., 1765.

C. Lucilius, 105 B.C.

With a great knowledge of language he combined a great talent for satire, of which he was the founder among the Romans.—*Eschb.*

Best edition, Patavii, Jos. Cominus, 1735, 8vo, $1 25.

T. Lucretius Carus, 90 B.C.

He wrote a philosophical poem on the Nature of Things, which represents the philosophy of the Epicurean sect in its most imposing features. The composition in particular passages is very rich in scenery, and florid, and bursts, at turns, like the lightning from a cloud.—*Eschb.*

Best edition, D. Brown, Edinb., 1812. Best translation, J M. Good, 2 vols., Lond., 1805.

Albius Tibullus.

He combined soft, tender feeling, with the noblest and most expressive diction, with the most elegant variety of invention, of images and allusions, without any far-fetched art and unnatural ornament of style.—*Eschb.*

Transl., James Granger, 2 vols. 12mo, $1 75, London, 1720.

Sextus Aurelius Propertius, 701 A.U.

The chief merits of his remaining elegiac poems are passionate expression, rich poetical diction, and correctness of style; but he often transgresses the limits of nature and decorum, and is too prodigal in the use of poetical ornament. —*Eschb.*

Best edition, Tibulli and Propertii opera, ex editione J. Broukhusii fideliter expressa, 18mo, $2 25, Glasgow, 1753.

Publius Virgilius Maro, 684 A.U.

He was the greatest of the Roman poets in pastoral, didactic, and epic poetry.—*Eschb.*

Best edition, Virgilii Opera, Heynii editio, quarto, 8 vols. 8vo, $50 00, Lips., 1830-39. Good edition, V. Opera notis ex editione Heyniana excerptis illustrata, 8vo, $6 50, Oxon., 1830. For translation, see third part.

Q. Horatius Flaccus, 688 A.U.

His satires and epistles converse with external and internal life, delineate man and human nature, and, while seeming to teach only the arts of luxurious living and courtly flattery, gently guide to a self-dependant life, adorned with arts and sciences.—*Wachler.*

Best edition, Horatius, recensuit et illustravit F. G. Döring, 8vo, $4 00, Oxon., 1838. For transl., see third part.

Catullus (Caius Valerius), born 86 B.C.

His poems are usually published with those of Tibullus

and Propertius. He was the friend of Cicero, Cinna, and Cornelius Nepos. He was the first of the Romans who imitated successfully the Greek lyric poetry. He succeeded also in heroic verse, but was most happy in epigrams and sportive composition. Martial, in one of his epigrams, grants to Catullus alone a superiority over himself. Two editions of his works, one by Volpius (Padua, 1737), the other by Döring, (Leipsic, 1788–90), deserve mention.

P. Ovidius Naso, 43 B.C.

His principal work is the "Fasti," as giving, in the familiar garb of light versification, a complete view of the connexion of the Roman state, religion, and history with daily life. His "Metamorphoses," a species of epic, has exercised a highly important influence on the arts and cultivation of more recent times.—*Wachler*.

Good edition, Ovidius Naso, ex recensione Heinsio—Burmanniana—Parisiis, 1820–24, 9 vols. Best translation, Dryden, Pope, Congreve, &c., &c., 2 vols., 90 cts. Harper & Brothers, New-York.

Marcus Manilius, 1st century.

His work "Astronomicon" is more valuable for the history of Astronomy it contains than for intrinsic poetical excellence.—*Eschb.*

Good edition, Richard Bentley, London, 1739, $2 75.

Phædrus, 1st century.

He is celebrated for his five books of Æsop's Fables, related with all the natural ease and simplicity of which fable is capable in a poetical dress.—*Eschb.*

Good edition, Fred. Henr. Bothe, Paris, 1821, $2 50.

Lucius Annæus Seneca, 1st century.

His tragedies are in general removed from the noble simplicity of Grecian tragedy, and are mostly of very defective plot and execution, though not without single poetical beauties.—*Eschb.*

Good edition, Torkill Baden, Lips., 1821, 2 vols., $3 75.

M. Valerius Martialis, end of the 1st century.

The most of his epigrams are uncommonly acute and appropriate; their multitude and proportionate excellence render the almost inexhaustible and always lively wit of this poet admirable.—*Eschb.*

Best edition, Martialis Epigrammata ad optimas editiones collata, 8vo, $1 62, Bipont, 1784.

Juvenal, 1st century.

He wrote 16 satires, in which he chastises the follies and vices of his times. His style is not so elegant, nor his disposition so mild and humorous as that of Horace, nor yet so gloomy and stern as that of Persius, and he often betrays the rhetorician.

Best edition, that of Henninius (Utrecht), 1685, 4to. Gifford's translation is very valuable.—*Enc. Am.*

Aurelius Prudentius, 4th century.

A Christian poet, whose hymns are distinguished for their good poetical expression, but still more for their pious and devotional contents.—*Eschb.*

Good edition, Rome, 1789, 2 vols.

(B.) MEDIÆVAL.

From the 5th to the 14th century.

1. FRENCH.

The Norman Alexander, 1180.

The Alexandrine verse derived its name from him.—*Eschb.*

Doëte de Troyes, 13th century.

A celebrated poetess.

Jean Froissart, 1337.

His poems are distinguished by the most graceful simplicity and loveliness.—*Enc. Am.*

Coinsi and Farsi.

These were two monks, who distinguished themselves by their moral and satirical *fabliaux*.

2. GERMAN.

The heroic songs, of which Tacitus speaks, are lost.

Ottfried's Harmony of the Gospels, 840.

It is the most important biblical poem. The language is rich and fluent, and the whole stands in high estimation. —*Wachler.*

It may be found in "Schill Thesaurus Antiquitatum Teutonicarum," Ulm., 1727, 3 vols., $3 75.

The earliest German ballad, 881,

celebrates the victory of Louis III. over the Normans; it is a beautiful production, breathing a poetical and pious spirit. —*Wachler*.

The Minnesingers,

amatory poets, who began with Henry of Veldeck (1170). The most celebrated are Wolfram of Eschenbach, Walter von der Vogelwaide, Henry of Ofterdingen, &c., &c.—*Enc. Am.*

L. Tieck has published two hundred and twenty poems, modernized, from that great collection, under the title of Minnelieder aus dem Schwabischen Zeitalter, Berlin, 1803.

The Niebelungenlied, 1207.

A romantic epic of great merit, both in regard to the plan and the execution. Characters are developed in it as in a drama of Shakspeare.—*Enc. Am.*

Best edition, Vonder Hagen, with notes, Frankfort on the Maine, 1824, 2 vols.

The Heldenbuch.

A celebrated collection of old German poems, drawn from national traditions of events which happened in the time of Attila and the irruption of the German nations into the Roman Empire.—*Enc. Am.*

"Heldenbuch in der Ursprache," Berlin, 1820-24, 2 vols., 4to.

3. ITALIAN.

Dante Alighieri, 1265.

(See third part.)

Cino da Pistoria, 1266.

He ranks among the best of the early Italian poets, and resembles Petrarca more than any of the other predecessors of this poet.—*Enc. Am.*

The most complete edition is that of Ciampi, Florence, 1812.

Petrarca.

(See third part.) Good edition, Padua, 1819-20, 2 vols., 4to.

Boccacio, 1313.

He appears, in all his productions, to be a poet of the richest invention, the most lively imagination, and the tenderest and warmest feeling.—*Enc. Am.*

3 vols. 8vo, $8 50.

4. SPANISH.

El Poema de Cid, 12th century.

This is a collection of ballads commemorating the deeds of a Spanish hero Cid, and is very striking for the simplicity and poetical colouring. A great number have been published in the Collection of the best Ancient Spanish Historical, Chivalrous, and Moorish Poems, by Depping (Altenburg and Leipzic, 1817).—*Enc. Am.*

El Poema de Alexandro Magno, 12th century.

Much inferior to the former.

5. ENGLISH.

Robert Langland, 14th century.

Author of the curious poems, "The Vision of Pierce Plowman," and "Pierce Plowman's Creed." They are satires on the vice and luxury of the monastic orders and Romish clergy in general. Editions have been published by Dr. T. D. Whitaker.—*Enc. Am.*

Chaucer, 14th century.

(See third part.)

John Gower, 14th century.

The language is tolerably perspicuous, and the versification often harmonious.—*Enc. Am.*

(C.) MODERN.

1. ENGLISH AND AMERICAN.

Alexander Barclay, 16th century.

He is remarkable for his "Ship of Fools," for the greater part a translation from the German.—*P. Enc.*

Sir Thomas Wyatt, 1503.

His poetical works evince more elegance of thought than imagination, while his mode of expression is artificial and laboured.—*Enc. Am.*

Henry Howard, Earl of Surrey, 1520.

As a poet he is very respectable. The harmony of his

numbers and the purity of his language have been deservedly commended by Pope and others.

His works, and those of Wyatt, edited by Dr. Nott, 2 vols. 4to, $10 00, London.

Thomas Sackville, 1527.

As a poet, he was the first who approached to perfection in the English heroic stanza, and gave the first example of regular tragedy in blank verse. The language is pure and perspicuous.—*Enc. Am.*

Spenser, 1553.

(See third part.) Whole poems, 5 vols. 12mo, $7 50.

Samuel Daniel, 1562.

He employed his brilliant talent in writing an epic on the most remarkable occurrences in the history of his country. He contributed much to the improvement of the poetical diction in England.—*P. Enc.*

Shakspeare, 1564.

(See third part.)

Ben Jonson, 1566.

He demands our particular notice, as the chief advocate and practiser, among the old English dramatists, of the imitation of the ancients.—*P. Enc.*

7 vols., $7 50.

George Chapman, 1568.

He possessed some poetical powers, and was a man of genius. He translated Homer.

12mo, $2 50.

Hall's Satires, 16th century.

Warton praises in them "a classical precision to which English poetry had yet rarely attained," and calls the versification "equally energetic and elegant."—*Hallam.*

8vo, $1 25.

Drayton, 1580.

His "Polyolbion" is a poem which, of the kind (topographical and legendary), probably never has been equalled in any other language, both in extent and elegance; nor can any one read a portion of it without admiration for its learned and highly gifted author. It contains thirty thousand lines, written in Alexandrine couplets.

8vo, $2 75.

Fairfax, 1580.

His reputation rests on his version of Tasso's "Godfrey of Bouillon." It is written in the same stanza with the original, and combines fidelity to the sense of the author with harmony of versification.—*Enc. Am.*

$5 00, London.

Drummond, 1585.

The sonnets of Drummond are polished and elegant, free from conceit and bad taste, in pure, unblemished English.—*Hallam.*

12mo, $1 50, London.

Beaumont and Fletcher, 1585 *and* 1576.

They were men of the most distinguished talents: "they hardly wanted anything but a more profound seriousness of mind, and that sagacity in art which observes a due measure in everything, to deserve a place beside the greatest dramatic poets of all nations."—*Schlegel.*

3 vols., 4to, $12 00.

Waller, 1605.

His verse is more polished and harmonious than that of any of the preceding or contemporary poets, but his compositions have a great deal of that quaintness and trifling witticism which was in fashion in his age, and he possesses no genius either for the sublime or pathetic.—*Tytler.*

4to, $2 75.

Fanshaw, 1607.

His poetry is far above mediocrity.—*Enc. Am.*

12mo, $1 50, London.

Milton, 1608.

(See third part.)

Cowley, 1618.

In his poems there is a redundancy of wit; yet many of his poetical pieces, where the subject restrained these faults, display the highest beauties.—*Tytler.*

2 vols. 8vo, $2 75.

Herrick, 1620.

The most amorous of our amorous poets. He has as much variety as the poetry of kisses can well have; but his love is in a slight degree that of sentiment; his mistress-

es have little to recommend them save their beauties, and none of these are omitted in his catalogues.—*Hallam.*
2 vols. 4to, $9 00.

Dryden, 1631.

(See third part.)

Wycherley, 1640.

A dramatic writer, remembered for two comedies, the "Plain Dealer" and "The Country Wife:" the latter has probably never been surpassed.—*Hallam.*
For edition, see Congreve.

Lee, 1650.

A dramatic writer, who, in spite of his proverbial extravagance, is a man of poetical mind and some dramatic skill. —*Hallam.*

Otway, 1651.

The "Orphan" of Otway and his "Venice Preserved" have both a deep pathos, springing from the intense and unmerited distress of woman; both have a dramatic eloquence, rapid and flowing, and sometimes with very graceful poetry. —*Hallam.*
2 vols. 8vo, $5 50.

Southern, 1660.

A dramatic writer, who deserves the praise of having first of any English writers denounced the traffic in slaves, and the cruelties of their West Indian bondage.—*Hallam.*
2 vols. 12mo, $2 50, London.

Prior, 1664.

As a poet his reputation has declined of late years, the humour in which he principally excels being overlooked on account of the character of his serious performances, which, although splendid and correct in diction, harmonious in versification, and copious in poetical imagery, fail in moving either the feelings or the fancy. His great art consists in telling a story with a degree of poetical ease and vivacity which perhaps never has been excelled.—*Enc. Am.*
2 vols. 8vo, $2 25.

Swift, 1667.

His style forms the most perfect example of easy familiarity that the language affords; but although admirable for its pureness, clearness, and simplicity, it exhibits none of the glow of genius, its highest merit consisting in its extreme accuracy and precision.—*Enc. Am.*

2 vols. 12mo, $3 75.

Congreve, 1670.

A dramatic writer, who, more than any preceding writer among us, kept up the tone of a gentleman; his men of the world are profligate, but not coarse; he gave, in fact, a tone of refinement to the public taste which it never lost.—*Hallam.*

Wycherley, Congreve, and other dramatic works, 1 vol. 8vo, $5 00, London.

Ambrose Philips, 1671.

The verses which he composed, not only to young ladies in the nursery, but to Walpole when minister of state, and which became known by the ludicrous appellation of namby-pamby, are easy and sprightly, but with a kind of infantile air which fixed upon them the above name.

Addison, 1672,

by a decent mediocrity of poetic language, rising occasionally to superior efforts, has deserved a high degree of praise. His celebrated tragedy of "Cato," equally remarkable for a correctness of plan, and a sustained elevation of style, was farther distinguished by the glow of its sentiments in favour of political liberty, and was equally applauded by both parties.—*Aikin.*

3 vols. 8vo, $5 50.

Rowe, 1673.

His principal efforts were in poetical translation, and his version of Lucan's "Pharsalia" has been placed among the greatest productions of English poetry.—*Aikin.*

2 vols. 12mo, $2 50, London.

Young, 1681.

(See third part.)

Pope, 1688.

(See third part.)

Gay, 1688.

His pictures of rural life were so extremely natural and amusing, and intermixed with circumstances so beautiful and touching, that his pastorals proved the most popular works of the kind in the language.—*Aikin.*

2 vols. 8vo, $2 00.

Thomson, 1700.

His poetical merit undoubtedly stands most conspicuous in his "Seasons." Its diction is somewhat cumbrous and laboured, but energetic and expressive. Its versification does not denote a practised ear, but is seldom unpleasantly harsh. Upon the whole, no poem has been more, and more deservedly, popular.—*Aikin.*

2 vols. 12mo, $2 50.

Fielding, 1707.

As a dramatic writer he did not generally succeed; for, although no man possessed a stronger feeling of the ridiculous, or executed detached scenes with greater humour, he took too little time to construct his dramas, with a view to plot and effective development.—*Enc. Am.*

8vo, $4 50.

Johnson, 1709.

No writer delivers moral maxims and dictatorial sentences with more force. He also excels in giving point to sarcasm, and magnificence to imagery and abstraction.—*Enc. Am.*

The deep and pathetic morality of the *Vanity of Human Wishes* (by Johnson) has often extracted tears from those whose eyes wander dry over pages professedly sentimental. —*Walter Scott.*

"I asked him," says James Ballantyne, speaking of W. Scott, "what was the poetry from which *he* derived most pleasure. He answered, Johnson's; that he had more pleasure in reading *London* and the *Vanity of Human Wishes* than any other poetical composition he could mention."

Lord Byron's Diary for 1821 contains the following entry: "Read Johnson's *Vanity of Human Wishes.* All the examples, and mode of giving them, sublime, as well as the latter part, with the exception of an occasional couplet. 'Tis a grand poem—and so *true!* true as the 10th of Juvenal himself." "Yet it is the cant of our day," adds Lockhart, "above all of its poetasters, that Johnson was no poet. To be sure, they say the same of Pope, and hint it occasionally even of Dryden."

Armstrong, 1709.

Of his "Art of Preserving Health" it may be affirmed that, of the class to which it belongs, scarcely any English performance can claim superior merit. Its topics are judiciously chosen from all those which can add grace or beauty to a difficult subject; and, as he was naturally gifted with a musical ear, his lines are scarcely ever harsh.—*Aikin.*

Shenstone, 1714.

His "School Mistress," written in Spenser's style, through the vein of benevolence and good sense, and the touches of the pathetic, by which this performance is characterized, it is rendered extremely pleasing, and he stands, perhaps, at the head of his competitors.—*Aikin.*

Garrick, 1716.

An actor and dramatic writer. As an actor, he has rarely been equalled for truth, nature, and variety and facility of expression. His literary talents were respectable. His principal piece, which he composed jointly with Colman, is the Clandestine Marriage.—*Enc. Am.*

2 vols. 12mo, $2 50.

Collins, 1720.

He must be acknowledged to possess imagination, sweetness, bold and figurative language. His numbers dwell on the ear, and easily fix themselves in the memory. His originality consists in his manner, in the highly figurative garb in which he clothes abstract ideas, in the felicity of his expressions, and his skill in imbodying ideal creations.—*Aikin.*

1 vol. 12mo, $1 37.

Akenside, 1721.

Respecting his poem "On the Pleasures of Imagination," it would be an injury to deny him the claims of an original writer, which he merited by the expansion of the plan of his prose original, and by enriching its illustrations from the stores of philosophy and poetry.—*Aikin.*

1 vol. 12mo, $1 25.

Home, 1724.

A dramatic writer. His "Douglas" became a stock piece. -*Enc. Am.*

Mason, 1725.

As a poet he excels more in lyric than in dramatic composition; he often exhibits a minute learning, which borders upon pedantry, and displays more of the artificial mechanism of poetry than of its genuine spirit. In all his productions he breathes the purest spirit of morality and the warmest zeal for liberty.—*Edinb. Enc.*

4 vols., $7 50.

Goldsmith, 1729.

(See third part.)

Churchill, 1731.

The "Rosciad" is his best poem: the delineations are drawn with equal energy and vivacity; the language and versification, though not without inequalities, are superior to the ordinary strain of current poetry, and many of the observations are stamped with sound judgment and correct taste.—*Aikin.*

4 vols. 12mo, $5 00.

Cowper, 1731.

Though he has not aspired to the first-rate powers of creation in inventing incident and imbodying characters, his pages are full of scenery and pictures of life and manners, dignified by the highest sentiments, and made interesting by the most tender touches of the social affections.—*Ed. Enc.*

8vo, $3 50.

Beattie, 1735.

Of his "Minstrel," his principal piece, Dr. Aikin says, "Whatever may be its defects, it possesses beauties which will secure it a place among the approved productions of the British muse."

12mo, $1 37.

Holcroft, 1744.

He is stated to have been the first who introduced on the stage those, since popular, entertainments termed melodrames. He possesses strong natural abilities, and, considering that he was self-taught, his attainments were very considerable.—*Enc. Am.*

Sheridan, 1751.

As a dramatist, he may be considered at the head of the department of that line of comedy which exhibits the polite malice, the civil detraction, the intrigue, persiflage, and lurking irony which characterize a social intercourse in the more cultivated ranks of life.—*Enc. Am.*

Crabbe, 1754.

The rough energy of his descriptions, the vigorous and manly style of his versification, the deep though oppressive interest of his stories, and his stern maxims of morality, must have secured for him universal admiration.—*Mrs. Hall.*

8 vols, 12mo, $10 00.

Burns, 1759.

(See third part.)

Rogers, 1762.

(See third part.)

Wordsworth, 1770.

(See third part.)

Scott, 1771.

(See third part.)

Montgomery, 1771.

Those who can distinguish the "fine gold from the sounding brass" of poetry, must place his name high in the list of the British poets, and those who consider that the chiefest duty of such is to promote the cause of religion, virtue, and humanity, must acknowledge in him one of their most zealous and efficient advocates.—*Mrs. Hall.*
4 vols. 16mo, $6 00.

Coleridge, 1772.

Some of the most perfect examples that our language can supply are to be found among his poems; full of the simplest and purest nature, yet pregnant with the deepest and most subtile philosophy.—*Aikin.*
3 vols. 8vo, $2 33.

Southey, 1774.

(See third part.)

Lamb, 1775.

His poetical productions are very limited, but they are sufficient, both in quality and quantity, to secure for him a prominent station among the poets of Great Britain.—*Mrs. Hall.*
8vo, $3 75.

Campbell, 1777.

(See third part.)

Moore, 1780.

(See third part.)

Cunningham, 1784.

His ballads and lyrical pieces are exquisite in feeling, chaste and elegant in style, graceful in expression, and natural in conception; they will bear the strictest and most critical inspection of those who consider elaborate finish to be, at least, the second requisite of the writers of song.—*Mrs. Hall.*

2 vols. 12mo, $2 50.

Henry Kirke White, 1785.

A collection of British poets would be imperfect if it did not contain the poems of this "marvellous youth." "His death," says Dr. Southey, "is to be lamented as a loss to English literature."—*Mrs. Hall.*

Byron, 1788.

The amazing power he possessed of searching into and portraying character; his prodigious skill in versification; his fine perception of the sublime and beautiful in nature; his graceful and unforced wit; his deep readings of human passion; his accurate knowledge of the secret movements of the human heart, were so many keys to his wonderful and universal success.—*Mrs. Hall.*

1 vol. 8vo, $5 00.

Wilson, 1789.

His poems are full of beauty: they have all the freshness of the heather; a true relish for nature breaks out in all of them; they are the earnest breathings of a happy and buoyant spirit; a giving out, as it were, of the breath that has been inhaled among the mountains.—*Mrs. Hall.*

2 vols., $3 50.

Croly, 1790.

Dr. Croly is a writer of tragedy and comedy; an almost universal poet. He is grand and gorgeous, but rarely tender and affectionate; he builds a lofty and magnificent temple, but it is too cold and stately to be a home for the heart.—*Mrs. Hall.*

2 vols. 8vo, $4 50.

Milman, 1791.

His poems are fine examples of sound intellect and cultivated taste, but we look in vain through them for evidence of inventive power and originality of thought. He has little skill in mastering the heart or in contr[illegible] the feelings.—*Mrs. Hall.*

Shelley, 1792.

His poetry resembles the creation, for the moral harmony of which he was so anxious. It is wonderfully flowing and energetic, round and harmonious as the orb, no less conversant with seas and mountains than with flowers and the minutest beauty; and it hungers and thirsts after a certain beauty of perfection, as the orb rolls in loving attraction round the sun.—*Mrs. Hall.*

8vo, $2 75.

Mrs. Felicia Hemans, 1793.

(See third part.)

Clare, 1793.

The most accomplished of British poets will not complain at finding him introduced into their society; setting aside all consideration of the peculiar circumstances under which he wrote, he is worthy to take his place among them.—*Mrs. Hall.*

Keats, 1796.

(See third part.)

Hood, 1798.

More tender, more graceful, or more beautifully-wrought lyrics, are scarcely to be found in our language.

1 vol. 12mo, $2 00.

Pollok, 1799.

(See third part.)

Procter.

He cannot be said to equal in energy the older writers, who have been his models, but at times he approaches them very nearly in deep feeling, in true pathos, and in fine and delicate delineation of human character.—*Mrs. Hall.*

Joanna Baillie.

Her "tragedies" will be classed among the most admirable in the English language. They are elegant and classical, stately, with occasional touches of natural passion; but her tragedy, with every advantage of taste and study, has the port and flexure of female genius.

8vo, $2 50.

L. E. Landon.

(See third part.)

Mary Howitt.

Her poems are always graceful and beautiful, and often vigorous, but they are essentially feminine: they afford evidences of a kindly and generous nature, as well as of a fertile imagination, and a safely-cultivated mind.—*Mrs. Hall.*

Bayley.

He is natural in all his songs: they make their way to the heart; they are understood and appreciated by the unlearned; they speak the thoughts and describe the feelings of the great mass of mankind, who have no idea of relating their woes and pleasures, in splendid diction, or delicately-turned sentiment.—*Mrs. Hall.*

Tennyson.

His poems are so thickly studded with evidences of manly force and exquisite tenderness, with feelings so true, and fancies so felicitous, clothed in a music often peculiar in its flow, but never cloying, as to substantiate Mr. Tennyson's claim to a high place among modern poets.—*London Athen.*

AMERICAN.

John Trumbull, 1750, died 1831.

His most finished poems are "M'Fingal" and the "Progress of Dulness." The latter was as serviceable to the cause of education as the former was to that of liberty. M'Fingal is in three cantos, written in the Hudibrastic vein, and considered much the best imitation of the cruel satire of Butler that has been written. It is never tedious, and few commence reading it who do not follow it to the end, and regret its termination. Throughout the three cantos, the wit is never separated from the character of the hero.

Philip Freneau, 1752, died 1832.

He was of French extraction, a revolutionary patriot, room-mate of Madison, friend of Jefferson, and editor. His patriotic songs and ballads, which are superior to any metrical composition then written in this country, were everywhere sung with enthusiasm.

Timothy Dwight, 1752, died 1817.

An eminent divine, and president of Yale College. His "Conquest of Canaan," an epic poem, in eleven books, is his principal production. It was commenced when he was twenty-three years old: though generally deficient in spirit and distinctive features, there are passages not inferior to any American poet of the same period.

David Humphreys, 1753, died 1810.

He wrote many fugitive pieces, much admired at the ime. Mr. Griswold characterizes them as simple and correct in thought and language, and aiming only at an elegant mediocrity.

Joel Barlow, 1755, died 1812.

His principal work, the "Columbiad," is an enlargement and improvement of his "Vision of Columbus," the production of his earlier years. Though lacking unity of fable and interest both of incident and character, it has, says Mr. Griswold, "many bursts of eloquence and patriotism, which should preserve it from oblivion."

Robert Treat Paine, 1773, died 1811.

His "Adams and Liberty," with a few other short pieces, has gained a place in American literature. "He had a brilliant fancy, and a singular command of language; but he was never content to be simple and natural."

Washington Allston, 1779.*

The oldest of living "Poets of America." His "Sylphs of the Seasons," "The two Painters," and the "Paint King," "though very different in object and vein, are all original in their fable, style, and cast of thought, and all have the purest and most cheerful influence upon the mind."

John Pierpont, 1785.

"Mr. Pierpont has written in almost every metre, and many of his hymns, odes, and other brief poems, are remarkably spirited melodies." His "Airs of Palestine" is his longest poem, and was received with great applause.

Richard H. Dana, 1787.

The largest and most remarkable of his poems is his "Buccaneer," a poem in which he has depicted with singular power the strange and darker passions. He is the oldest representative of the more spiritual school of poets and scholars, which has arisen, in this country, under the auspices of Wordsworth, Coleridge, &c., &c. "His prose and poetry will every year find more and more readers."

James A. Hillhouse, 1789, died 1841.

The author of several fine pieces both in prose and poetry. His "Hadad" has generally been regarded as his master-

* Alas! no longer living (July 18, 1843).

piece. "As a poet," says Mr. Griswold, "he possessed qualities seldom found united: a masculine strength of mind and a most delicate perception of the beautiful. With an imagination of the loftiest order, still the grand characteristic of his writings is their classical beauty."

Charles Sprague, 1791.

He is the author of several brief pieces, and one or two poems of more pretensions. They show great skill in the use of language, and prove him to be a master of the poetic art. They are especially distinguished for good taste.

Carlos Wilcox, 1794, died 1827.

The general character of this poet is religion and sincerity. He was a lover of nature, and described rural sights and sounds with peculiar clearness and fidelity.

William Cullen Bryant, 1794.

As remarkable for his literary precocity as for his genius. When 13 years old, he wrote the "Embargo" and "Spanish Revolution," which were published, and greatly admired. Indeed, a piece of his written when he was nine, was thought worthy of being printed in the columns of a newspaper at the time. He ranks with the first poets of his time. "No poet has described with more fidelity the beauties of the creation, nor sung in nobler lay the praises of the Creator. He is a translator of the silent language of the Universe to the World."

Joseph R. Drake, 1795, died 1820.

Author of a considerable portion of the once celebrated series of humorous and satirical pieces known as the "Croaker Pieces." His largest serious poem is the "Culprit Fay," a story exhibiting the most delicate fancy, and much artistic skill.

James G. Percival, 1795.

Author of "Clio," "Zamor," "Classic Melodies," &c., &c. "He has all the natural qualities of a great poet, but lacks the active skill, or declines the labour, without which few authors gain immortality. His genius is versatile, and he possesses, in an eminent degree, the creative faculty. He is also an admired and successful painter of nature."

Fitz-Greene Halleck, 1795.

Author of the celebrated ode "Marco Bozzaris,," "Connecticut," &c., &c., &c. Whether serious or satirical, his pieces are admirable. There are few finer martial lyrics than his Marco Bozzaris.

John G. Brainard, 1796.

He has deep feeling, delicate fancy, but fails in humorous pieces.

Mrs. L. H. Sigourney, 1797.

She has surpassed all the poets of her sex in this country in the extent of her productions. They are often vigorous, and always characterized by a religious and domestic piety.

Robert C. Sands, 1796, died 1832.

A man of most playful and fertile talent, cut off before he reached an early meridian, and leaving behind him some beautiful memorials of his genius, both in prose and poetry.

Grenville Mellen, 1799, died 1841.

The author of several pretty pieces, which were received by the public with much favour. He was somewhat deficient, however, in vigour and creative genius.

N. P. Willis, 1807.

"Dana and Bryant," says Mr. Griswold, "are teachers of high religious philosophy; Halleck and Holmes excel in human and delicate satire; Longfellow has a fine imagination, and is unequalled as an artist; but Willis, more than any other among us, is the poet of the world. His tastes lead him to cultivate a knowledge of social life and its secret springs."

J. G. Whittier, 1800.

The poet of freedom and humanity. His verses are characterized by a manly vigour of thought and language, and breathe the true spirit of liberty.

Oliver W. Holmes, 1809.

One of our most promising young poets, sufficiently characterized in the extract from Mr. Griswold, given above.

Willis G. Clark, 1810, died 1841,

distinguished for graceful and elegant diction, thoughts morally and poetically beautiful and chaste, and appropriate images. His strains are sad, but not misanthropic.

The sisters (Lucretia and Margaret M.) Davidson.

Two rarely-gifted and most precocious spirits, cut off in the bloom of early youth, but bequeathing to our time impassioned and beautiful strains, which the world will not willingly let die.*

2. FRENCH.

Charles, Duke of Orleans, 1420.

His poems excel those of his contemporaries in tenderness and depth of feeling.—*Penny Cyc.*

Francis I., 1494.

His poetry, though of a light description, is by no means devoid of ease and grace.—*Penny Cyc.*

Marot, 1505.

Among the authors of the reign of Francis I., Marot deserves the first place.—*Penny Cyc.*
$1 50.

Jodelle, 1532.

He was the first Frenchman who wrote plays in his own language, and with chorus in imitation of the Greek.—*Blake.*
4to, $1 50.

Mary Stuart, 1542.

She composed some beautiful verses.—*Penny Cyc.*

Margaret of Valois, 1552.

She is well known by her attainments and literary labours. —*Penny Cyc.*

La Peyrouse, 1555.

He was the author of the first tragedy in Alexandrines. *Enc. Am.*

Malherbe, 1555.

His odes have all the ease of Horace, as well as his incidental strokes of the sublime.—*Tytler.*
8vo, $2 00.

* The above notices of American poets are necessarily very brief, and are chiefly taken from Mr. Griswold. They are confined to those who have lived since the opening of the War of Independence, and who have either paid the debt to nature, or attained a clear and well-defined position among the bards of America. Many of great merit, and yet greater promise, are omitted, and perhaps more than one who ought to have been included by the rule within which we have restricted ourselves.

Hippolyte, 1573.

A dramatic writer, who eclipsed all his predecessors by the harmony of his verse.—*Enc. Am.*

Regnier, 1573.

His satires are the principal basis of his reputation: his colouring is vigorous, but his style is incorrect; yet he is not destitute of true poetical turns, delicate wit, and a pleasing humour.—*Enc. Am.*

8vo, $1 00.

Hardy, 1580.

A dramatist, who, possessed of very extensive reading, made some efforts to deviate from the beaten track of his predecessors; but his genius was not equal to his boldness and facility.—*Enc. Am.*

6 vols., $8 00.

Dufresny, 1610.

He wrote good conversational pieces.—*Enc. Am.*

Molière, 1620.

His comedies, properly read, may supply experience, because he has not depicted mere passing events, but human nature, which does not change. He is a writer for those of riper age and the gray-haired; their experience corresponds to his observations, and their memory to his genius.—*Enc. Am.*

4 vols. 18mo, $2 00.

La Fontaine, 1621.

See third part.)

Corneille, 1625.

He is allowed to have brought the French dramatic poetry to the highest pitch of excellence which it has ever attained. We cannot say that Corneille has not availed himself of the compositions in other languages; for, besides that the correct regularity of his pieces demonstrates a thorough acquaintance with the rules of the drama, he has borrowed some of his plots both from the Greek tragedians, and some of the dramatists of Spain. The tragedy of the Cid, Rhodogune, Cinna, Les Horaces, have never been surpassed by any dramatic writer of the French.—*Tytler.*

2 vols. 8vo, $4 50.

Madame Deshoulières, 1634.

She wrote with feminine tenderness.—*Enc. Am.*
2 vols., $2 00.

Boileau, 1636.

His poems display a graceful versification, a natural and sustained style, vigorous and well-connected ideas.—*Enc. Am.*
Boileau, Malherbe, and Rousseau, 1 vol. 8vo, $2 25.

Racine, 1639.

Corneille, with more of the sublime of poetry, had less acquaintance with the tender passions. It is here that the forte of Racine lay. The pathetic of Britannicus is superior to anything that Corneille has attempted in the same style. Athalie is full of grandeur and dignity of sentiment; and the comedy of the Plaideurs shows that the genius of Racine was as universal as that of Corneille.—*Tytler.*
8vo, $2 25.

Reynard, 1647.

He has some celebrity as a comic writer.—*Enc. Am.*

Fénélon, 1651.

(See third part.)

Fontenelle, 1657.

His idyls are written with a cold elegance.—*Enc. Am.*
3 vols., $4 00.

Chénier, 1664.

He possessed a brilliant imagination and a philosophical mind, and has infused much grace and elegance into all his compositions. His dramatic pieces are highly praised, of which "Tiberius" is his best effort.—*Am. Quart. Rev.*

J. B. Rousseau, 1669.

Celebrated as a lyric writer, who treats every subject with ease.—*Enc. Am.*

Voltaire, 1694.

Among his works, his dramas hold the first place. Among all the French writers, he perhaps displays in the fullest degree the peculiarities of his nation.—*Enc. Am.*
8vo, $5 00.

Crebillon, 1707.

He is the only one of the French poets of the stage, if we

except Voltaire, who has drawn his images from the sources of terror. In all his pieces virtue and morality are powerfully inculcated.—*Tytler.*
3 vols., $2 75.

Diderot, 1713.

He was a man of brilliant talent and warm imagination, but his works are deficient in plan and connexion, yet are characterized by energy and eloquence.—*Enc. Am.*

Le Brun, 1729.

His odes rise to a higher flight than most of the French poems.—*Enc. Am.*
8vo, $1 50.

Beaumarchais, 1732.

He was a singular instance of versatility of talent, being at once an artist, politician, projector, merchant, and dramatist.—*Enc. Am.*
7 vols., $3 50.

Delile, 1738.

Lively feelings, richness of conception, animated description, purity and great elegance of expression, harmonious and easy versification are his chief excellences.—*Enc. Am.*

Andrieux, 1759.

A distinguished dramatic poet, alike for his easy wit, the striking characters, and beautiful language of his pieces.—*Enc. Am.*
4 vols., $3 50.

Ducis, 1759.

He has introduced with eminent success upon the French stage the tragedies Hamlet, Romeo, King Lear, Macbeth, Othello. For vigorous description and the art of exciting tender emotions, qualifications so essential for the tragic author, he is thought to have few equals, and perhaps no superior, among the modern French writers.—*Am. Quart. Rev.*

Arnault, 1766.

He has gained some celebrity as a tragic poet.—*Enc. Am.*

Picard, 1769.

On account of his skilful delineation of character, was styled "Le petit Molière."—*Enc. Am.*

Chateaubriand, 1769.

His writings breathe a poetical spirit. They are composed with warmth, replete with images, spirited, and not without power; many of his descriptions may be called excellent.—*Enc. Am.*

Le Mercier, 1770.

A poet, and the most talented dramatic writer of his age. In his tragedy of "Agamemnon," he strove, with signal success, to combine with felicity of plot and purity of style more original and striking attractions.—*Penny Cyclop.*

Béranger, 1780.

The man of letters must set a high value upon his works, for he is aware that the national song, a portion of the French literature, which may be said to have taken its rise in the Chant Marseillais and the Chant du Départ, owes the prolongation of its existence almost entirely to the talents of Béranger.

Lamartine, 1802.

The best of the late lyric writers.—*Enc. Am.*
1 vol., $3 50.

Victor Hugo.

Most of his odes are sufficiently happy in poetical conception, but frequently disfigured by unnatural refinement, by vague and enigmatic phraseology.—*Am. Quart. Rev.*
$6 00.

3. GERMAN.

Martin Luther, 1483.

His excellent hymns are well known.—*Enc. Am.*

Hans Sachs, 1494.

His poems are distinguished for naiveté, feeling, invention, wit, and striking description.—*Enc. Am.*

Fischart, 1560.

In the broad comic he is not to be surpassed; and even in his most satirical effusions there is an honesty and good nature always observable.—*Enc. Am.*

Opitz, 1597.

He was the creator of a new and more correct poetical style in Germany, founded on the model of the ancient classics.—*Enc. Am.*

Hagedorn, 1708.

A celebrated poet; his style is pure and flowing.

Gellert, 1715.

He wrote fables, stories, didactic poems, with several pieces intended for the improvement of the stage.—*Enc. Am.*

Kleist, 1715.

His idyls are much admired for their elegance and simplicity.—

Gleim, 1719.

His poems are very numerous, and contain successful attempts in almost every species of poetry.

A. W. Schlegel, 1721.

He has become celebrated for his translation of Shakspeare, which may well be called a German reproduction of the original.—*Enc. Am.*

Klopstock, 1724.

He gained the brightest and quickest fame by his "Epopee," the first cantos of which, by their prophetic grandeur and the magnificence of their description, their genuine patriarchal tone and unfeigned sincerity of love and devotion, announced him a rival of Milton.—*Enc. Am.*
Compare Coleridge, Biog. Lit.
8vo, $5 00.

Lessing, 1729.

One of the greatest dramatic writers Germany has produced.—*Enc. Am.*
8vo, $4 00.

Wieland, 1733.

He has enriched German literature with works, which have made known to his countrymen the merits of the French and English writers.—*Enc. Am.*
36 vols., $13 50.

Herder, 1744.

He contributed much to a more active study of nature, brought before the public the poetry of past times of Europe and Asia, and awakened a taste for national song. He effected more by his various accomplishments and fine taste than by his creative power, yet he has produced fine songs.—*Enc. Am.*
7 vols., $6 00.

Hoelty, 1748.

A lyric poet, who excelled particularly in the elegy and idyl.

Bürger, 1748.

He was more at home in ballads and simple songs than in the higher lyrical poetry, yet in some of his productions he appears as a true poet of the people, and his style, with some faults, is clear, vigorous, and tender.—*Schlegel.*

$2 00.

Goethe, 1749.

Goethe is the most universal poet, thoroughly modern in some of his inimitable songs, in which he gives vent to the tenderest emotions of the heart with a sincerity at times almost childlike, while in other productions he exhibits the spirit of ancient literature to a degree which, probably, no modern poet of any nation has reached, as the resemblance is not merely in the form, but in the very conception of the ideas.—*Enc. Am.*

2 vols., $12 00.

Schiller, 1759.

His inspiration exhibited the struggle of human nature and human will with life and fate. His ideas are as holy and elevated as Klopstock's, but they appear clothed in reality and truth.—*Enc. Am.*

1 vol., $4 75.

Kotzebue, 1761.

The dramatical muse of Kotzebue was fertile, but without dignity, and frequently without good morals.

Jean Paul F. Richter, 1763.

He seems to have liked particularly to analyze emotions, to dissect individual character in every station, even the humblest. He does not exhibit man under those general influences which operate on large masses of men, but deals almost exclusively with the individual, considered as such.

Tieck, 1773.

He possesses poetical resources hardly inferior to Goethe, and his productions, moreover, are distinguished for virtue and purity, as well as for poetical spirit. He is one of the most learned commentators in Shakspeare.

1 vol. 12mo, $1 75.

Uhland, 1787.

He is undoubtedly one of the best lyric poets of Germany. There is a truth, a warmth, and intensity of feeling in his poems which stir the heart.—*Enc. Am.*

Körner, 1791.

He is particularly celebrated for the spirited poems which he composed in the campaign against Napoleon (1813). They all have become national.

$3 00.

A copious selection of extracts from all the German poets will be found in *Poetischer Hausschatz des Deutschen Volkes, by Dr. G. L. B. Wolf, Leipzig*, 1841.

German books of all descriptions may be obtained in New-York of Messrs. Eichthal and Bernhard, proprietors of the "Deutsche Schnellpost."

Heyne, 1797.

He is one of the most popular poets of Germany, and undoubtedly possesses great talent, although his style is full of inequalities, frequently passing from sublimity to vulgarity, and from deep feeling to an extreme frivolity.—*Py. Cyc.*

4. ITALIAN.

Boccacio, 1313.

5 vols. 8vo, $8 50. (See third part.)

Lorenzo de Medici, 1448.

He had attempted to restore the poetry of Italy to the state in which Petrarch had left it; but this man, so superior by the greatness of his character, and by the universality of his genius, did not possess the talent of versification in the same degree as Petrarch. Yet his ideas are natural, and often accompanied by a great charm of imagination.—*Sismondi.*

Machiavel, 1469.

His comedies, by the novelty of the plot, by the strength and vivacity of the dialogue, are far superior to anything Italy has produced. His poems are more remarkable for vigour of thought than for harmony of style or grace of expression.—*Sismondi.*

Ariosto, 1474

(See third part.)

Tasso, 1544.

(See third part.)

Chiabrera, 1552.

The vigour, the vivacity, and the inspired character of his genius carried Italian poetry to a very high pitch. Though his expressions are not always the most elegant, yet the elevation of thought, the vivacity of the images, and a certain divine enthusiasm, the very soul of lyrical composition, leave us little inclination to dwell upon his faults.—*Sismondi.*

3 vols. 8vo, $5 50.

Metastasio, 1698.

His dramas invariably open with striking and imposing effect, and are full of magnificence and attractions calculated to rivet the attention of the audience. It would be quite impossible to convey an idea in feeble prose of the united effect of the finest poetry and music in his pieces.—*Sismondi.*

12 vols. 8vo, $12 00.

Alfieri, 1749.

He has united the beauties of art, unity, singleness of subject, and probability, the properties of the French drama, to the sublimity of situation and character, and the important events of the Greek theatre, and to the profound thought and sentiment of the English stage.—*Sismondi.*

4 vols. 8vo, $9 00.

5. SPANISH AND PORTUGUESE.

Gil Vincente, 1480.

He may be considered in some measure the founder of the Spanish theatre, and the earliest model upon which Lope de Vega and Calderon proceeded to form a yet more perfect drama.—*Sismondi.*

Boscan, 1490.

Vega, 1494.

These poets brought from Italy the softer beauties of amorous poetry, imbodied in the regular sonnet, which had hitherto been little employed in the Peninsula.—*Hallam.*

Mendoza, 1500.

Though full of philosophical discussions, his poems are yet written in a neat and easy style.—*Sismondi.*

Camoens, 1524.

A celebrated Portuguese poet. The versification of his Lusiad has something so charming and splendid, that not only cultivated minds, but even the common people are enraptured by its magic, and learn by heart, and sing its beautiful stanzas.—*Enc. Am.*

Cervantes, 1549.

To "Don Quixote" he owes his immortality.—*Sismondi.*

Of his dramas, we may observe that they are curious specimens of the character, which that great genius gave to the national drama of Spain, at a period when it was in his power to model it according to his will.—*Enc. Am.*

8vo, $2 50.

Lope Felix de Vega Carpin, 1562.

The inconceivable fertility of invention of L. F. de Vega Carpin supported his dramatic fame, notwithstanding the little care and time which he gave to the correction of his pieces; but his other poems, the offspring of hasty efforts, are little more than rude sketches.—*Sismondi.*

Gongora, 1562.

The effect produced by his poetry on a people eager after novelty, impatient for a new career, and who on all sides found themselves within the bounds of authority, of the laws, and the Church, presents a remarkable phenomenon in literature.—*Sismondi.*

Calderon, 1601.

He may be considered as placed on the highest pinnacle of romantic poetry, and all her brilliancy was lavished on his works, as, in a display of fireworks, the brightest colours and the most striking lights are reserved for the last explosion.—*Schlegel.*

17 vols., $15 00.

Yriarte, 1752.

He attained, in some degree, to the grace and simplicity of La Fontaine; and his merit was the most felt, as at that period no good fabulist had appeared in Spain.—*Sismondi.*

6 vols. 8vo, $5 00.

II. PHILOSOPHERS

(A.) ANCIENT.

1. GREEK.

Pythagoras, 584 B.C.

The theoretical philosophy of Pythagoras, which treats of nature and its origin, was enveloped in the most profound obscurity, and we know nothing of it but what may be conjectured from single intimations of the ancients.—*Enc. Am.*

Socrates, 469 B.C.

Socrates claims our highest respect, alike for the powers of his highly-cultivated mind, the purity of his sentiments, the excellence of his instructions, the extent of his influence, and the end of his godlike life. Xenophon says of him, "All who knew him found in him the best guide to virtue." —*Anthon.*

The best edition of Xenophon's Memoirs of Socrates is that of Reading, Cant., 1720.

Xenophon, 450 B.C.

The discrimination, solidity, precision, and mildness of manner so remarkable in his master, Socrates, he acquired himself, and transfused into his writings; from them we may learn the true spirit of the Socratic philosophy.—*Anthon.*

A good edition of his works is by Passow, Leipzig, 1833, 12mo.

Plato, 430 B.C.

He laid the first foundation for a scientific treatment of philosophy. His works are exceedingly valuable both for style and matter, rich in thought, and adorned with beautiful and poetical images.—*Eschenburg.*

Best edition, J. Bekker, Greek and Latin, Berlin, 1816–18, 10 vols. 8vo. Best translation, Sydenham and Taylor, London, 1804, 5 vols. 4to.—*Anthon.*

Aristotle, 385 B.C.

His works contain a great mass of clear thought and solid matter, although his insatiable love of inquiry was often betrayed into abstruse subtleties, as idle as they were dark.—*Eschenburgh.*

The best edition is that by Tauchnitz, Leipzig, 16 vols. 18mo, 1832.

Theophrastus, 321 B.C.

He possessed eminent powers, both in eloquence and philosophy; distinguished for watchful observation, he placed more reliance on experience than on speculation.—*Eschenburg.*

The best edition is that of Schneider, Leipzig, 1818, 5 vols. 8vo.—*Anthon.*

Translated by H. Gally, London, 1725.

Plutarch, A.D. 50.

In numerous philosophical pieces we find an eloquent diction and a rich fertility of thought, together with various knowledge and real prudence. They are important sources for learning the history of philosophy and of the human mind.—*Anthon.*

Best edition is that of Reiske, Leipzig, 1774–82, 12 vols. 8vo. English translation, M. Morgan and others, London, 1718, 5 vols. 8vo.

Sextus Empiricus, 190.

His works are very valuable in illustrating the history of philosophy, especially that of the skeptical school. The first edition was printed at Paris, 1621, folio.—*Anthon.*

Plotinus, 203.

One of the earliest teachers of the Alexandrian or Græco-Oriental school of philosophy. He laboured much to attain the comprehension of the absolute, and was learned and enthusiastic. The most celebrated of his works is the Enneades.

Best edition of his works is Creuzer, Oxon, 1835, 3 vols. Tenneman gives a good synopsis of his philosophy.

Porphyry, 233.

A disciple of Plotinus, and a bitter adversary of Christianity. He believed himself, like his master, to be in direct communication with the gods. His principal works are, *Life of Pythagoras*, *Life of Plotinus*, *A Treatise of Predicables*, and one on *Pythagorean Abstinence.*

Iamblichus, 4th century.

Notwithstanding the extravagance, mysticism, and fable with which his works abound, they are yet a valuable help in getting an idea of the philosophy of the later Platonists. There has been no edition of his entire works.—*Anthon.*

Proclus, 412.

Of the Alexandrian school; lost in mystical reveries, but greatly admired in his day.

A recent edition of his works, more complete than any previous one, has been published by M. Cousin.

Stobæus, 450.

His collection from a multitude of philosophical writers is valuable, both on account of the contents themselves, and also of the numerous passages rescued from destruction only by being inserted therein.

The best edition, Heeren, Goettingen, 1792, 2 vols. 8vo.

2. ROMAN.

M. T. Cicero, 106 B.C.

He was a Platonist in philosophy, although he set forth the principles of almost every school of philosophy except the Epicurean. Of his philosophical works, the "Academical Investigations," in two books, are the most valuable.—*Enc. Am.*

Annæus Seneca, 58 B.C.

In his philosophical writings, there is much acumen and matter for reflection; the style, however, is too often artificially elaborate, and tiresome by its antitheses.—*Eschb.*

The best edition is Seneca, cum notis variorum, Amst., 1672, 3 vols. 8vo. Translation of Seneca's Epistles by F. Morell, 2 vols. 4to, $5 50.

3. CHRISTIAN PHILOSOPHERS.

Justin Martyr, A.D. 103.

He combined with Christianity a portion of the *Greek* philosophy, endeavouring to purify the latter. Tatian (a contemporary) attempted, on the other hand to Christianize the ORIENTAL philosophy. The conversion of J. Martyr is an instructive commentary on the condition of thoughtful minds in his time.

Irenæus, 108.

Fragments of his works in Greek are preserved, which prove that his style was simple, though clear and often animated. His opinions concerning the soul are curious. He set himself to refute the Oriental errors which had crept into the

West, and which were attempting to corrupt Christianity.—*Anthon.*

The best edition, Grabe, Oxon, folio, 1702.

Clement of Alexandria, 180.

Some parts of his *Stromata* are rich in historical notices of philosophy, as well as in *logical* and *theoretical* views.

Origen, 185.

He is undoubtedly one of the most remarkable men among the Christian writers His talents, eloquence, and learning have been celebrated not only by Christian writers, but by heathen philosophers.—*Anthon.*

The best edition is that of De la Rue, Paris, 1733-59, 4 vols. folio, reprinted at Wuertzburg, 15 vols. 8vo, 1780.

Eusebius, 264.

His "Præparatio Evangelica," though its subject is one entirely sacred in its nature, yet contains a great number of valuable notices respecting the mythology of the pagan nations, and the philosophy of the Greeks in particular.—*Anthon.*

Best edition, Vigier, Paris, 1628, folio, reprinted Leipz., 1688, folio.

Lactantius and Arnobius.

These Numidian philosophers and fathers have both left able attacks on the philosophy of the Gentiles. That of Lactantius, called the *Divine Institutes*, and which treats of the excellence of Christianity as compared with *philosophy* and *idolatry*, is admirable.

Athanasius, 296.

Villemain says of him: "If he often contended on points of deep obscurity, his aim was to establish that religious unity of which he well understood the value and the power. He has justly been pronounced one of the greatest men of whom the Church can boast."—*Eschb.*

The best edition of his works is that of Montfaucon, Paris, 1698, 3 vols. folio.—*Anthon.*

St. Augustine, 354.

In his controversial works he enters deeply and with great sagacity into philosophical questions, while in his *Confessions* and *Retractions* he opens the inmost workings of his own mind.

Chrysostom, 354.

For overpowering popular eloquence Chrysostom had no equal among the fathers. His style is elevated, yet natural and clear. He transfuses his own glowing thoughts and emotions into all his hearers, seemingly without effort, and without the power of resistance.—*Murdock.*

Chrysostom's Golden Book on the Education of Children, London, 1559, 12mo.—*Anthon.*

(B.) MEDIÆVAL.

Boethius, 455.

The most learned Latin philosopher of this period. His most celebrated work is "De Consolatione Philosophiæ." It is an imaginary conversation between the author and philosophy personified, who endeavours to console and soothe him in his afflictions. The topics of consolation are deduced from the tenets of Plato, Zeno, and Aristotle, but without any notice of the sources of consolation which are peculiar to the Christian system, which circumstance has led many to think him more of a Stoic than a Christian. It is partly in prose and partly in verse.—*Penny Enc.*

8vo, London, 1785, translated.

John of Damascus, 730.

Like Boethius of the West, he, in the East, forms a link which unites the ancient philosophy with that of the Middle Ages. He helped preserve a knowledge of Aristotelianism, and was also devoted to theology.

Erigena, 840.

He took up that remarkable system which has from time immemorial prevailed in some schools of the East, wherein all external phenomena, as well as all subordinate intellects, are considered as *emanating* from the Supreme Being, into whose essence they are hereafter to be absorbed. A treatise, written by him with great acuteness and subtlety, "De Divisione Naturæ," was published at Oxford by Dr. Gale, in 1681.—*Enc. Am.*

St. Anselm, 1033.

He originated the attempt, which was afterward renewed by Des Cartes, to constitute the true principle of all science, and which has been justly characterized as one of the boldest ever made in the philosophical world. In this point of view, his works called *Monologium* and *Prosologium* are the most remarkable.

Roscellin, 1060.

He was the founder of *Nominalism*. This sect is memorable in the history of philosophy in the Middle Ages, since from them proceeded a spirit which opened the way to the higher philosophy of subsequent times.—*Enc. Am.*

Abelard, 1079.

There are few lives of literary men more interesting, or more diversified by success and adversity, by glory and humiliation, by the admiration of mankind and the persecution of enemies, nor from which more impressive lessons of moral prudence may be derived.—*Hallam.*

The most complete edition of his works was published at Paris, 1616, in 4to.

Peter Lombard, 1100.

His "Master of Sentences," a collection of the opinions of the Fathers upon the principal points of theology and philosophy, had a great influence on the prevailing studies of the learned, especially in the next and following ages.

John of Salisbury, 1110.

He attacked the vicious modes of instruction then current, and protested against a barren dialectics. His works contain, also, valuable materials for a history of scholasticism.

Albertus Magnus, 13th century.

Besides theological learning, he was well versed in mechanics, natural history, and natural philosophy.—*Enc. Am.*

Bonaventura, 1221.

He has been praised for having avoided scholastic cavils and ambiguities in his style, and for having spoken the language of earnest faith and sincere piety.

His works have been collected in 13 vols. 4to, Venice, 1751, to which edition a well-written life of Bonaventura is affixed.—*Penny Enc.*

Thomas Aquinas, 1227.

The rival, but also the friend of Bonaventura. His writings all bear the impress of a powerful mind. His *Summa Theologica*, his *Commentaries* on Aristotle, and various *special* treatises, are full of philosophical speculation.

(C.) MODERN.

1. ENGLISH AND AMERICAN.

Francis Bacon, 1561.

The great reformer of philosophical methods, especially in physics. His *Novum Organum Scientiarum* and *De Dignitate et Augmentis Scientiarum* are his most memorable philosophical works.

Hobbes, 1588.

The metaphysical philosophy of Hobbes, always bold and original, often acute and profound, struck deep root in the minds of reflecting men, and has influenced more extensively the general tone of speculation. In nothing does he deserve more credit than in having set an example of close observation in the philosophy of the human mind.—*Hallam.*

5 vols. 8vo, $16 00.

Cudworth, 1617.

He is celebrated for his grand work, "The True Intellectual System of the Universe," a work of great power and erudition, although the attachment of the author to the Platonism of the Alexandrian school has led him to advance some opinions which border on incomprehensibility and mysticism.—*Enc. Am.*

4to, $4 00.

Locke, 1632.

In the estimation of Sir J. Mackintosh, Locke's Essay still stands the most conspicuous landmark in the progress of metaphysical philosophy for the last two centuries. He adds, "If Locke made few discoveries, Socrates made none; yet both did more for the improvement of the understanding, and not less for the progress of knowledge, than the authors of the most brilliant discoveries."

8vo, $3 00.

Shaftesbury, 1671.

He was the first philosopher who propounded the theory of a *moral sense* in ethics, and by him that term was first introduced.

Samuel Clarke, 1675.

A profound metaphysician, who made virtue to consist in a conformity with the essential relations of things. He wrote against Leibnitz and Hobbes, and was the friend of Newton.

Berkeley, 1684.

The works of this great metaphysician are, beyond dispute,

the finest models of philosophical style since Cicero. Perhaps they surpass those of the great orator in the wonderful art by which the fullest light is thrown on the most minute and evanescent parts of the most subtle of human conceptions. —*Sir J. Mackintosh.*

8vo, $2 50.

Butler, 1692.

He was the first to vindicate the disinterested nature of our affections. His sermons on Human Nature, as well as his great work, "The Analogy," are full of profound remarks and suggestions.

Edwards, 1703.

The metaphysician of America. His power of subtle argument, perhaps unmatched, certainly unsurpassed among men, was joined, as in some of the ancient mystics, with a character which raised his piety to fervour. He composed two famous works: "On the Freedom of the Will," and "On the Origin of Sin." The first is his master-piece, and worthy of the powers of Locke.—*Sir J. Mackintosh.*

2 vols. 8vo, $12 00.

Hartley, 1705.

His fame as a philosopher and a man of letters depends on his work, "Observations on Man." He exhibits the outlines of connected systems of physiology, mental philosophy, and theology. The doctrine of association which he adopted and illustrated explains many phenomena of intellectual philosophy.—*Enc. Am.*

8vo, $2 50.

Reid, 1710.

His doctrine of the immediate or intuitive knowledge of mind and matter, which involved the overthrow of the ideal system, and the skepticism deduced from it, was an important step in the progress of philosophy.—*Enc. Am.*

2 vols. 8vo, $5 50.

Hume, 1711.

Notwithstanding some considerable defects, his proof from induction of the beneficial tendency of virtue, his conclusive arguments for disinterestedness, and his decisive observations on the respective provinces of reason and sentiment in morals, concur in ranking his *Enquiry* with the ethical treatises of the highest merit in our language.—*Sir J. Mackintosh.*

2 vols. 8vo, $4 00.

Adam Smith, 1723.

Perhaps there is no ethical work, since Cicero's Offices, of which an abridgment enables the reader so inadequately to estimate the merit as the "Theory of Moral Sentiments." This is chiefly owing to the variety of explanations of life and manners which embellish the book, often more than they illuminate the theory.—*Sir J. Mackintosh.*

Hutchinson, 1729.

He gave full development to the system indicated by Shaftesbury and Butler. His earliest work was an "Inquiry into our Ideas of Beauty and Virtue;" his last, a "System of Moral Philosophy."

Priestley, 1733.

As a metaphysician, his elucidation of Hartley's theory of association, his works upon philosophical necessity, and upon materialism, will always ensure attention.—*Enc. Am.*

Paley, 1743.

The practical bent of his nature is visible in the language of his writings, which, on practical matters, is as precise as the nature of the subject requires, but in his rare and reluctant efforts to rise to first principles, becomes indeterminate and unsatisfactory; though no man's composition was more free from the impediments which hinder a writer's meaning from being quickly and clearly seen. His style is as near perfection in its kind as any in our language.—*Sir J. Mackintosh.*
6 vols. 8vo, $5 00.

Bentham, 1749.

His "Letters on Usury" are perhaps the best specimens of the exhaustive discussion of a moral and political question, leaving no objection, however feeble, unanswered, and nc difficulty, however small, unexplained; remarkable, also, for the clearness and spirit of the style, for the full expression which suits them to all intelligent readers, for the tender and skilful hand with which prejudice is touched, and for his admirable apology of projectors.—*Sir J. Mackintosh.*

Stewart, 1753.

It would be difficult to name works in which so much refined philosophy is joined with so fine a fancy; so much elegant literature with such a delicate perception of the distinguishing excellences of great writers; and with an estimate, in general, so just of the services rendered to knowledge by a succession of philosophers. They are pervaded by a philosophical benevolence, which keeps up the ardour of his genius, without disturbing the serenity of his mind.—*Sir J. Mackintosh.*

7 vols. 8vo, $8 50.

Mackintosh, 1765.

He is eminent as a jurist, a statesman, and a writer, equally distinguished for his extensive learning, his large views, and his liberal principles in law, politics, and philosophy. He is the author of a celebrated review (Edinburgh Review, vols. xxvii. and xxxvi.) of Stewart's Discourse on the Progress of Metaphysical Science, and of a Discourse on the Progress of Ethical and Political Science, published separately. In this last he brings out an ethical system of his own, somewhat peculiar, in which he makes conscience a secondary principle.—*Enc. Am.*

4to, 1830. Ethical Philosophy, 8vo, $2 00.

Brown, 1778.

His speculative philosophy involves many radical inconsistencies, and would hardly deserve to be mentioned in so general a sketch, were it not remarkable as an open revolt against the Scotch system at the moment the latter seemed to be developed with new power, and to acquire new authority on the European Continent, and for the temporary popularity it possessed in Great Britain, and particularly in this country.—*Enc. Am.*

2. GERMAN.

Leibnitz, 1646.

He was in favour of rationalism in the sense in which it was manifested by Plato, and the system of demonstration, which prevented him from entirely rejecting the scholastic philosophy. The principal characteristics of his philosophy are a peculiar theory of knowledge, the doctrine of monadology, and the doctrine of optimism.—*Enc. Am.*

The most complete and accurate edition of his works was published by Lewis Dutens, Geneva, 1768, 6 vols. 4to.

Wolff, 1679.

He was in general but a continuator of the philosophy of Leibnitz, adding less to it in the way of substance than of form.

Kant, 1724.

Besides the great merit of Kant in regard to intellectual philosophy, we owe him much for his views of virtue and inflexible morality, which he placed again on their true elevated basis, after they had been referred exclusively to interest by others. To the inquirer into his philosophy, we would say, that he should be careful not to reject immediately what he cannot understand, and ought not expect to understand without deep study and strict mental discipline.—*Enc. Am.*

A very good enumeration of his works is to be found in Cousin's Manuel de l'Histoire de la Philosophie, traduit de l'Allemand de Tenneman, Paris, 1829, 2 vols.

Mendelsohn, 1729.

A celebrated Jewish philosopher. He established no new system, but was, nevertheless, one of the most profound and patient thinkers of his age, and the excellence of his character was enhanced by his modesty, uprightness, and amiable disposition. He wrote several philosophical works; his master-piece, "Phædon," or "On the Immortality of the Soul," has been translated into most modern languages.—*Enc. Am.*

Jacobi, 1743.

His works are rich in whatever can attract elevated souls, yet the opinions respecting him are very different. He has been called the "German Plato," on account of the religious glow in his metaphysical writings. His philosophy, among other traits, is characterized by an aversion to systems, all of which, he maintains, when consistently carried out, lead to fanaticism. His works were published by Fleischer, Leipzig, 6 vols.—*Enc. Am.*

Fichte, 1762.

Fichte admitted the absolute existence only of the thinking individual, by which he considered even the objects of thought to be produced; he denied the reality of an exterior world. This system atoned for its exclusive character by the high standard to which this vigorous spirit raised the moral dignity of man.—*Enc. Am.*

Krug, 1770.

Krug has written a great deal on philosophical and political subjects; he has united all the principal doctrines of Kant systematically, in transcendental synthetics.—*Enc. Am.*

Fries, 1773.

He was distinguished for the moral tendency of his philosophy. He published at Heidelberg, in 1807, his New Critique of Reason, 3 vols., and in 1811 his System of Logic.—*Enc. Am.*

Schelling, 1775.

To him mind and nature are only manifestations of the Divine principle, and the knowledge of this identity between thought and outward existence rests on intellectual intuition. The principal of his works are, "On the Possibility of a Form of Philosophy in General" (Tuebingen, 1795); "Of the Soul of the World" (Hamburg, 1798); "On the I (ego) as a Principle of Philosophy" (Tuebingen, 1795).—*Enc. Am.*

3. FRENCH.

Montaigne, 1533.

Montaigne is the earliest classical writer in the French language. So long as an unaffected style and an appearance of the utmost simplicity and good nature shall charm, so long as the lovers of desultory and cheerful conversation shall be more numerous than those who prefer a lecture or sermon, so long will Montaigne be among the most favourite authors of mankind.—*Hallam.*

1 vol. 8vo, $3 50.

Gassendi, 1592.

His works against the philosophy of Aristotle and that of Des Cartes, as well as his *Syntagma Philosophiæ Epicuri*, and his book on the *Life of Epicurus*, merit special attention.

Des Cartes, 1596.

He developed his system with much ingenuity, in opposition to the empirical philosophy of the English and the Aristotelian scholastics, and adopted the rigorous systematic or mathematical mode of reasoning.—*Enc. Am.*

His works published by Victor Cousin, 1824–26, 11 vols., Paris, $16 00.

Arnauld, 1612.

He was a man of vigorous and consistent mind, full of solid knowledge and great thoughts; in his writings bold and violent, undaunted in danger, and of irreproachable morals.

Paris, 1770, 12 vols., $12 00.

Malebranche, 1638.

As a philosopher, although he agreed with those who preceded him in conceiving ideas to be the immediate objects of perception, he has distinguished more than any previous metaphysician the object from the sensation which it creates, and thereby led the way to a right understanding both of our external senses and mental powers.

Montesquieu, 1689.

(See third part.)

Voltaire, 1694.

The principal writer of the eighteenth century, who may be considered as the representative and the personification of the age, on which he exercised a most extraordinary influence. He was the leader of the so-called philosophers of France, and was regarded as an infallible oracle in literature.—*Penny Enc.*

Œuvres complètes, 13 vols. 8vo, $28 00, Paris, 1835.

Rousseau, 1712.

That he was a man of powerful talent, an elegant writer and acute reasoner, cannot be denied, but we look in vain through his pages for traces of that original and inventive faculty which constitutes genius and secures immortality.—*Enc. Am.*

Œuvres complètes, 25 vols. 8vo, $20 00, Paris, 1826.

Diderot, 1713.

As a philosopher, he followed the dictates of an intemperate imagination rather than those of a sound reason. His works are deficient in plan, and disfigured with pretensions, obscurity, and arrogance, but, nevertheless, are characterized by energy, and sometimes even bold eloquence.—*Enc. Am.*

15 vols. 8vo, Paris, 1798, $16 00.

Helvetius, 1715.

In his work an "Essay on the Mind and its Faculties," he developed with much eloquence, and followed to some bold conclusions, the principles which he had imbibed from Locke, that all thought is a modification of physical sensation. He makes this the foundation of a system of public and private morals. His work "On Man" may be considered a continuation of the former, and contains a fuller development of the doctrines laid down in it; but, at the same time, many new ones, particularly such as relate to the science of education.—*Edinb. Enc.*

The tendency of his writings is bad.

Translated by Dr. Hooper, London, 1810, 2 vols. 8vo, $5 00.

Condillac, 1715.

His "Essai sur l Origine des Connaisances humaines"

1746, 2 vols., first drew the attention of the world to a thinker who, with much acuteness of mind, sought to explain by the law of the association of ideas almost all the phenomena of the human mind.—*Enc. Am.*

Paris, 1827, 16 vols. 8vo, $9 00.

Lavater, 1741.

His great work, under the modest title "Physiognomical Fragments," made him known all over Europe. He has added explanations in a poetical style, full of enthusiastic exclamations.—*Enc. Am.*

Translated by Holcroft, London, 1840, $5 00.

Bonstetten, 1745.

This philosopher strives more particularly to defend the emotions of the heart, the feelings, against the coldness of logicians, who derive all the operations of the mind from ideas only. His "Etudes de l'Homme" (Geneva, 1821, 2 vols.) is a valuable work, written in the spirit of the higher psychology, but more in the shape of sketches and hints than of a methodical system.—*Enc. Am.*

Benjamin de Constant, 1767.

His works are distinguished by perspicuity and liveliness of style, richness of imagination, and often by depth of knowledge and acute observation, although he cannot entirely divest himself of his propensity for declamation, witticisms, and sophisms.

Royer Collard, 1768.

The eloquent and able expounder of the philosophy of Reid in France, and the successful opponent of the sensual school, which, up to the time when he began his lectures in 1811, was the ruling philosophy in that country. Fragments of his lectures, published by his pupil Jouffroy, are all that remain.

De Gerando, 1770.

His leading idea is, that all the course of man's life should be a continued self-education, embracing all his faculties, and directing all his actions; and he has developed these principles in his works.—*Penny Cyc.*

Brussels, 1839, 2 vols. 8vo, $5 00.

Victor Cousin, 1791.

His opinions are likely to have much influence on the philosophy of France, as they rest on different principles from the sensual system, which his countrymen had derived from

Condillac and Locke. His system, of which an outline may be found in his "Fragments," coincides, in some respects, with the German metaphysics.—*Enc. Am.*

Œuvres de Cousin, Brussels, 1840, 3 vols. 8vo, $10 00.

Jouffroy, 1796.

A disciple of Cousin, of eminent abilities. He has laboured to illustrate and establish the true psychological method of observation, and has also entered into ethical speculations. His views are not always very definite.

III. MATHEMATICAL AND PHYSICAL SCIENCES, CHEMISTRY, AND NATURAL HISTORY.

(A.) ANCIENT.

Thales, 640 B.C.

He first observed the apparent diameter of the sun, and divided the year into 365 days. Of his works none are extant. —*Enc. Am.*

Pythagoras, 584 B.C.

He rendered essential services to the mathematical sciences, and first established a mathematical philosophy.—*Enc. Am.*

Euclid, 300 B.C.

He was a teacher of geometry, in which branch he was the most thorough and distinguished scholar among the Greeks.—*Eschb.*

The best edition is by J. Williamson, London, 1781, 2 vols. 4to.

Archimedes, 287 B.C.

We cannot fully estimate his services to mathematics, for want of an acquaintance with the previous state of science; still, we know that he enriched it with discoveries of the highest importance, upon which the moderns have built.—*Eschb.*

Best edition by Robertson, Oxford, 1792. French translation by Peyrard, Paris, 1807.

Aristarchus, 267 B.C.

His work on the magnitude and distance of the sun and moon is still extant. He invented the sundial.—*Enc. Am.*

Ptolemy, 70 A.D.

He is considered the first astronomer of antiquity. The system of the world which he exhibits in his work is known under the name of the Ptolemaic; a Latin version of it was made in 1230.—*Enc. Am.*

Galen, 131 A.D

A Greek physician. His writings give evidence of deep reflection as well as historical knowledge of the old Greek systems of philosophy, and extend to every department of medicine.—*Enc. Am.*

Best edition is that of Chartier, Paris, 1679.

Roger Bacon, 1214.

His writings are wonderful, not only on account of the new and ingenious views which they present on many points in optics, &c., &c., but also on account of the prophetic insight which he seems to have had into the future triumphs of science.

(B.) MODERN.

Copernicus, 1473.

Copernicus was a mathematician of the first order, a sincere lover of truth, a mind free from trammels to an extent which was then almost unknown, and which we should have deemed almost incredible had we not had the proof before us. He immortalized himself by his work "De Orbium Cœlestium Revolutionibus," Amsterdam, 1670.—*Penny Enc.*

Leonardo da Vinci, 1452.

An illustrious painter and fine writer, who, in some fragments of his writings recently published for the first time, seems (according to our common estimate of the age in which he lived) to have far outstripped all his contemporaries even in physical discoveries. "The discoveries," says Hallam, "which made Galileo, and Kepler, and Mæstlin, and Maurolycus, and Castelli, and other names illustrious, the system of Copernicus, the very theories of recent geologers, are anticipated by Da Vinci within the compass of a few pages, not, perhaps, in the most precise language, or on the most conclusive reasoning, but so as to strike us with something like the awe of preternatural knowledge."

Tycho Brahe, 1546.

A celebrated astronomer. We are indebted to his observations for a more correct catalogue of the fixed stars, for several important discoveries respecting the motions of the moon and the comets, and the refraction of the rays of light, &c., &c.—*Enc. Am.*

An account of his life and writings is to be found in a work "Tycho Brahe," &c., &c., an essay by Helfrecht, Hafn., 1798.

Napier, 1550.

A distinguished mathematician. To him is to be ascribed the admirable invention of logarithms, and of the five circular parts in trigonometry, and the mode of calculation by rods, &c. His life has been written by Lord Buchan.—*Enc. Am.*

Galileo, 1564.

Galileo discovered the gravity of the air, invented the cycloid and the simple pendulum, and was the first who clearly explained the doctrine of motion.—*Enc. Am.*

A complete edition of his works, in 13 vols., appeared at Milan, 1803.

Kepler, 1571.

He first proved that the planets do not move in circles, but in ellipses, and that in their motions they describe equal areas in equal times, and that the squares of their periodical times are equal to the cubes of their distances.

The most important of his works, which is still regarded as classical by astronomers, is his "Astronomia Nova" (Prague, 1609, folio).—*Enc. Am.*

Harvey, 1578.

An English physician. His "Exercitationes de Generatione Animalium" is a curious work; but his great achievement for science and his own fame was the discovery and clear demonstration, for the first time, of the double or general circulation of the blood.

Pascal, 1623.

In early youth he gave proofs of extraordinary talents, and showed a decided inclination for geometry. He made several useful inventions and discoveries. His works appeared at the Hague in 1779, in 5 vols.—*Enc. Am.*

Boyle, 1626.

A celebrated English natural philosopher. We are indebted to him for the first certain knowledge of the absorption of air in calcination and combustion, and of the increase of weight which metals gain by oxydation. His works were published in 5 vols. folio, London, 1744.

Huygens, 1629.

In 1658 appeared his system of Saturn, in which he discovered a satellite attending that planet, and he ascertained the existence of its permanent ring. His works have been collected in 6 vols. 4to.—*Blake.*

His speculations in Optics, Dynamics, &c., were very acute and original.

Hooke, 1635.

An eminent English natural philosopher. A man of undoubted talents; published a number of papers in the Philosophical Transactions.

Willoughby, 1635.

An eminent naturalist. His principal work was "Ornithologiæ Libri tres," which has been translated into English.

Newton, 1642.

With great powers of mind, and with a comprehension which embraced at one view the meaning of every subject to which he directed attention, and overleaped as trifling all the difficulties which had arrested the progress of other philosophers, he was enabled to shed lustre on the age in which he lived, and the country which gave him birth; and to introduce such astonishing improvements, and make such stupendous discoveries in science, in mathematics, and astronomy, as would, each of them individually, have bestowed immortality. His most valuable works have been collected and published, together with an excellent commentary, 1784, in 5 vols. 4to, by Bishop Horsley.

Leibnitz, 1646.

(See above.)

Des Carles, 1650.

It is to his geometrical and algebraic discoveries, perhaps, that he is indebted for the most solid part of his fame, though to him more than to any other one philosopher is the science of dynamics indebted. His works were published at Amsterdam, 1692, 9 vols. 4to.—*Enc. Am.*

Tournefort, 1656.

An eminent French botanist. He travelled over the Levant, and published a work with the title of "Rélation d'un Voyage du Levant" (2 vols. 4to). Of this work, which stands high among books of the class, there have been several editions, and it has been translated into English.—*Enc. Am.*

Halley, 1656.

His reputation was widely extended, both as a profound philosopher, and as a man of taste; and almost every department of physical science received some improvements from his labours. In 1752 appeared his "Astronomical Tables for computing the places of the Sun, Moon, Planets, and Comets."—*Enc. Am.*

L'Hopital, 1661.

Such was his reputation, that Huygens, profound as was his acquaintance with science, did not disdain to apply to him for information relative to the nature of the differential calculus. He was the author of Les Sections Coniques, Les Lieux Géométriques, La Construction des Equations, and Une Théorie des Courbes Mechaniques.—*Enc. Am.*

Celsius, 1672.

A Swedish Orientalist. His "Hierobotanicon" is a learned work on the plants mentioned in the Bible.—*Enc. Am.*

Bradley, 1692.

From his "Astronomical Observations made at the Observatory at Greenwich, 1750–62" (Oxford, 1805, 2 vols. folio) thousands of observations on the sun, moon, and planets have been taken, which, properly arranged, have brought our astronomical tables to great accuracy.—*Enc. Am.*

Simpson (*Robert*), 1695.

He published a treatise on Conic Sections, and a valuable edition of Euclid.

Bernard de Jussieu, 1699.

A French botanist. Cuvier says of him, "The most modest, and, perhaps, the most profound botanist of the eighteenth century, who, although he scarcely published anything, is, nevertheless, the inspiring genius of modern botanists."—*Enc. Am.*

Franklin, 1707.

To this American philosopher we owe the discovery of the identity of lightning and electricity, and the invention of lightning rods.

Euler, 1707.

He distinguished himself particularly by his endeavours to perfect the analytic mode, according to the system of the Leibnitzian school, and to complete its separation from pure geometry, which Newton's disciples principally employed in their investigations. He wrote a famous "Théorie Complète de la Construction et de la Manœuvre des Vaisseaux," which has been translated into English, Italian, and Russian. His greatest production was "Institutiones Calculi Integralis," Berlin, 1755. His remarkably clear Introduction to Algebra must also be remembered.—*Enc. Am.*

Haller, 1708.

A German physician. He published a large work on Botany of the Plants of Switzerland.—*Enc. Am.*

Simpson (*Thomas*), 1710.

A renowned English mathematician, who wrote a New Treatise on Fluxions, a Treatise on Algebra, &c., &c.—*Blake.*

Cullen, 1712.

A celebrated English physician. His "First Lines of the Practice of Physic" must be considered his "*magnum opus,*" and which, amid all the recent fluctuations of opinion, has retained its value.—*Enc. Am.*

D'Alembert, 1717.

One of the most distinguished French mathematicians of the eighteenth century. He published two famous works on Dynamics, "*Traité de Dynamique,*" and on Fluids, "*Traité des Fluides.*" Among his communications to the academy at Berlin, two are highly distinguished: that on Pure Analysis, and the one which treats of the vibration of strings.—*Enc. Am.*

His works, Paris, Berlin, 1821-22, 5 vols., $4 50.

Mayer, 1723.

A celebrated German astronomer. About his time astronomers were employed on the theory of the moon, to assist in finding the longitude at sea. He overcame all difficulties, and prepared the excellent lunar tables by which the situation of the moon may at any time be ascertained to a minute, and which have immortalized him.—*Enc. Am.*

A part of his MSS. have appeared: "Opera inedita," edition of Lichtenberg, Goettingen, 1774, folio.

Hunter, 1728.

An English physician. His fame chiefly rests on his researches concerning comparative anatomy. He published a celebrated work, "Observations on various Parts of the Animal Economy," 1 vol. 4to.—*Enc. Am.*

Black, 1728.

A celebrated English chemist. He enriched the science with his doctrine of latent heat, which has led to such important results. He wrote "Lectures on Chemistry."
2 vols., 1803.

Lalande, 1732.

In 1764 he published his "Astronomie," a classical work, which was afterward printed in 3 vols. 4to, and reached the third edition, and of which he made an abridgment. It is a work which cannot be too highly recommended to the lovers of this science.—*Enc. Am.*
3 vols. 4to, $12 00.

Lagrange, 1736.

One of the most consummate mathematicians of modern times. Of his well-known works, his "Mechanique Analytique" is one of the most celebrated.
2 vols. 4to, $7 50, Paris, 1811.

Lavoisier, 1743.

A celebrated French chemist, whose name is connected with the antiphlogistic theory of chemistry, to the reception of which he contributed by his writings and discoveries. In 1774 appeared his "Opuscules Chymiques," comprising a general view of what was then known relative to gaseous bodies, with several new experiments, remarkable for ingenuity and accuracy.—*Enc. Am.*

Volta, 1745.

He turned his attention to the subject of Galvanism, and to his researches is due the discovery of what has been termed the principle of electro-motion, or the excitement of electricity by the contact of heterogeneous substances, as exhibited in the phenomena of the Voltaic pile, or electric column. —*Blake.*

Laplace, 1749.

A celebrated French astronomer and geometrician. His two greatest works, which would suffice to immortalize his name, are, "An Exposition of the System of the World," 2 vols. 8vo, and "A Treatise on Celestial Mechanism," 5 vols. 4to.

Werner, 1750.

A celebrated German mineralogist. He published a work on mineralogy, which has been considered as the basis of his oryctognostic, or mineralogical system. It has been translated into various languages, and adopted and commended by other writers.—*Enc. Am.*

Rumford, 1752.

He was familiar with the discoveries and improvements of modern science, and the industry and perseverance with which he pursued his inquiries enabled him to make some considerable additions to our knowledge of chemistry and practical philosophy. He published four volumes of Essays, experimental, political, economical, and philosophical.—*Enc. Am.*

Bell, 1763.

An eminent English physician. He published a celebrated work on "Anatomy." The first volume consists of a description of the bones, muscles, and joints; the second, the anatomy of the heart and arteries. The work was completed by his brother.—*Penny Enc.*

Wollaston, 1766.

Though almost every branch of science, at different times, occupied his attention, chemistry was that to which he seems to have been most ardently devoted, and it was by his investigations in that department of philosophy that he attained the most distinguished reputation.

Leslie, 1766.

A Scottish mathematician, inventor of the differential thermometer, and author of various scientific works.

Mohs, 1774.

A celebrated German mineralogist. His principal works are his "Charakteristic des Naturhistorischen Mineralsystem," Dresden, 1820, and "Grundriss der Mineralogie," 1822-26.—*Enc. Am.*

Gauss, 1777.

One of the first mathematicians of the age. He gave a brilliant display of his powers in his "Disquisitiones Mathematicæ," Leipzig, 1801, a work full of the most refined mathematical speculation, by which the higher arithmetic has been enriched with beautiful discoveries. He also published "Theoria Motus Corporum Cœlestium," Hamburg, 1809, 4to, a work which contributed much to give a right direction to the efforts made about this time for a more exact and proper use of astronomical observations.

De Candolle, 1778.

A celebrated French botanist. His "Théorie Elémentaire de la Botanique" is well known.—*Enc. Am.*

Sir H. Davy, 1779.

The discovery of the metallic basis of the alkalis and earths, the creation of the science of electro-chemistry, the invention of the safety-lamp, and of the mode of preserving the copper-sheeting of ships, form a part of his labours.

His works, 9 vols. 8vo, $28 00, London, 1840.

Berzelius, 1779.

He has enriched chemistry, which, in our times, has become a perfectly new science, by the most important discoveries and profound works, and he has proved himself one of the best chemical analysts.—*Enc. Am.*

Legendre, 1787.

He has made very important and profound researches respecting the attraction of elliptic spheroids, and has the glory of having been the first to prove that the ellipse is the only form that can preserve the equilibrium of a revolving liquid mass, and that the particles of the mass attract each other according to the square of their distances.

Among his more important works are, Théorie des Nombres, Paris, 1830, 2 vols., $7 00. Exercise de Calcul Intégral, &c., &c., Paris, 1811, 3 vols., $15 00.

IV. HISTORIANS.

(A.) ANCIENT.

1. GREEK.

Hecatæus, 550 B.C.

The fragments of this writer that have reached our times were collected by Creuzer, and published in his "Historicorum Græcorum Antiquit.—*Anthon.*

Fragmenta, 8vo, Heidelberg, 1806.

Pherecydes, 530 B.C.

A celebrated sage of ancient Greece. He is regarded as the first who wrote on philosophy and religion. The fragments of his works were collected by Sturz.—*Enc. Am.*

Second edition, Gera, 1798.

Herodotus, 484 B.C.

(See third part.) Best edition, Schweighäuser, Greek and Latin, Strasburg, 1816, 6 vols. 8vo.

Thucydides, 471 B.C.

(See third part.) Best edition, Becker, Greek and Latin, Oxford, 1821, 4 vols. 8vo.

Hellanicus of Mytilene, 460 B.C.

He made the first attempt to employ chronology in history. The fragments which remain of his writings were published in Leipzig, second edition, 8vo, 1826.—*Anthon.*

Xenophon, 450 B.C.

(See third part.)

Herodotus, 7 vols., Thucydides, 6 vols., Xenophon, 10 vols., Opera Omnia, Greek and Latin, 23 vols., Edinburgh, 1804-11, $50 00.

Ctesias, 400 B.C.

He wrote a work on the Assyrian and Persian History, in twenty-three books, and also *one* book on India. We have only some fragments, preserved in Photius. They were published by Bähr, Frankfort, 1824.—*Eschenburg.*

Theopompus, 360 B.C.

Dionysius says of this historian, "Not content with relating whatever has passed before the eyes of the world, Theopompus penetrates to the inmost souls of his principal actors, scrutinizes narrowly their most secret intentions, removes the mask from them, and brings forward into open day those vices which their hypocrisy had hoped to conceal. Hence some have charged him with calumniating, because he has blamed boldly what deserved to be blamed, and has lessened the glory which surrounded some individuals."

In 1829 the first complete edition of all the fragments appeared, from the Leyden press, with Notes, a Life of Theopompus, &c., &c., by Wichers, 8vo.

Polybius, 203 B.C.

(See third part.) Best edition, "Historiarum Reliquiæ," Greek and Latin, 8vo, Paris, 1839, $4 75.

2. ROMAN.

Julius Cæsar, 100 B.C.

(See third part.) His complete works by Oberlin, 8vo, $2 50, London, 1825.

Sallustius Crispus, 100 B.C.

(See third part.) 1 vol. folio, $3 25, Venice.

Cornelius Nepos.

Of his writings, we have only the biographies of distinguished Grecian generals. They are models of the biographic style, on account of their concise, and yet clear and full dress, and elegance of diction.—*Eschb.*

Best edition, Fischer, Lips., 1806, 8vo.

Dionysius, 60 B.C.

His narrative is not wholly impartial, being often too favourable to the Romans, and his style is not unexceptionable; yet we may obtain from this work the best insight of the Roman system and constitution, because the author was led, in explaining to the Greeks a novel and strange subject, to enter into particulars much more than the Roman writers needed to do.—*Eschenburg.*

Livy, 59 B.C.

(See third part.) Best edition, Homeri, London, 8vo, 1794, 3 vols., $7 50.

Velleius Paterculus, 19 B.C.

He is the author of a summary history of Rome. It comes down from the commencement of Rome to his own times, and deserves commendation more for its style than historical verity, as he was evidently swayed by partiality and a servile adulation towards Tiberius and Sejanus.—*Eschb.*

Best edition, Lemaire, Paris, 1822, 8vo. Translated by Baker, 8vo, $1 50, London, 1814.

Suetonius, A.D. 50.

He gives a plain and candid account of facts, many of them otherwise not known, but of the greatest importance for history. His style is simple, concise, and correct, without either ornament or affectation.—*Anthon.*

Opera edit., F. A. Wolf, 4 vols., Leipz., 1802, $4 50. A good translation by Dr. A. Thomson, London, 8vo, 1796.

Curtius Rufus.

He wrote a history of the deeds of "Alexander the Great." His style differs much from the noble simplicity of most of the Greek and Roman historians, and often sinks into the extravagant and romantic; his style is also frequently elaborate, and abounds too much in ornament. Notwithstanding this, his narrative is not deficient in suavity and interest.

Diodorus, first century.

We are indebted to him for many particulars which, but for him, we never should have known; and we must regret that we have lost the last, and, probably, the most valuable portion of his works, as even by the fragments which remain, we are enabled in many places to correct the errors of Livy. The style of Diodorus, though not very pure or elegant, is sufficiently perspicuous, and presents but few difficulties, except where the MSS. are defective, as is frequently the case.—*Anthon.*

Best edition, Bipont, 8vo, 1793, Greek and Latin, Heynii, 11 vols.

Valerius Maximus, first century.

Notwithstanding the faults of this historian, his work is interesting both for the history and the study of antiquity, and contains a number of little facts taken from authors whose works have not reached us.

Best edition, Hare, 3 vols. 8vo, Paris, 1822.

Tacitus, first century.

(See third part.) Best edition, Leipz., 8vo, 1801, Oberlin, 4 parts, 2 vols., $11 00.

Appianus, first century.

His Roman History abounds with valuable information respecting the history of those times, and on many points of ancient geography. Though evidently a compilation, it is not the less important, however, on this account, since many of the sources whence he derived his information are completely lost to us, while, for some epochs of Roman history, he is the only authority we possess.—*Enc. Am.*

Best late edition is that of Schweighäuser, Leipzig and Strasburg, 1785, 3 vols.

Plutarch, end of first century.

(See third part.) Best edition, Coray, Paris, 1809–15, 6 vols. 8vo. Good translation by Langhorne, 8vo, $3 50, London, 1840.

Florus, end of first century.

He has left us an Abridgment of Romar History. This work is an extract, not merely from Livy, but from many other ancient historians, no part of whose works any longer remain. It is less a history than a eulogium on the Roman people, written with elegance, but, at the same time, in an oratorical style, and not without affectation.—*Anthon.*

Best edition is that of Duker, Lugd. Bat., 1722 and '44, 2 vols. 8vo.

Justinus, second century.

He made an Epitome of the History of Trogus Pompeius. To judge from the epitome, there were many errors in the work, especially in the Jewish history; but this epitome, which corresponds to the original in its title and arrangement, has obtained a considerable reputation, and even now is often used in schools. The style is, on the whole, elegant and agreeable, but it is destitute of that noble simplicity and classical correctness which distinguish the work of a master.

Best edition is that of Hearne, Oxford, 1705.

Dion Cassius, A.D. 155.

He wrote the Roman History in eighty books, of which only those from the thirty-sixth to the fifty-fourth are extant complete. He gives an impartial account of events which he witnessed, but is often influenced by jealousy or servility. His style is too rhetorical for history.

Herodianus, 240 A.D.

We see the importance of his work in its forming a grave, and almost solitary chronicle of a part of Roman history; for the writers of the Augustan age, who lived long after him, hardly do more than copy his narrative. His style is plain and unaffected, and his narrative, in general, seems written in a spirit of sincerity, but it has no claims to philosophical or critical art. His greatest fault is having neglected chronology.

The best edition is that of Becker, Berlin, 1826, 8vo.

Scriptores Historiæ Augustæ.

Spartianus, Capitolinus, Trebellius Pollio, Flavius, Vopiscus, are collectively called by that name.—*Eschenburg.*

Ammianus Marcellinus, 4th century.

No writer was ever more entitled to praise for candour and impartiality. He understood well the art of clearly showing the connexion of events, and of painting in striking colours the characters of those individuals whom he introduces into his narrative. He is one of the principal sources that we have for the geography and history of ancient Germany.—*Anthon.*

Best edition, Gronovius, Lugd. Bat., 1693, 4to.

Aurelius Victor, 380 A.D.

His History of the Origin of the Roman People, according to its title, from Janus until the tenth consulate, under Constantine, but, as we have it, only to the first year after the foundation of Rome, contains many circumstances not mentioned by others, or, at least, not so minutely.—*Anthon.*

Best edition is that of Arntzenius, Amst., 1733, 4to.

Eutropius, 4th century.

He wrote an abridgment of the Roman History. It is a brief and dry outline, without either elegance or ornament, yet containing certain facts which are nowhere else mentioned.—*Anthon.*

Best edition, Tzschucke, Leipzig, 1797, 8 vols.

(B.) MEDIÆVAL.

Gregory of Tours, 593.

His "Historiæ Eccles. Francorum Libri X.," which, notwithstanding its marvellous tales and want of method, has much interest, as being the only historical work of the time.—*Enc. Am.*

Opera, ex edit., Theod. Ruinart, Parisiis, 1699, fol., $6 50.

Bede, 672.

The writings of Bede were numerous and important, considering the time in which they were written. His English Ecclesiastical History is the greatest and most popular of his works, and has acquired additional celebrity by the translation of King Alfred.—*Enc. Am.*

Bede's Ecclesiastical History of the English Nation, carefully revised and corrected from the translation of Mr. Stevens, by the Rev. J. A. Giles, 8vo, $2 62, London, 1840.

Eginhardt, about 790.

He is the oldest German historian, and we have from him a full and well-written History of the Life of Charlemagne, which was published by Schmink, 1711, 4to, with illustrations and biography. His letters, which are of much importance as contributions to the history of his age (Frankfort, 1714, fol.), are still extant.—*Enc. Am.*

Gulielmus Tyrius, 12th century.

One of the best historians of the Crusades, having been an eyewitness of a part of the events which he relates. An edition of his works was published by Henrico Pantaleone, Basil, 1564, in folio.

Geoffrey of Monmouth, 12th century.

Among his various productions, his Chronicle, or History of the Britons, is the only one which requires notice. It contains a pretended genealogy of the kings of Britain from the time of the fabulous Bruce. The wonderful stories told of King Arthur also take their rise in this work.—*Enc. Am.*

His history was published by Commeline, Heidelberg, 1587, folio, Latin. An English translation by Aaron Thompson, London, 1718, 8vo.

William of Malmsbury, 12th century.

Finding that a satisfactory account of his own country was wanting, he determined to write one. His "De Regibus Anglorum" is a general history of England, in five books, from the arrival of the Saxons, in 449, to the 26th Henry I., in 1126; a modern history, in two books, from that year to the escape of the Empress Maud from Oxford, in 1143; with a Church history of England, in four books, published in Sir H. Savile's collection (1596). He discovers great diligence, good sense, and modesty.—*Enc. Am.*

Matthew of Westminster, 13th century.

An English chronicler. He compiled a chronicle, commencing from the creation, and extending to the year 1307, which he entitled "Flores Historiarum," Frankfort, 1601.

Giovanni Villani, 13th century.

An Italian historian. He wrote the History of Florence, from its foundation to 1348. This work is extremely valuable; it deserves full credit wherever the author, whose veracity and honesty are everywhere visible, speaks as an eyewitness. It is simple and inartificial, but not without interest, on account of its naïveté and vigour.—*Enc. Am.*

Last edition, 1729, 2 vols. folio.

Matteo Villani.

He continued the work of his brother to 1363. The book treats of contemporaneous events, and is characterized by the same love of truth which is found in the work of Giovanni.

(C.) MODERN.

1. ENGLISH AND AMERICAN.

Thomas Walsingham, fifteenth century.

An English chronicler; he also styles himself royal historiographer. His works are "Historia Brevis," containing the annals of England from the end of Henry III.'s reign, and "Hypodigma Neustriæ," giving an account of the occurrences in Normandy from the time of Rollo to the sixth year of Henry V.—*Enc. Am.*

London, 1574, folio.

Buchanan, 1506.

As an historian, he is considered to have united the beauties of Livy and Sallust as to style; but he discovered a great lack of judgment and investigative spirit, taking up all the tales of the chronicles as he found them, and affording to their legendary absurdities the currency of his own eloquent embellishment.

History of Scotland, translated, &c., &c., $3 00, London, 1831.

Camden, 1551.

His life of Elizabeth is a solid and valuable history.—*Hallam.*

Raleigh, 1552.

Among his valuable works his "History of the World" stands pre-eminent; the Greek and Roman story is told more fully and correctly than by any earlier English writers, with a plain eloquence, which has given this book a classical reputation in our language. The author has intermingled political reflections, and illustrated the history by episodes from modern times, which now, perhaps, are the most interesting passages.—*Hallam.*

History of the World, folio, $6 00, London, 1614.

Francis Bacon, 1561.

His life of Henry VII. is the first instance, in our language, of the application of philosophy to reasoning on public events in the manner of the ancients. Praise upon Henry is too largely bestowed; but it was in the nature of Bacon to admire too much a crafty and selfish policy, and he thought, also, no doubt, that so near an ancestor of his own sovereign should not be treated with severe impartiality.—*Hallam.*

Lord Herbert of Cherbury, 1581.

His History of Henry VIII. ought here to be added to the list, as a book of good authority, relatively, at least, to any that preceded, and written in a manly and judicious spirit.—*Hallam.*

4to, $2 00, London, 1740.

Clarendon, 1608.

(See third part.)

Fuller, 1610.

His "Worthies of England" is a production valuable alike for the information it affords relative to the provincial history of the country, and for the profusion of biographical anecdote and acute observation on men and manners. His History of the Church is also very interesting.—*Enc. Am.*

Lyttleton, 1708.

His History of Henry II. contains the elaborate result of the researches and deliberations of twenty years.—*Edinburgh Encyclopædia.*

5 vols. 4to, $7 50, London, 1767.

Watson, 1710.

He published the History of Philip II. of Spain (2 vols., 1777), and undertook that of Philip III., which, being left imperfect at his death, was completed and published by D. Wm. Thomson, 1783.—*Enc. Am.*

1 vol. 4to, $1 50, London.

Hume, 1711.

(See third part.)

Henry, 1718.

His laborious History of England contains much historical information properly arranged, and is to be read without difficulty.—*Smyth.*

12 vols. 8vo, $16 00, London.

Ferguson, 1724.

He composed a History of the Roman Republic. This work is not so much a regular narrative of the events of the Roman history as a commentary on that history; its object is to elucidate the progress and changes of the internal policy of the Roman commonwealth, the successive conditions of its social state, as well as the progress of the milita-

ry system of the Romans. This work, therefore, forms a kind of introduction to that of Gibbon.—*Penny Cyclopædia.*
3 vols. 8vo, $5 00.

Goldsmith, 1731.

(See third part.)

Robertson, 1733.

(See third part.)

Milford, 1734.

(See third part.)

Warton, 1734.

"History of English Poetry." What the author has done of this great work exhibits an extent of research and reading, and a correctness of taste and critical judgment, which render it a subject of regret that he should have been diverted from completing his design.—*Enc. Am.*
3 vols. 4to, $7 50, London.

Gibbon, 1737.

(See third part.)

Stuart, 1742.

He is the author of "History of the Reformation in Scotland" (1784), and "History of Scotland" (1782). His works display erudition, industry, and sound judgment, wherever the latter quality is not influenced by his jealousy and hatred of contemporary writers.—*Enc. Am.*

Russell, 1746.

He was the author of the "History of America from its discovery by Columbus to the conclusion of the late War," 1778, 2 vols. 4to, and the "History of Modern Europe, with an Account of the Decline and Fall of the Roman Empire," in a series of letters, 1779, 4 vols. 8vo.—*Blake.*

Cox, 1747.

His "History of Austria" is executed with every appearance of diligence, and furnishes the English reader with a complete account of the political history of that celebrated state. By his labours we may consider ourselves as furnished with information, which we must otherwise have extracted with great pain and labour, if at all, from those documents and historians in different languages to which they refer.—*Smyth.*

Roscoe, 1752.

(See third part.)

Belsham, 1752.

His historical works were published in a uniform edition in 12 vols. 8vo, under the title of "History of Great Britain to the Conclusion of the Peace of Amiens in 1802."—*Penny Enc.*

London, 1805, 5 vols. 4to, $10 00.

Sir J. Mackintosh, 1765.

(See third part.)

Lingard, 1780.

(See third part.)

Hallam's Constitutional History of England.

This work is eminently judicial; its whole spirit is that of the bench, not of the bar. He sums up with a calm, steady impartiality, turning neither to the right nor to the left, glossing over nothing, exaggerating nothing. On a general survey, we do not scruple to pronounce the constitutional history the most impartial history that we ever read.—*Enc. Am.*

4 vols. 8vo, $7 50.

Turner.

(See third part.)

Prescott's Ferdinand and Isabella

(See third part.)

Bancroft's History of the United States.

(See third part.)

Irving's Conquest of Grenada.

(See third part.)

2. FRENCH.

Froissart, 1337.

His historical writings, which reach down to 1400, are precious documents, exhibiting the character and manner of his age.—*Enc. Am.*

By his picturesque description and fertility of historical invention, he may be reckoned the Livy of France.—*Hallam.*

Froissart's Chronicles of England, France, Spain, translated from the French by Johnes, London, 1838, 2 vols. 8vo, $10 00.

Philip de Comines, 1445.

He is the first of modern writers who in any degree has displayed sagacity in reasoning on the characters of men and the consequences of their actions, or who has been able to generalize his observations by comparison and reflection. He is free from that pedantic application of history, which became common with those who passed for political reasoners in the next two centuries.—*Hallam.*

Monstrelet, 15th century.

He was the author of a history of his own time in French. It extended from 1400 to 1467, but the last fifteen years were furnished by another hand.

Chronicles of England, France, Spain, &c., &c., translated from the French by Johnes, London, 1840, 2 vols. 8vo, $9 50.

De Thou, 1553.

He composed in the Latin language a voluminous history of his own times. It comprises the years from 1545 to 1607. Accurately acquainted with the politics, revolutions, and geography of modern Europe, the narrative of De Thou is at once copious and exact, while his native candour and love of truth ensured all the necessary freedom and impartiality.—*Enc. Am.*

De Thou, Histoire Universelle, London, 1734, 16 vols. 4to, $20 00.

Duchesne, 1584.

He has been called the father of French history. His most important works are, his Collection of French Historians, his Historiæ Normanorum Scriptores ab Anno 838–1220, and his genealogical works, which throw much light on the history of France.

Paris, 1636, 5 vols., $12 00.

Dufresne, or *Ducange*, 1610.

He did much for the history of the Middle Ages, especially as regards France, as well as for the Byzantine history. He wrote "Historia Byzantina," Paris, 1680, folio.—*Enc. Am.*

Montfaucon, 1655.

Among his numerous works, we here only mention his "Monumens de la Monarchie Françoise." Of an author who has left 44 vols. folio, it may be expected that elegance will not be a characteristic; accordingly, his writings are blamed for their cumbrous style and defective arrangement, but his erudition has never been questioned, and his works are still looked up to as guides through that obscure and intricate department of knowledge, which he devoted his life to study.—*Edinburgh Enc.*

The above-mentioned work, Paris, 1729–33, 5 vols., folio.

Vertot, 1655.

(See third part.)

Rapin, 1661.

His great work, L'Histoire d'Angleterre (Hague, 10 vols. 4to, 1725–26), has been twice translated. It is prolix and unanimated, but impartial, and contains much solid information.—*Enc. Am.*

Rapin's History of England, from Julius Cæsar to the Revolution, 1688, translated by N. Findall, second edition, 2 vols. folio, $7 50, London, 1732.

Rollin, 1661.

(See third part.)

Count de Caylus, 1692.

Among his principal works is his "Recueil d'Antiquités Egyptiennes," Paris, 1752–67, 7 vols. If he has sometimes misunderstood the ancient authors, and committed some errors with respect to ancient monuments, he has, nevertheless, treated with great success of the processes and materials employed in the arts by the ancients.—*Enc. Am.*

Voltaire, 1694.

Among his historical works, "Le Siècle de Louis XIV. et Louis XV.," and the History of Charles XII., &c., &c., abound in penetrating views. His merits are not those of thorough investigation, but of striking and happy description and sagacious observation. His prevailing defect is the exaggerated estimation of the superiority of the French over other modern nations.

Mably, 1709.

His style is easy, pure, often elegant, but tame; his views often partake of the asperity of his temper. His complete works appeared at Paris, 1794, 15 vols.

Goguet, 1716.

He was the author of that excellent work entitled "L'Origine des Loix, des Arts, des Sciences, et de leur Progrès chez les Anciens Peuples," 1758, 3 vols. 4to. The author has done the most he could with the scanty materials within his reach.—*Penny Cyc.*

Barthelemy, 1716.

(See third part.)

Raynal, 1718.

Though he is to be censured for his opinions, which are often licentious and skeptical, his writings possess vigour, clearness, and elegance, and exhibit the nervous powers of an ardent imagination, and the striking features of a rapid invention. Some of his works are, History of the English Parliament, 2 vols. 12mo; Historical Anecdotes from the Age of Charles V., 3 vols. 12mo; Historical Memoirs of Europe; History of the Revolution of the English American Colonies.—*Brunet.*

Millot, 1726.

Some of his works are much esteemed for the spirit and elegance of their style. The following were published together: "Elémens de l'Histoire Générale, Ancienne et Moderne;" Elémens de l'Histoire de France; de l'Histoire d'Angleterre.—*Brunet.*

Paris, 1800, 15 vols. 8vo.

Daru, 1767.

We are indebted to him for two important works, the Life of Sully, and the History of Venice. The last of these is one of the most important productions of modern literature in the department of history. It appeared in a third edition in 1825, in 8 vols.—*Enc. Am.*

Sismondi, 1773.

(See third part.)

Michaud, 1775.

He was the author of an Historical View of the First Wars of Napoleon, 2 vols., and a History of the Crusades.

Guizot, 1787.

(See third part.)

Lacretelle, 1790.

As an historical writer he has a peculiarly brilliant diction, although his ideas want force and profundity. He wrote Histoire de France pendant les Guerres de Religion; Histoire de France depuis la Restauration, 3 vols., not completed.—*Enc. Am.*

Villemain, 1791.

Histoire de Cromwell, d'après les Mémoires du Temps,

et les Recueils Parlementaires, 2 vols. 8vo, Paris, 1819. In all respects a very good book.—*Quart. Rev.*

Michelet.

(See third part.)

Augustin Thierry.

He has pointed out with great sagacity the defects of the existing French historians. The work which has established his reputation is, "History of the Conquest of England by the Normans, its Causes and Consequences on England, Scotland, and Ireland, and on the Continent."

Third edition, Paris, 1830, 4 vols., $3 50.

Amadée Thierry.

History of the Gauls from the distant Times to the entire Submission of Gaul under the Roman Dominion.

Paris, 1828, 3 vols. 8vo, $3 00.

Capefigue.

History of Philip Augustus, Paris, 1829, 4 vols. 8vo. Constitutional and Administrative History of France from the Death of Philip Augustus, Paris, 1831, 8vo.

Mignet.

History of the French Revolution from 1789 to 1814, fifth edition, Paris, 1833, 2 vols. 8vo.

The author has drawn from every source, has neglected no kind of testimony, but perhaps the best claim to confidence lies in his not having witnessed the scenes which he relates. He depicts in the most vivid colours its disorders and its triumphs; he develops its mischiefs and its benefits, and judges all in a spirit of impartiality.—*Edinb. Rev.*

Thiers.

History of the French Revolution, second edition, Brussels, 1838, 4 vols. Translated, with notes, by F. Shoberl, 5 vols. 8vo, $15 00, London, 1840.

3. ITALIAN AND SPANISH.

Poggio, 1380.

His sentiments are, in general, liberal and manly, and he may be deemed the most elegant composer in Latin (the language of his works). His "Historia Florentina," which comprises the period from 1350 to 1455, is to be found in the collection of Grævius and Muratori.—*Enc. Am.*

Valla, 1406.

Among the revivers of literature he has always held a high rank, which he merited by unwearied application and an enlarged course of study, including history, criticism, &c., &c. His works were published together at Basil, in 1543.—*Enc. Am.*

Platina, 1421.

He wrote the "Lives of the Popes," printed first at Venice, 1479, folio; History of Mantua, &c., &c., all in Latin, and collected in folio, 1752.—*Blake.*

Lives of the Popes, 1 vol. 8vo, $2 00, London, 1704.

Politianus, 1454.

A learned Florentine scholar. Among the most esteemed of his writings is an Account of the Conspiracy of the Pazzi. —*Enc. Am.*

Pactianæ Conjurationis Commentariolum Anno 1478, 4to.

Mirandola, 1463.

He was considered by his contemporaries a miracle of learning. He published a mystical or cabalistic explanation of the history of the creation, in which he derives Plato's doctrines from Moses. In judging of this work, it is necessary to remember the state of letters at the time when he lived.—*Enc. Am.*

Machiavelli, 1469.

His eight books on the History of Florence are among the first historical works of modern times, which deserve to be placed side by side with the beautiful remains of antiquity. The history is distinguished for its pure, elegant, and flowing style; its impartiality is doubtful. Some of the best observations on Machiavel are to be found in a work probably little known to our readers, Professor Ranke's "Zur Kritik neuerer Geschichtschreiber," Berlin and Leipzig, 1824.—*Enc. Am.*

Works of Machiavel translated, $5 00.

Guicciardini, 1482.

His History of Italy is well known for the solidity of the reflections, the gravity and impartiality with which it is written, and the prolixity of its narration; a fault, however, frequent, and not unpardonable in historians contemporary and familiar with the events they relate. Guicciardini has generally held the first place among Italian historians, though he is by no means equal, in literary merit, to Machiavel.—*Hallam.*

Guicciardini's History, containing the Wars of Italy and other parts, reduced into English by Jeffrey Fenton, folio, $4 50, London, 1618.

Mendoza, 1503.

His History of the Wars of Grenada is placed, by the Spaniards themselves, on a level with the most renowned of the ancients.—*Hallam.*

Baronius, 1538.

His Annals (Rome, 1588–1607, 12 vols. folio) comprise a rich collection of genuine documents from the papal archives, and are therefore of great use to the student of ecclesiastical history, but contain many false statements and unauthentic documents, and the air of sincerity which prevails throughout is calculated to give very erroneous ideas of the papal administration of the Church.—*Enc. Am.*

Sarpi, 1552.

In his "History of the Council of Trent," he has developed the intrigues connected with the transactions of the famous assembly with a degree of boldness and veracity which renders the work one of the most interesting and important productions of the class to which it belongs.—*Enc. Am.*

4to, $6 50, Helmstaedt, 1761.

Bentivoglio, 1579.

In his History of the Civil Wars of Flanders he has united great political knowledge with perspicuity of narrative and force of language. He is often wonderfully eloquent. As a model of the perfect historical style, we cannot recommend a finer example than Bentivoglio's Introduction to the work we have mentioned.—*Tytler.*

1 vol. folio, Paris, $2 25.

Davila, 1579.

He is principally celebrated for his History of the Civil Wars of France, from 1559 to 1598. This has been translated into several languages, and deserves a place near the works of Guicciardini and Machiavelli.—*Enc. Am.*

2 vols. folio, $7 50, Paris.

Muratori, 1672.

Annali d'Italia dal principio dell' Era volgare sino all anno 1750, e continuati sino all anno 1827. 40 vols. 8vo, $40 00,

Firenze, 1827. A valuable work, which has often been reprinted.—*Enc. Am.*

Botta, 1766.

(See third part.)

4. GERMAN.

Centuriæ Magdeburgenses, 1540.

Under this title a regular and copious history of the Church, from the primitive ages to the Reformation, was compiled. Mosheim, or his translator, calls this an immortal work; and Eichhorn speaks of it in strong terms of admiration for the boldness of the enterprise, the laboriousness of the execution, the spirit with which it cleared away a mass of fable, and placed ecclesiastical history on an authentic basis.—*Hallam.*

Basil, 1559, folio, $3 00.

Puffendorf, 1632.

He wrote a History of Sweden, from the campaign of Gustavus Adolphus in Germany to the abdication of Queen Christine; and the History of Charles Gustavus; and, lastly, an Introduction to the History of the Principal Kingdoms and States of Europe (translation, 8vo, $1 00, London, 1740). Puffendorf is a host in himself; no historical collection can be complete without his works.—*Dibdin.*

Mosheim, 1694.

(See third part.)

Schlegel, 1721.

(See third part.)

Pfeffel, 1726.

His principal works are, "Abrégé Chronologique de l'Histoire et du Droit publique d'Allemagne;" Recherches Historiques, concernant les Droits du Pape sur la ville et l'Etat d'Avignon; Etat de la Pologne.—*Enc. Am.*

All his works are of great ability and skill, and of value to the historian.

Adelung, 1732.

His work on the History of the Civilization of Mankind is a production of considerable merit.—*Penny Cyc.*

8vo, $2 00.

Herder, 1744.

He strove to discover a point of union where science, religion, history, poetry, and art should meet; and in order to take one comprehensive view of all the tendencies of man, he made himself acquainted with the literature of a variety of countries, Oriental as well as European, ancient as well as modern. His "Philosophy of the History of Man" has been translated.—*Penny Cyc.*

Herder, Philosophie und Geschichte, 14 vols. in 7, $6 00, 1827.

Tenneman, 1748.

A Manual of the History of Philosophy (translated by Rev. A. Johnson). A work which marks out all the leading epochs in philosophy, and gives minute chronological information concerning them, with biographical notices of the founders and followers of the principal schools, and ample texts of their works.—*Hayward.*

8vo, $4 00.

Müller, 1752.

To the study of the ancient classics he is indebted for that love of liberty and moral grandeur, that clearness and method of thought, elegance and energy of expression, which early distinguished him. His great work, "Geschichte Schweitzerischer Eidgenossenschaft," is distinguished for accuracy of research, profound and broad views, and, although minute, is not dry.—*Enc. Am.*

His Universal History, see below (third part).

Eichhorn, 1752.

He has composed several valuable works, of which, among others, his Ancient History of the Greeks and Romans, consisting entirely of extracts from the original historians, is in high repute (Antiqua Historia, ex ipsis veterum Script. Roman. Narrationibus contexta, Goett., 1811, 2 vols.). He afterward published a history of the last three centuries, considered in a general view, and in relation to the changes that have occurred in the particular countries of Europe, Asia, Africa, and America; in 1818 he brought it down to the latest period.—*Enc. Am.*

Schiller, 1759.

He added greatly to his reputation by his "History of the Revolt of the Netherlands," but his "Thirty Years' War" is deemed his chef d'œuvre in history.—*Penny Cyc.*

Heeren, 1760.

(See third part.)

Bouterweck, 1766.

He has gained a permanent reputation by his "History of Modern Poetry and Eloquence," published 1801–1821, a work which, though unequal in some respects, also partial and superficial, is an excellent collection of notices and original observations, and may be considered one of the best works of the kind in German literature.—*Enc. Am.*

Wachler, 1767.

Some of his works have great merit, though the writer may sometimes fall into indistinct generalities. "Manual of the History of Literature" (4 vols., 1822–24). History of Historical Inquiry and Art since the Revival of Letters in Europe, (1812–20).

Rotteck, 1775.

Rotteck is distinguished from all other German historians by the circumstance that his works, in addition to deep research and critical acuteness, display a civic spirit, if we may call it so. Though born in a country where civil liberty was so little understood at the time of his education, he has, nevertheless, learned to understand it, and to trace its development in history. His chief work is his Universal History, which has lately been translated.—*Enc. Am.*

Schlosser, 1776.

His works, "Universal History," "General View of the History and Civilization of the Ancients," and his history of the 18th century, display extensive acquaintance with the subjects, and much vigour and independence of thought.—*Enc. Am.*

Niebuhr, 1776.

(See third part.)

Raumer, 1781.

He is considered as Heeren's rival by his "History of the Sixteenth and Seventeenth Centuries," translated from the German, 2 vols. 8vo, $3 50. History of Queen Elizabeth, and Mary Queen of Scots, 8vo, $2 25. History of Frederic II. and his Times, 8vo, $2 25. The last two works are from original documents in the British Museum and state paper office.

Menzel, 1784.

His works, though not equal in deep research to those of many contemporary writers of Germany, are valuable for their descriptive merit, particularly his History of the Germans, Breslau, 1815-23, 8 vols. 4to.—*Enc. Am.*

History of German Literature, translated, 4 vols. 8vo, $9 00.

Neander, 1789.

(See third part.)

Busch.

He wrote in the style of a chronicler with great impartiality and research, but in rather a dry manner, and in an imperfect style, his " Outline of the History of the most Remarkable Events of Modern Times since 1440."—*Penny Cyc.*

Wachsmuth.

What other writers have done in subjecting the complicated events of modern times to a criticism, searching and minute as to details, and rich in results and general principles, the same patient investigation has been carried by Wachsmuth to the study of antiquity. In his hands it has become a rich and instructive study, peculiarly adapted to form the youthful mind to habits of careful investigation and accurate appreciation of evidence.—*Penny Cyc.*

Historical Antiquities of the Greeks, translated, 2 vols. 8vo, $8 00, Oxford.

Boëckh.

(See third part.)

V HISTORICAL MEMOIRS.

Xenophon's Anabasis, 450 B.C.

Xenophon describes his retreat, and at the same time the whole expedition of the younger Cyrus, in his Anabasis. His style in general, and particularly in this work, is a model of elegant simplicity.—*Enc. Am.*

A good translation by Spelman, London, 1742.

Cæsar's Commentaries, 100 B.C.

The Commentaries, written in a plain, perspicuous style, entirely free from all affectation, place him in the same class with Xenophon, and those few individuals who have successfully united the pursuit of letters and philosophy with the business of active life.—*Penny Enc.*

Best edition, Oudendorp, Leyden, 1757, 4to; translated by Duncan, 8vo, $1 75, London, 1832.

Brantome, 1157.

His Memoirs are a living picture of his age: for Brantome was personally acquainted with all the great characters of the times, and an eyewitness of all the important events which then took place, and in some was an actor. He places us in the middle of that century when expiring chivalry was contending with the forming, and, as yet, unsettled manners of later times.—*Enc. Am.*

8 vols. 8vo, Paris, 1822–24.

Comines, 1445.

His Memoirs contain the history of his own time, from 1464 to 1498. The great value of them consists in his frankness and sincerity. He is a matter-of-fact historian; he paints men and politics such as he found them to be, with all their selfishness, craft, and evil doings, which he relates with great imperturbability.—*Penny Cyc.*

The Memoirs translated by Danet, $2 75, London.

Las Casas, 1474.

His short "Narrative of the Destruction of the Indies" is justly celebrated. In it he gives a frightful account of the acts of oppression and barbarity committed by the conquerors.—*Penny Cyc.*

Margaret of Valois, 1492.

She related the history of her youth with much, although somewhat artificial elegance, and feminine adroitness, but, at the same time, evident good nature.—*Enc. Am.*

Montluc, 1500.

His Memoirs are deserving of being read, not only for their relation of events, but for a lively style, and occasionally for good sense and acute thinking.—*Penny Cyc.*

Du Bellay, 1513.

His Memoirs, relating to the period from 1513 to 1516 (Lambert, Paris, 1753, 7 vols.), are distinguished for vigorous delineation and the national feeling which they display.—*Enc. Am.*

Sully, 1559.

(See third part.)

Lord Herbert of Cherbury, 1581.

His character is strongly marked in his memoirs, which show him to be vain, punctilious, and fanciful, but open, generous, brave, and disinterested. His style is manly, strong, and free from the quaint pedantry of his age.—*Enc. Am.*

8vo, $2, London, 1826.

Winthrop, 1588.

(See third part.)

Rochefoucault, 1613.

He described the disturbances of the Fronde (1648–52) with the hand of a master, and has, notwithstanding his obvious partiality, great clearness and sagacity in relating and developing events, furnishes admirable portraits of the principal personages described, and is distinguished for animation and natural colouring.—*Enc. Am.*

De Retz, 1614.

(See third part.)

Pepys, 1620.

On the accession of William and Mary, he published his memoirs relating to the navy for ten years preceding. His diary affords a curious picture of the dissolute court of Charles II.—*Penny Cyc.*

2 vols., $9, London, 1825.

Burnet, 1643.

"History of his Own Times." With rarely anything like elegance, there is a fluency, and sometimes a rude strength in his style, which makes his work readable enough. Although it shows him to have been possessed of vanity and bustling officiousness, its testimony is very favourable to the excellence of his heart and moral nature, to his disinterestedness, his courage, his public spirit, and even to his ability and talent, within the proper range of his powers.—*Penny Cyc.*

8vo, $5.

Mather, 1663.

(See third part.)

Calamy, 1675.

He is the author of "Baxter's Life and Times." This work abounds in notices of the men, the transactions, the habits, and the opinions of the stirring period in which he lived.—*Penny Cyc.*

2 vols. 8vo, $2 50.

Duclos, 1705.

He is the author of Memoirs on the Manners of the Eighteenth Century. Though he took Tacitus for his model, he resembles him little in his delineation of character and the interest of his narrative.

Madame d'Epinay, 1712.

Her Memoirs give a true picture of the refined, but corrupt, manners which prevailed among the higher classes in France during the government of Louis XV.—*Enc. Am.*
Paris, 3 vols., 1818.

Walpole, 1718.

His Memoirs of the last ten years of the reign of George II. (2 vols. 4to, 1822) are of the highest value for the domestic history of that period.—*Enc. Am.*

Marmontel, 1723.

He holds a high rank among modern French authors. Warm and eloquent on elevated subjects, easy, lively, inventive, and ingenious on light ones, he addresses himself with equal success to the imagination, the judgment, and the heart.—*Enc. Am.*
2 vols. 12mo, $1 00.

Castelneau.

His Memoirs (1559–70, Brussels, 1731, 3 vols. folio) are distinguished for the highest political honesty, for the soundness, maturity, and clearness of his judgment, as much as for his dignified and tranquil manner.—*Enc. Am.*

Watson, 1737.

The volume entitled "Anecdotes of the Life of Bishop Watson" were written by himself, and contain much useful and interesting information.—*Edinb. Enc.*
8vo, $1 50, Philadelphia, 1818.

Madame Campan, 1752.

Her Memoirs respecting the private life of Marie Antoinette, with Recollections of the Times of Louis Fourteenth, Fifteenth, and Sixteenth, in 4 vols., contain interesting contributions to the History of the French Revolution.—*Enc. Am.*

Dohm, 1752.

His highly valuable Memoirs consist of a series of historical treatises upon the events of our times, in which Dohm has taken more or less part, or respecting which he has made investigations.—*Enc. Am.*

Madame Roland, 1754.

The best edition is that, "Memoirs de Madame Roland, avec une notice sur sa Vie" (1820). In them she gives an interesting account about her husband, his conduct, his ministry, and their private life.—*Blake.*

8vo, $1 50, Paris.

Madame La Roche Jacqueline.

She has written memoirs on the war in La Vendée, which contain vivid pictures of the events.—*Enc. Am.*

Wraxall, 1760.

"Memoirs of his Own Times." The author, a native of Bristol, in England, spent part of his life in the East Indies, and then travelled on the Continent to a great extent. His Memoirs are full of interesting incident.—*Enc. Am.*

7 vols., $14 00.

Wakefield, 1776.

He wrote "Memoirs of his Own Life," 2d edition, 1804, 2 vols. 8vo, a characteristic performance.—*Enc. Am.*

Bourrienne.

Highly entertaining Memoirs of Napoleon Bonaparte, translated. 18mo $1 75.

VI. BIOGRAPHY.

Cicero, 106 B.C.

"Middleton's Life of Cicero." Cicero's life, interesting on many accounts, is particularly so to the historical politician, as showing the consequences of the deplorable state of the Roman Republic in the case of so distinguished an individual, as well as the impossibility of preserving its liberty.—*Enc. Am.*

8vo, $2 50.

Philostratus, third century.

He wrote a valuable and interesting work entitled "Lives of the Sophists." It contains a fund of anecdotes illustrating the manners and morals of these ostentatious pretenders, and gives a vivid picture of the decline of eloquence.—*Enc. Am.*

A good English translation by Edw. Berwick, London, 1812, 8vo.

Plutarch, second century.

(See third part.)

Diogenes Laertius, third century.

His "Lives of the Philosophers" contains the biography of the principal philosophers of the various sects, together with their most remarkable apophthegms.—*Eschb.*

The best edition, M. Meibomius, Greek and Latin, Amsterdam, 1692, 2 vols. 4to; English translation, London, 1688, 2 vols. 8vo.

Petrarch, 1304.

The best of his biographers is the Abbé de Sade, a descendant of his Laura.

Chaucer, 1360.

Godwin's Life of Chaucer. A more honest and sincere votary of truth never existed than Mr. Godwin.—*Penny Cyc.* 4 vols. 8vo, $7 50, London.

Joan of Arc, 1410.

The story of her is, throughout, disgraceful to every one, friend or foe; it forms one of the most curious enigmas in historic record. It has sometimes been suggested that she was merely a tool in the hands of the priests; but these suppositions will hardly satisfy those who read with attention the history of Joan of Arc.—*Penny Cyc.*

A good account of her is given in Lebrun des Charmettes, Histoire de Jeanne d'Arc (Paris, 1817, 3 volumes).

Wolsey, 1471.

Cavendish's Life of Wolsey seems to have been written with great regard for truth, the author frequently stating facts which leave upon the reader an impression very different from the spirit in which the author gives them.—*Lieber.*

Knox, 1505 (M'Crie's Life of).

This work contains a copious narrative of the private life and public labours of the great founder of the Protestant faith in Scotland. The materials of the work are derived from a diligent collection of the different writers on that part of ecclesiastical history of which he treats, and from a considerable number of manuscript letters of the reformer.—*Christian Observer.*

$2 00, Edinburgh, 1841.

Vasari, 1512.

His "Lives of the most eminent Painters, Sculptors, and Architects" are highly esteemed, both on account of the facts the work contains, and for the scattered remarks in regard to the progress of the arts. It, however, has fallen into many errors respecting the earlier masters, a circumstance owing to the imperfections of existing accounts; and it is also guilty of partiality towards the Tuscan artists.—*Enc. Am.*

2 vols. 8vo, $12 00, Florence, 1832.

Fox's Book of Martyrs, 1517.

(See third part.)

G. Ridley's Life of the Reformer Ridley, 1538.

Tasso, 1544.

His life, with an historical and critical account of his writings, by John Black, 2 vols. 4to, $4 50, Edinburgh, 1810.

Mirror for Magistrates, 1559.

2 vols. 4to, 1815.

Cecil, 1563 (Nare's Life of).

Walton, 1593.

His Lives of Donne, Wotton, Hooker, Herbert, and Sanderson, exhibit a most pleasing picture of the abilities of the indefatigable author, and abound with interesting and curious anecdotes of men eminent in rank, in talent, and in learning. —*Blake.*

12mo, $2 83.

Ruinart, 1617.

He gives accounts of the lives and deaths of the early Christian martyrs, folio, Amsterdam, 1713.—*Penny Cyc.*

Ashmole, 1617.

His work "The History of the Order of the Garter" procured him great fame, and shows a vast amount of study and research into antiquity.—*Penny Cyc.*

Sir William Temple, 1628.

His Life and Times, with his unpublished Essays and Correspondences, by R. P. Courtenay, 2 vols. 8vo, $5 00.

Wood, 1632.

He wrote "Athenæ Oxonienses," an exact history of all the writers and bishops who have had their education in the University of Oxford from 1500 to 1690, &c., &c., &c. It is an invaluable work, both as respects biography and bibliography, and should be in every English library.—*Dibdin.*
2 vols. folio, $8 00.

James II., 1633.

Clarke's Life of James II., from authentic sources.
2 vols. 12mo, $2 50.

Strype, 1643.

A voluminous contributor to English biography; he wrote the Lives of Cranmer, Parker, Grindal, &c., &c.—*Enc. Am.*

He is the most valuable contributor to ecclesiastical history and biography that ever appeared in this country.—*Chalmers.*

Stanley, 1644.

His "History of Philosophy," containing the lives and opinions of philosophers of every sect, is a composition of great acknowledged merit.—*Blake.*

He brought a good deal from an almost untrodden field.—*Hallam.*
$7 50.

Duke of Marlborough, 1650.

Memoirs by William Coxe, with his Original Correspondence. An elaborate and valuable work.
3 vols. 4to, 1817–19.

Ben Jonson, 1674.

His works, with Notes and a Biographical Memoir of his Life, by Barry Cornwall.
8vo, $5 50.

Wesley, 1703 (Southey's Life of).

Few persons, we think, could have been found better qualified for this undertaking than Mr. Southey, as, in the collection of his facts and the comparison of his evidence, he has displayed his usual industry and discrimination; his narrative, as to the faithful record of singular and important occurren-

:es, can hardly fail to be read with interest and instruction, even by those who are little inclined to concur in his sentiments on Christian doctrine or ecclesiastical policy.—*Quart. Rev.*

2 vols. 8vo, $3 00.

William Pitt, 1708.

His Life, by Rev. F. Thackeray, 2 vols. 4to, London, 1827. The narrative between the reported speeches, which latter form a great proportion of the work, goes forward in a plain, straight road; and the style, although not very ornate, is too good to provoke fastidiousness, and too clear to produce embarrassment. As an honest chronicler, he quietly and unpretendingly conducts us from one event to another, and seldom interrupts the continuous chain by digressive remarks. —*Am. Quart. Rev.*

Johnson, 1709.

His "Lives of English Poets," with an occasional exhibition of political bias and strong prejudices, form a valuable addition to British biography and criticism.—*Enc. Am*

75 vols. 12mo, $50 00.

Turgot, 1727.

Condorcet's Life of Turgot.

Burke, 1730.

Among the many biographies of him, that by J. Prior, Esq., is by far the most accurate and complete.—*Penny Cyc.*

2 vols. 8vo, 1826.

Fuseli, 1739.

His Life and Writings, by John Knowles. These volumes are perhaps the most valuable, as regards the fine arts, ever published in England. They must be invaluable to the student, and to the innumerable lovers of whatever is great and beautiful in art, and cannot be too highly estimated as a guide for the collector of works of the old masters.—*Monthly Rev.*

3 vols. 8vo, $7 00.

Nichols, 1744.

Literary Anecdotes of the Eighteenth Century, 9 vols. 8vo, $54 00, London, 1812-16. A highly important and interesting work.—*Penny Cyc.*

Sir William Jones, 1746.

Teignmouth's Life of.

Canova, 1757.

The biography is a judicious, unpretending narrative of the leading incidents in a life of exclusive and untiring devotion to art, and of which the best and only faithful record is to be found in the productions of the artist.—*N. Am. Rev.*

Cicognara, 1758.

"History of Modern Sculpture." Although fastidious criticism has taxed it with some defects, it is undeniably a performance of great research and erudition.—*Penny Cyc.*

Wilberforce, 1759.

Life and Correspondence, by his son.
(See third part.)

Sir J. Mackintosh, 1765.

(See third part.)

Captain Beaver, 1766.

This individual will be known by name to a very small portion of our readers, though an abler, braver, more accomplished, or more high-minded officer never trod the deck of a British ship. Captain Smyth has rendered a service to his profession and his country by publishing the memoirs of his friend.—*Quart. Rev.*
8vo, London.

Ecclesiastical Biography, by Dr. Wordsworth, 1770.

"Lives of Eminent Men connected with the History of Religion in England from the Commencement of the Reformation to the Revolution." It is a valuable work.

Lives of the Novelists, by Walter Scott, 1771.

The author writes like a quiet, sober, sensible sort of a man, too rational to suffer himself to get in raptures about anything, and too little of a coxcomb to affect a fervour that he does not feel. It almost seems, while we are reading these volumes, as if we are admitted into the intimate and unreserved society of their celebrated author, and hear him expatiating at his ease on the subject of those writings, with whose merits and whose faults he was alike familiar.—*N. Y. Rev.*
2 vols., Philadelphia, 1825.

Sir W. Scott, 1771.

Life of, by Lockhart. (See third part.)

Sir Humphrey Davy, 1778.

A very correct account of his life is by Dr. Davy.—*Penny Cyc.*

Life of Black Hawk.

This book is a curiosity, an anomaly in literature. It is the only autobiography of an Indian extant. It is an autobiography of a wild, unadulterated savage, gall yet fermenting in his veins, his heart still burning with the sense of wrong, the words of wrath and scorn yet scarce cold upon his lips, and his hands still reeking with recent slaughter.—*North Am. Rev.*

Napoleon (Sir Walter Scott's Life of).

A work of partial views, and executed with too little care and research to add to the brilliant reputation of the author.—*Enc. Am.*

Portraits of Illustrious Personages of Great Britain, with Biographical and Historical Memoirs, by Edmund Lodge, Esq.

A work of considerable value.—*Penny Cyc.*
8vo, $5.

Emma Roberts's Memoirs of the Rival Houses of York and Lancaster.

Historical and biographical. Full of interesting and valuable matter.
2 vols. 8vo, $6 00, London, 1827.

Biographie Universelle.

We have no English biographical dictionary to be compared with this great work. Among its contributors, above 300 are the names of the most eminent French writers.—*Penny Cyc.*
26 vols. 8vo, $100, Paris, 1812–28.

Gorton's Biographical Dictionary.

(See third part.)

Blake's Biographical Dictionary.

Sir Egerton Brydges's Imaginary Biography.

2 vols. 12mo, $2 25, London, 1834.

Landor's Imaginary Conversations.

VII. GEOGRAPHY, TRAVELS, AND VOYAGES.

Eratosthenes, 230 B.C.

He gained great renown by his investigations of the size of the earth. Of his geographical works, which were long in high repute, the scattered remains were collected and published by Leidel.—*Eschenburg*.

Goett., 1789, 8vo.

Strabo, 19 A.D.

His Geography is a rich store of interesting facts and mature reflections, and of great utility in the study of ancient literature and art; it contains descriptions of particular countries, their constitutions, manners, and religion, interwoven with notices of distinguished persons and events.—*Esch.*

Best edition, Paris, 1816–19, 4 vols. 8vo.

Diodorus, first century.

(See his History.)

Pausanias, second century.

His work "Itinerary of Greece" is full of instructive details for the antiquarian, especially in reference to the history of art, as the author makes a point of describing the principal temples, edifices, statues, and the like.

Best edition, Siebelis, Greek and Latin, Leipzig, 1822–28, 5 vols. 8vo. English translation, Th. Taylor, London, 1793. 3 vols. 8vo.

Marco Polo, thirteenth century.

He not only gave a better account of China than any previously afforded, but likewise furnished an account of Japan, of several islands in the East Indies, of Madagascar, and of the coast of Africa.—*Enc. Am.*

1556, Paris, 4to.

Mandeville, fourteenth century.

A celebrated English traveller. He visited the greater part of Asia, Egypt, and Libya, making himself acquainted, according to his own account, with many languages, and collecting much information, true and false.—*Enc. Am.*

8vo, $2 25.

Columbus, 1435.

Irving's Life of Columbus. In the requisites of a judicious selection and disposition of the materials, a correct, striking, and discriminating picture of the different personages, a just and elevated tone of moral feeling, and, above all, the charm of an elegant, perspicuous, and flowing style, Mr. Irving leaves nothing to desire.—*North Am. Review.*

2 vols. 8vo, $2 75.

Drake, 1546.

Though the reputation of Drake as a skilful seaman and a bold commander was deservedly great, still, unless we judge him by the circumstances and the standard of the times, he must appear in many of his exploits in no other light than that of a daring and skilful bucanier.—*Penny Cyc.*

1741, London, 8vo.

Frobisher, 1585.

An account will be found of him in "A true Discourse of the last Voyages of Discoveries for the finding of a Passage to Cathay by the Northwest."—*Brunet.*

London, 1578, 4to.

Dampier, 1652.

(See third part.)

Dobrizhoffer.

An account of the Abipones, an equestrian people of Paraguay in South America. This work is replete with romantic incidents, and of all books on savage life, the most curious and interesting.—*Southey.*

3 vols. 8vo, $6 00.

Kæmpfer, 1657.

Of his writings, his history and description of Japan is deserving of mention. It was translated into English in 1727. *Enc. Am.*

2 vols. folio, $12 00.

Harris, 1667.

A complete collection of voyages and travels, consisting of above six hundred of the most authentic writers from every European language.

2 vols. folio, $10 00.

Charlevoix, 1720.

Travels in Canada from Quebec to New-Orleans. This

is a most valuable work; the author was a Jesuit, and a learned and pious man, of great simplicity and integrity.—*Charles Kent.*
2 vols. 8vo, $3 25.

Cook, 1728.

(See third part.)

Ulloa, 1735.

Voyages to South America. Admirable. They contain a picture of Peru as it was before the violence of the earthquake, and the tenfold more violent passions of man had consigned it to desolation.—*Charles Kent.*
2 vols. 8vo, $3 00.

Anson, 1740.

(See third part.)

Dupaty, 1746.

He wrote, among other works, "Letters on Italy," which appeared 1788, in 2 vols. Among many prejudicial views, they contain some excellent observations on the arts, and interesting descriptions of natural scenery.—*Enc. Am.*

Shaw, 1746.

Travels relating to several parts of Barbary and the Levant. His work is not disposed in the usual method of a journal, but arranged systematically, according to the nature of the subjects treated. It is a rich treasure of geographical, physical, and antiquarian knowledge, most of it referring more or less directly to the Sacred Scriptures.—*N. A. Review.*
4to, $5 00.

Russel, 1756.

Natural History of Aleppo. His remarks exhibit a thorough knowledge of the plants, animals, climate, diseases, &c., &c., of that Oriential region.—*N. A. Review.*
London, 1794, 2 vols.

Pinkerton, 1758.

A general collection of the best and most interesting voyages and travels in all parts of the world. A valuable work, from which much information can be derived.
17 vols. 4to, $75 00.

Bougainville's Voyages, 1766–69.

Bruce, 1768.

(See third part.)

Humboldt, 1769.

(See third part.)

Kalm, 1772.

Travels into North America. They contain its natural history, and an account of its plantations, and agriculture in general.

2 vols., $4 25.

Niebuhr, 1779.

Description of Arabia. Niebuhr has been regarded by all competent judges as one of the most sober, judicious, authentic, and instructive of all the travellers whose works have appeared for the last half century. This work is a kind of classic in respect to the country of which it treats.—*N. A. Review.*

Krusenstern, 1780.

His Voyage round the World surpassed those of his predecessors in its extent and results. No navigator has combined more philanthropy, care, and sacrifice of his own convenience, with a comprehensive knowledge of his own department.—*Enc. Am.*

Burckhardt, 1784.

He is celebrated for his travels in Nubia. He was the first modern traveller who succeeded in penetrating to Schendy in the interior of Soudan, the Meroë of antiquity, and in furnishing exact information of the slave-trade in that quarter.

La Perouse, 1785

(See third part.)

Remusat, 1788.

His "Mélanges Asiatiques," Paris, 1825, 2 vols., contain treatises upon the religion, morals, language, history, and geography of the nations of the East.—*Anc. Am.*

Mackenzie, 1789.

Voyage through North America to the Frozen and Pacific Oceans, with an Account of the Rise and Progress of the Fur-trade of that Country.

4to, $5 50.

Champollion, 1790.

Travels in Egypt. The result of them is of great importance in the history of hieroglyphics.—*Enc. Am.*

Parry, 1790.

(See third part.)

Eustace, 1802.

A Classical Tour through Italy, exhibiting a view of its scenery, antiquities, and monuments.
London, 1814, 2 vols., $10 00.

Chateaubriand's Travels in Greece, Palestine, and Egypt, 1806–7.

A most fascinating work, adorned with taste, elegance, and learning, and full of the descriptive and pathetic eloquence which the fire of genius and the ardour of Christian enthusiasm inspire.—*Chancellor Kent.*
8vo, $1 50.

Humboldt on New Spain.

2 vols., 1811.

Belzoni, 1812.

He made a tour to Egypt. He was certainly one of the most enterprising and sagacious of modern explorers. His narrative of the operations and recent discoveries within the Pyramids appeared in London, 4to, 1820.—*Brunet.*

Henderson, 1814.

He made a missionary tour in Iceland, and gives a deal of information concerning that island.—*Enc. Am.*

Salt, 1814.

He published a volume containing an account of a voyage to Abyssinia, and travels in the interior of that country in 1809. London, 1814.

Morrison, 1816.

He was sent by the English Bible Society to China for the purpose of acquiring the language of the Chinese, in order to make a correct translation of the Bible into it. He returned in 1826, and published "Horæ Sinicæ," or "Translations from the Popular Literature of the Chinese."—*Enc. Am.*

Dupin, 1816.

Voyages dans la Grande Bretagne, 1816–19, 2 vols. 4to, Paris, 1820. It is highly to the credit of M. Dupin, as a man of quick perception and talent, that he has compressed more important and more correct military information into these two volumes than any foreigner could be expected to gain on such subjects, and it is surprising to us to find so few errors in his work.—*Quart. Rev.*

Hall, 1816.

Voyage to the Eastern Seas. We could hardly name a better mode of journal writing than these volumes, and whoever would read for the double purpose of instruction and amusement, will find themselves richly compensated for the time they may give to their perusal.—*N. Am. Rev.*
2 vols. 12mo, $1 50, New-York.

Ker Porter, 1817.

From 1817–20, he was engaged in travelling through the East, and in the course of his travels, explored the countries from the banks of the Polar Sea to the Euphrates, and from the Euphrates to the mouth of the Persian Gulf. Travels in Georgia, Persia, and Armenia, 1822.—*Blake.*

Buchanan, 1817.

Journey from Madras through Mysore, Canara, and Malabar. A highly authentic and valuable work, containing much information on the production, climate, manufactures, as also on the manners, religion, &c., &c., of these districts.—*Lowndes.*
4to, 3 vols., $18 00, London.

Ross, 1818.

(See third part.)

Caldcleugh, 1819.

Travels in South America. Though the book is heavy and languid, and they who read for the sake of deep research or glowing narration will be disappointed, yet it is but fair to add that the author has seen and heard much, and has added considerably to our stock of information concerning several parts of South America.—*Quart. Rev.*
2 vols. 8vo, $3 50, London.

Brookes, 1820.

Travels to the North Cape. Abating a leaning to the credulous, we consider the work as a valuable acquisition to the stock of travels.—*Quart. Rev.*

Schmidtmayer, 1820.

Travels into Chili over the Andes. The author relates

what he saw with every mark of veracity, and with becoming simplicity, and, with some slight censures, we can cheerfully recommend the work; we deem its scattered hints most valuable assistants in forming a just idea of the real state of the countries through which he travelled.—*Quart. Rev.*
4to, $6 00, London.

Klaproth, 1820.

His inquiries were directed to the history and geography of the interior of Asia. In 1824 appeared his "Historical Tables of Asia, from the Monarchy of Cyrus to our own Time," 4 vols. 4to; also, Historical, Geographical, and Statistical Description of China, 2 vols. 4to.—*Enc. Am.*

Dwight (Timothy), 1821.

Travels in New-England and New-York. These volumes derive much value from the author's unpretending fidelity; it gives his testimony that weight which the evidence of an honest and sensible man must always carry with it.—*Quart. Rev.*
4 vols. 8vo, $5 00, New-York.

Schoolcraft, 1821.

Travels in the Central Portions of the Mississippi Valley. We cheerfully recommend these travels to our readers, as a work full of various and useful information. His style has roundness, fulness, dignity, and strength, but is often deficient in simplicity, propriety, purity, and grace.—*New-York Rev.*
8vo, $2 00, New-York.

Scoresby, 1823.

The celebrated Greenland voyager wrote a "Journal of a Voyage to the Northern Whale Fishery, including Researches and Discoveries on the Eastern Coast of West Greenland." Edinburgh, 1824.

Kotzebue, 1823.

In his narrative he gives an account of a voyage round the world, in which it was intended that he should penetrate beyond the Icy Cape which had been discovered by Cook, but the ice obliged him to return. and he arrived at Cronstadt in 1826.—*Enc. Am.*

Cochrane, 1823.

Journal of a Residence and Travels in Colombia during 1823–24. Although too diffuse, and carrying with it too

much of the air of book-making, the narrative is not wholly without interest.—*N. Am. Rev.*
2 vols. 8vo, $5 00, London.

Leslie and Jameson, 1823.

They have given a compendious view of the attempts to explore the Polar regions and seas.—*Enc. Am.*

Franklin, 1825.

Narrative of a Second Expedition to the Shores of the Polar Sea, in the years 1825, 1826, and 1827. It is difficult to do sufficient justice either to the skill and intelligence displayed in its conduct, or the information to be derived from it.—*Am. Quart. Rev.*

Dwight (*Henry C.*), 1825.

Travels in the North of Germany, in the years 1825 and 1826, $2 50, New-York.
This work contains many valuable details, not unmingled, however, with mistakes, which a longer residence, a closer observation, or more preparatory study, might have enabled a foreign tourist to avoid.—*N. Am. Rev.*

Head, 1827.

Rough Notes taken during some Rapid Journeys across the Pampas. They are written in a hurried, unpolished style, but with a good deal of animation, and occasionally with a graphic power of description. Every reader may derive entertainment and instruction from this book.—*N. Am. Rev.*
1 vol. 12mo, $1 50, Boston.

Malcolm, 1828.

Hagi Baba of Ispahan. We may safely say that not amusement only, but instruction of a very serious kind is to be derived from considering the nature of some of the materials which are here under the management of a master.—*Quart. Rev.*
2 vols., London.

Malcolm, 1828.

Memoirs on Central India, and Travels in Persia. (See third part.)

Bigelow, 1828.

Travels in Malta and Sicily. We can recommend the work as one which contains a mass of useful information, as well as a fund of liberal and rational entertainment for the intelligent reader. The style is animated, and generally correct, though at times a little too ambitious. The tone of thinking is manly and liberal.—*N. Am. Rev.*

The Kuzzilbach.

A tale of Khorasan, 3 vols., London, 1828.

This Oriental romance displays an accurate and intimate acquaintance with the manners and customs, as well as the history of Persia. The power of description displayed in it is of a most picturesque and rich character. The author's pictures of natural scenery in the East show an eye familiar with its beauties and its terrors.—*Quart. Rev.*

Stewart, 1830.

(See third part.)

Dr. Johnson, 1834.

Excursions through France, Belgium, Germany, Switzerland, and Italy. Excellent.—*Chancellor Kent.*

Coxe, 1834.

Travels in Switzerland. They give the most thorough examination of that most picturesque and romantic of all civilized countries.—*Chancellor Kent.*

Reed and Mattheson, 1835.

A Narrative of the Visit to the American Churches by the Deputation from the Congregational Union of England and Wales. On the whole, we must say that these travellers, though strongly tinctured with some prejudices, which they have taken no pains to conceal, have written in a friendly spirit.—*N. Am. Rev.*

2 vols. 8vo.

Catlin.

North American Indians. (See third part.)

Wilbraham, 1838.

Travels in Georgia and Caucasian Russia. This traveller is distinguished for crossing and recrossing the snowy Caucasus.—*Chancellor Kent.*

Wilkinson, 1840.

Account of the Private Life, Manners, and Customs of the Ancient Egyptians, derived from the study of hieroglyphics, sculpture, &c., &c., still existing, compared with the accounts of ancient authors.

3 vols. 8vo, $16 00, London.

Robinson, 1840.

(See third part.)

Wilkes, 1840.

A History of the United States' Exploring Expedition to the South Pacific.

Rockwell, 1841.

Sketches of Foreign Travel and Life at Sea. Much labour has been bestowed upon this work, on one hand, to interest the general reader, by a lively and graphic description of objects of curiosity and taste, and striking incidents by land and sea; and, on the other, to imbody a large amount of information not accessible to those familiar only with our own language, and fitted to be useful and instructive to men of education and intelligence.—*Pref.*

2 vols., Boston.

Stephens.

(See third part.)

Ritter.

His Geography in relation to the Nature and History of Mankind, or General Comparative Geography, is a valuable work.—*Enc. Am.*

Oriental Translation Fund.

The society under this name have published thirteen works, containing interesting translations from Eastern languages. London, 1829–33. The cost is $44 50.

VIII. POLITE LITERATURE.

(PROSE.)

Lysias, 458 B.C.

The purity, the perspicuity, the grace and simplicity which characterize his orations would have raised him to the highest rank in the art, had they been coupled with the force and energy of Demosthenes. His style is elegant, without being overloaded with ornament, and always preserves its tone.—*Anthon.*

A good edition is that of Dobson, in the Oratores Attici, London, 1828, 2 vols. 8vo.

Isocrates, 436 B.C.

He is a perfect master in the style which he has adopted, and has well merited the high encomiums of Dionysius of Halicarnassus for the noble spirit and rectitude of purpose which pervade all his writings.—*Anthon.*

A correct edition of his Orations was published by Orellius in 1814, 8vo.

Demosthenes, 385 B.C.

His style is rapid harmony, exactly adjusted to the sense it is vehement reasoning, without any appearance of art; it is disdaining anger, boldness, freedom, involved in a continued stream of argument; and, of all human productions, the orations of Demosthenes present to us the models which approach the nearest to perfection.—*Hume.*

Best edition, Reiske, edited by Schaefer, London, 1822, 3 vols. 8vo.

Æschines, 385 B.C.

His orations are distinguished by a happy flow of words, by an abundance and clearness of ideas, and by an air of great ease, which arose less from art than nature.

Cicero, 106 B.C.

(See third part.)

Seneca, A.D.

A celebrated Roman rhetorician. He wrote on civil lawsuits, "*Controversiæ.*" They belong to the class of rhetorical works, because they review and compare the procedure of Greek and Latin orators with regard to invention, application, and style.—*Eschenburg.*

Best edition, that of Heinsius, Amsterdam, 1620, 8vo.

Longinus.

(See third part.)

Quintilian.

(See third part.) Best edition, Spalding, Leipzig, 1798-1834, 6 vols. 8vo.

Pliny the Younger.

Wherever he can indulge in general ideas or philosophic views his language assumes a tone of energy and vivacity, and his thoughts somewhat of unexpected boldness.

Best edition, Lemaire, Paris, 1823, 2 vols. 8vo.

Heliodorus.

A Greek romance writer, principally known by the "Adventures of Theagenes and Chariclea," of which Villemain says, "The style is pure, polished, symmetrical; and the language of love receives a character of delicacy and reserve, which is very rare among the writers of antiquity."—*Anthon.*

Best edition is that of Coray, Paris, 1804, 2 vols. 8vo.

Boccacio.

He was the earliest Italian writer who furnished models of grace and refinement in his own mother tongue. His principal prose works are the "Novels," the "Decameron," and his "De Casibus Virorum Illustrium." His Latin style is censured as hasty, crude, and constrained.

The Decameron, with Remarks on the Life and Writings of Boccacio, 2 vols. 8vo, $3 00, London.

Petrarch.

The first real restorer of polite letters. He awakened admiration for the ancient writers, and laboured untiringly to acquire a good style in Latin. In this last he was but partially successful. His Letters are much admired.

Epistolæ, 1 vol. 4to, $2 50, Paris.

Poggio Bracciolini.

He was indefatigable in recovering lost works of Roman literature that lay mouldering in the repositories of convents. We owe to him alone eight orations of Cicero, a complete Quintilian, Columella, part of Lucretius, three books of Valerius Flaccus, Silius Italicus, Ammianus Marcellinus, Tertullian, and several less important writers; twelve comedies of Plautus were also recovered in Germany through his directions. Poggio, besides this, was undoubtedly a man of considerable learning, and still greater sense and spirit as a writer, though he never reached a very correct or elegant style.

Gasparin of Barziza,

or, as he is often called, *Gasparin of Bergamo*, had the good fortune to find Cicero De Oratore, and, by incessantly turning over its pages, gained a propriety, regularity, and harmony of style till then unknown. Among his works are several orations, which probably were actually delivered; they are the earliest models of that classical declamation, which became so usual afterward, and are elegant, if not very forcible.

Leonardo Bruni, more usually called *Aretino*,

from his birthplace, held, during this period, the next highest place in politeness of style after Gasparin. "He was the first," says Paulus Cortesius, "who replaced the rude structure of periods by some degree of rhythm." His History of the Goths, which is chiefly translated from Procopius, though he is silent on the obligation, passes for his best work.

Paris, folio, $14 00.

Laurentius Valla,

who is ranked by Hallam as the head of the literary republic of his time. His most celebrated work is on the Graces of the Latin Language, "De Elegantiis Lat. Linguæ," and probably did more for philology than any of its predecessors, and as much as any that has succeeded.

Paris, 4to, $3 00.

Leo Baptista Alberti.

He was a painter and sculptor, and the author of the earliest modern writings on these subjects. He was also a poet, and a moral writer in the various forms of dialogue, dissertations, fable, and light romance. He had deeply meditated, says Mr. Hallam, the remains of Roman Antiquity, and endeavoured to design from them general theorems of beauty, variously applicable to each description of buildings. But for the fact that he wrote before his own language became polished, and that he was soon succeeded by men so illustrious as Leonardo da Vinci and Michael Angelo, he would occupy a high place in the temple of fame.

Politian.

He occupied the chair of Greek and Latin eloquence at Florence, and is regarded as the first who wrote the Latin language with much elegance. His "Miscellanies" consist of observations illustrating passages in Latin authors, and when put forth was considered an immortal work.

Erasmus.

The greatest scholar and critic of his time. In 1522 he published his Colloquies, a book even now much read, and deserving to be so. It was professedly designed for the instruction and amusement of youth; but both are conveyed at the expense of the prevalent usages in religion. In 1527 twenty-four thousand copies of this work were printed, and all were sold. It is but one of many works by Erasmus. His Epistles and Ciceronianus are worthy of special attention.

The Colloquies, London, 8vo, $2 00.

Vasco de Lobeyra.

His "Amadis de Gaul," the famous romance, was first published in four books. It afterward grew to twenty, in successive editions, which are held to be far inferior to the original. In its present state it could hardly be read with patience by any, except a very youthful reader.

Melancthon.

His style was so much admired, that to copy his manner (genus discendi Philippicum, as it was called) was more the fashion than to have recourse to his masters, Cicero and Quintilian. His "Loci Communes," and "Moralis Philosophiæ Epitome," are good specimens.

Paulus Manilius.

He was eminent for his scholarship and the fastidious purity of his Latin style. He went so far that he would employ no words unless used by Cicero; not even those of Cicero's correspondents who might be as highly accomplished and polite as himself.

Bembo (Cardinal).

He was surpassed by none of his time for elegance as a writer both in Italian and in Latin. It has been said that his efforts to give a perfect finish to his compositions was such, that he kept forty portfolios, into which every sheet entered successively, and was only taken out to undergo his corrections before it entered the next. His letters are most admired.

Rabelais.

He was the author of the most brilliant performance in fiction of the half century to which he belonged. Few books (though but few are less likely to obtain the praise of a fastidious critic) have more originality, or evince a more abundant fertility, always of language, and sometimes of imagination. He bears a slight resemblance to Lucian, and a considerable one to Aristophanes. The title of his work is Pantagruel.

Sir Thomas More's Utopia.

It is said by Mr. Hallam to be the only work of genius of

that age in England. He adds, "Perhaps we scarcely appreciate highly enough the spirit and originality of this fiction, which ought to be considered with regard to the barbarism of the times and the meagerness of preceding inventions. It is manifest that some of his most distinguished successors in the same walk of romance, especially Swift, were largely indebted to his reasoning, as well as inventive talents.

12mo, $1 00, London.

Machiavel.

The style of this writer is eminent for simplicity, strength, and clearness. It would not be too much to place him at the head of the prose writers in Italy.

The usual style of Italian prose in this, accounted by some its best age, is classical, elaborate, ornate, yet not to excess, with a rhythmical structure, apparently much studied, very rhetorical, and, for the most part, trivial, as we should now think, in its matter. The prose of Tasso is placed by some almost on a level with his poetry for beauty of diction. The "Galatea of Casa," "The Dialogue on the Beauty of Women" by Firenzuola, and a "Treatise on Painting" by Raphael Borghini, have also been much admired for beauty of style.

$5 00.

Montaigne.

His Essays, which appeared in 1580, exerted a great influence upon the taste and the opinions of Europe. Montaigne is superior to any of the ancients in liveliness, in that careless and rapid style where one thought springs naturally, but not consecutively, from another, by analogical rather than deductive connexion; so that, while the reader seems to be following a train of arguments, he is imperceptibly hurried to a distance by some contingent association.—*Hallam.*

3 vols. 12mo, $6 00, London.

George Herbert.

His "Country Parson" belongs to the few English writings of the practical class of the seventeenth century. It is a pleasing little book, but the precepts are sometimes so overstrained as to give an air of affectation.—*Hallam.*

18mo, $1 50, London.

Sir Philip Sidney.

His "Arcadia" appeared in 1590. It was the Arcadia which first taught to the contemporary writers that inimitable interweaving and contexture of words; that bold and unshackled use and application of them; that art of giving to language, appropriated to objects the most common and trivial, a kind of acquired and adventitious loftiness, and to diction, in itself noble and elevated, a sort of superadded dignity; that power of ennobling the sentiments by the language, and the language by the sentiments, which so often excites our admiration in perusing the writers of the age of Elizabeth.—*Hallam.*

See also Sidney's Defence of Poesy, &c.

Folio, $7 00.

Selden's Table-Talk.

The editor of this very short and small volume, which gives, perhaps, a more exalted notion of Selden's natural talents than any of his learned writings, requests the reader to distinguish times, and "in his fancy to carry along with him the when and the why many of these things were spoken." The sayings reported are full of vigour, raciness, and a kind of scorn of the half learned.—*Hallam.*

Galileo's Letters.

They are written with clearness, elegance, and spirit; no one among the moderns had so entirely rejected a dry and technical manner of teaching, and thrown such attractions round the form of truth as Galileo.—*Hallam.*

Bentivoglio's Letters.

Bentivoglio is reckoned as a writer among the very first of the seventeenth century. His Letters are commonly known; they are written with equal dignity and ease.—*Hallam.*

$2 25, Paris.

Mademoiselle Scuderi.

Her romances seem to have been remarkably the favourites of the clergy. "I find," says Mascaron, one of the chief ornaments of the pulpit, in writing to Mademoiselle Scuderi, "so much in your works calculated to reform the world, that, in the sermons I am now preparing for the court, you will often be on my table by the side of St. Augustine and St. Bernard."—*Hallam.*

$17 00, London.

Balzac.

His writings are not formed to delight those who wish either to be merry or wise, to laugh or to learn; yet he has real excellences besides those which may be deemed relative to the age in which he came (17th century). His language is polished; his sentiments are just, but sometimes common; the cadence of his periods is harmonious, but too artificial and uniform. His letters are in twenty-seven books; they begin in 1620 and end about 1653.—*Hallam.*

Cervantes.

Few books of moral philosophy display as deep an insight into the mechanism of the mind as Don Quixote, the first part of which appeared in 1605. And when we look also at the fertility of invention, the general probability of the events, and the great simplicity of the story, wherein no artifices are practised to create suspense or complicate the action, we shall think Cervantes fully deserving of the glory that attends this monument of his genius.—*Hallam.*

4 vols. 4to, $20 00, London.

Calderon.

In the twenty-fifth volume of the Quarterly Review an elaborate and able critique on the plays of Calderon seems to have estimated him without prejudice on either side. "His boundless and inexhaustible fertility of invention, his quick power of seizing and prosecuting everything with dramatic effect, the unfailing animal spirits of his dramas, if we may venture on the expression, the general loftiness and purity of his sentiments, the rich facility of his verse, the abundance of his language, entitle him to a high rank as to the imaginative and creative faculty as a poet, but we cannot consent to enrol him among the mighty masters of the human breast."

Shakspeare.

(See third part.)

Burton.

"Anatomy of Melancholy," written in English, and in a style not by any means devoid of point and terseness, with much good sense, and observation of men as well as of books; and the author having also the skill of choosing his quotations for their rareness, oddity, and amusing character, without losing sight of their pertinence to the subject, he has produced a work of which Johnson said that it was the only one which had ever caused him to leave his bed earlier than he intended.

8vo, $3 25, London.

La Fontaine.

Few writers have left such a number of verses which, in the phrase of his country, have made their fortune, and been, like ready money, always at hand for prompt quotation. His lines have at once a proverbial truth and a humour of expression which render them constantly applicable. This is chiefly true of his Fables; for his Tales, though no one will deny that they are lively enough, are not reckoned so well written, nor do they supply so much for general use.—*Hallam.*

8vo, $10 50, London.

Madame de Sevigné.

Her wit, and talent of painting by single touches, are very eminent; scarcely any collection of letters which contain so little that can interest a distant age are read with such pleasure; if they have any general fault, it is a little monotony and excess of affection towards her daughter, which is reported to have wearied its object; and, in contrast with this, a little want of sensibility towards all beyond her immediate friends, and a readiness to find something ludicrous in the dangers and sufferings of others.—*Hallam.*

9 vols. 12mo, $10 00, London.

Bossuet.

Maury says of him, "He was an orator whose discourses, animated by a most glowing and original genius, are classic works in eloquence, which ought to be perpetually studied; just as, in the arts, one goes to Rome to form his taste by tho master-pieces of Raphael and Michael Angelo. Behold the French Demosthenes! Behold Bossuet!" His sermon at the tomb of the great Condé is considered as a master-piece.

Flechier.

He devoted his talent to the study of eloquence, in which he became so eminent as to be reckoned the rival of the great Bossuet. Of his funeral orations, the finest was that which he delivered on the death of Marshal Turenne.—*Enc. Am.*

Bourdaloue.

"What I chiefly admire in him," says Maury, "is the inexhaustible fertility of his plans, which are never alike, and the happy talent of arranging his argument, his accurate and forcible logic, that redundancy of genius which, in his discourses, leaves nothing farther to be supposed; the simplicity of a style nervous and affecting, natural and noble. These are the talents which never permit me to think of this great man without saying to myself, See, then, to what an elevation genius may be raised when it is invigorated by study."

3 vols. 8vo, $6 75, Paris.

Dryden.

Every poem and play of Dryden was ushered into the world by those prefaces and dedications which have made him celebrated as a critic of poetry and a master of the English language. His style was very superior to any that England had seen. As a critic, he is not to be numbered with those who have sounded the depths of the human mind. He scatters remarks sometimes too indefinite, sometimes too arbitrary; yet his predominating good sense colours the whole; we find in them no perplexing subtlety, no cloudy nonsense, no paradoxes and heresies in taste to revolt us.—*Hallam.*

His prose works, 4 vols. 8vo, $3 00, London.

Pascal's Provincial Letters.

They are finely written, as all confess them to be, though too much filled with obsolete controversy; they quote books too much forgotten; they have too little bearing on any permanent sympathies to be read with much interest or pleasure.—*Hallam.*

8vo, $1 50.

Evelyn.

He wrote, in 1651, a little piece purporting to be an Account of England by a Frenchman. It is chiefly mentioned here on account of the polish and gentlemanly elegance of the style, which very few had hitherto regarded in such light compositions.—*Hallam.*

His "Sylva" is his great work.

Rochefoucault.

Among the books, in ancient and modern times, which record the conclusions of observing men on the moral qualities of their fellows, a high place should be reserved for "The Maxims of Rochefoucault."—*Hallam.*

8vo, $1 25, Paris.

La Bruyère.

His principal work is "The Characters of La Bruyère," published in 1687. His general reflections, like those of

Rochefoucault, are brilliant with antitheses and epigrammatic conciseness; sometimes, perhaps, not quite just or quite perspicuous; but he pleases more, on the whole, from his variety, his greater liveliness, and his gentler spirit of raillery.

2 vols. 8vo, $4 00, Paris.

Sir William Temple.

The style of his "Miscellanies" will be found, in comparison with his contemporaries, highly polished, and sustained with more equability than they preserve, remote from any thing either pedantic or humble. The periods are studiously rhythmical, yet they want the variety and peculiar charm that we admire in those of Dryden.—*Hallam.*

2 vols. folio, $4 00, London.

Cowley.

"His thoughts," says Johnson, "are natural, and his style has a smooth and placid equability which has never yet obtained its due commendation. Nothing is far-sought or hard-laboured, but all is easy without feebleness, and familiar without grossness."

8vo, $1 50, London.

Perrault.

He rendered his "Tales of Mother Goose" almost a counterpart in prose to the Fables of La Fontaine, by giving to them all a real interest, as far as could be, with a naturalness of expression, an arch naïveté, a morality neither too obvious nor too refined, and a slight poignancy of satire on the world. —*Hallam.*

Wotton.

He published, in 1694, his "Reflection on Ancient and Modern Learning." He draws very well, in this, the line between Temple and Perrault, avoiding the tasteless judgment of the latter in poetry and eloquence, but pointing out the superiority of the moderns in the whole range of physical science. Wotton had been a boy of astonishing precocity; at six years old he could readily translate Latin, Greek, and Hebrew; at seven he added some knowledge of Arabic and Syriac. He entered Catharine Hall, Cambridge, in his tenth year; at thirteen, when he took the degree of bachelor of arts, he was acquainted with twelve languages.—*Hallam.*

8vo, $1 00, London.

St. Evremond.

Nothing can be more trifling than the general character of his writings, but sometimes he rises to literary criticism, or even civil history; and on such topics he is clear, unaffected, cold, without imagination or sensibility; a type of the frigid being whom an aristocratic and highly-polished society is apt to produce. His chief merit is in his style and manner.—*Hallam.*

3 vols. 8vo, $3 50, London.

Congreve.

Though not the first among dramatic writers, he is undeniably among the first names. More than any preceding writers among us, he kept up the tone of a gentleman; his men of the world are profligate, but not coarse; he rarely caters for the populace of the theatre by such indecencies as they must understand; he gave, in fact, a tone of refinement to the public taste, which it never lost, and which, in its progression, has banished his own comedies from the stage.—*Hallam.*

2 vols. 8vo, $3 00, London.

Baxter.

His style, far from being correct, has, notwithstanding, in some of his practical pieces, and particularly in that entitled "The Saints' Everlasting Rest," many fine and affecting passages. He only wanted "his genius to be curbed by salutary checks" to have attained in his practical works the character of a most pathetic writer.—*Maury.*

His works, 4 vols. 8vo, $24 00, London.

Bayle.

He is admirable in exposing the fallacies of dogmatism, the perplexities of philosophy, the weaknesses of those who affect to guide the opinions of mankind. But, wanting the necessary condition of good reasoning, an earnest desire to reason well, a moral rectitude from which the love of truth must spring, he often avails himself of petty cavils, and becomes dogmatical in his very doubts.—*Hallam.*

His Dictionary is a very useful work for those to consult who love the biographical part of literature, which is what I love most.—*Dr. Johnson.*

The Dictionary, 4 vols. folio, $20 00, London; Miscellaneous Reflections, 2 vols. 8vo, $2 50, London.

Fénélon.

Télémaque. The beauties of this work are very numerous; the descriptions, and, indeed, the whole tone of the book, have a charm of grace something like the pictures of Guido; but there is also a certain languor which steals over us in reading, and though there is no real want of variety in the narration, it reminds us so continually of its source, the Homeric legends, as to become rather monotonous.—*Hallam.*

1 vol. 8vo, $1 50.

Massillon.

He discovers much knowledge both of the world and the human heart; he is pathetic and persuasive, and, upon the whole, is perhaps the most eloquent writer of sermons which modern times have produced.—*Blair.*

The Sermons translated, 8vo, $2 50, London.

Addison.

(See third part.)

Corneille.

The language in his plays is elevated; his sentiments, if sometimes hyperbolical, are generally noble, when he has not to deal with the passion of love; conscious of the nature of his own powers, he has avoided subjects wherein this must entirely predominate; it was to be, as he thought, an accessory, but never a principal source of dramatic interest.—*Hallam.*

2 vols. 8vo, $4 50, Paris.

Racine.

The style of Racine is exquisite. The female characters in his plays are of the greatest beauty; they have the ideal grace and harmony of ancient sculpture, and bear somewhat of the same analogy to those of Shakspeare which that art does to painting. They are the forms of possible excellence, not from individual models, nor likely, perhaps, to delight every reader, for the same reason that more eyes are pleased by Titian than by Raphael.—*Hallam.*

8vo, $2 25, Paris.

Steele.

In 1709 he began the periodical paper so celebrated under the title of "The Tatler," which included a portion of the information of a common newspaper, but, in raciness of humour and vivacity and urbanity of tone, was not, perhaps, exceeded by the most celebrated of its successors.—*Enc. Am.*

4 vols. 8vo, $4 00, London.

Swift.

As a writer he was original, and has, perhaps, never been exceeded in grave irony, which he veils with an air of serious simplicity, admirably calculated to set it off. He also abounds in ludicrous ideas, which often deviate into very unpardonable grossness. His style forms the most perfect example of easy familiarity that the language affords.—*Enc. Am.*

2 vols. 8vo, $10 00, London.

Gay.

His well known "Fables" were written professedly for the instruction of the Duke of Cumberland, and published in 1726. This performance exhibits great ease of narration, and much lively and natural painting.—*Enc. Am.*

2 vols. 8vo, $2 00, London.

Pope's Letters.

They are elegant and sprightly, although studied and artificial; but, as many characteristic epistles are given from those of his correspondents, the collection is interesting and valuable.—*Enc. Am.*

12mo, $1 25.

Samuel Richardson.

He appeared before the public in 1740 as the author of "Pamelia," "Clarissa Harlowe," and "Sir Charles Grandison." These works were particularly popular, and the author was regarded as a man of the most virtuous sentiments, of the most amiable modesty, possessed of the most dignified power of imagination.

His Correspondence from Original Sources, with a Biography and Observations on his Writings, by Mrs. Barbauld, 6 vols. 8vo, $7 50, London.

Lady Mary W. Montagu.

As a letter writer her fame stands very high; her letters obtained universal admiration for their wit, judgment, and descriptive powers.—*Enc. Am.*

3 vols. 8vo, $7 50, London.

Bolingbroke.

His "Letters upon History," published in 1735, are admired even at the present day; but in them the individual character of the author appears to the exclusion of general views, and, particularly, they are blamed for attacking revealed religion, which their author had once warmly defended.—*Enc. Am.*

8vo, $1 50, London.

Saurin.

He writes with ardour and vehemence. He does not make an ostentatious show of wit; he forcibly urges his arguments: he knows when to insist upon them; he is moved, and he inflames. He has the merit of being a natural orator, and he would have acquired the taste in which he is deficient, if he had joined to the study of examples the residence of Paris.—*Maury.*

London, 8 vols. 8vo, $8 00.

Bridaine.

He was born with a popular eloquence, abounding with metaphorical and striking expressions, and no one ever possessed in a higher degree the rare talent of arresting the attention of an assembled multitude.—*Maury.*

Warburton.

The English language, even in its widest extent, cannot furnish passages more strongly marked, either by grandeur in thought, or by felicity in expression, than are to be found in the works of Bishop Warburton.—*Dr. Parr.*

His works, London, $7 50.

Hurd.

Bishop Hurd (a friend of Warburton) was learned and accomplished.—*Bishop Warburton.*

London, 8 vols. 8vo, $12 00.

Molière.

In just and forcible delineation of character, skilful contrivance of circumstances, and humorous dialogue, his plays are unsurpassed. The powers of Molière are directed with greater skill to their object than those of Shakspeare; none of his energy is wasted; the spectator is not interrupted by the serious scenes of tragi-comedy, nor his attention drawn aside by poetical episodes.—*Hallam.*

Paris, 4 vols. 18mo, $2 00.

Fontenelle.

His best productions are, perhaps, the eulogies on the deceased members of the Academy of Sciences at Paris, which he pronounced during almost forty years; they are just and candid, with sufficient, though not very profound knowledge of the exact sciences, with a style pure and flowing, which his good sense had freed from some early affectation, and his cold temper as well as sound understanding restrained from extravagance.—*Hallam.*

Voltaire.

Though Corneille is deemed to have expressed heroic sentiments with greater sublimity, and Racine the natural emotions with greater sweetness, it is admitted that Voltaire introduced moral motives into the drama with greater effect, and displays a more intimate acquaintance with the original relations of the mind.—*Penny Cyc.*

Some of his other writings are licentious in the extreme.

His dramas, 9 vols. 12mo, $5 00.

De Foe.

It is unnecessary to dwell upon his "Robinson Crusoe," a work which everybody has read, and which has been translated into all the languages of Europe; but it may be proper to mention, that the imputation of his founding it upon the papers of Alexander Selkirk, left on the island of Juan Fernandez, appears to be untrue.—*Enc. Am.*

Chesterfield.

His Letters to his Son have been much censured for the loose morality which they are supposed to inculcate; but still, it must be admitted that they show a great knowledge of the world, and much practical good sense, expressed in an easy, agreeable, and correct style.—*Penny Cyc.*

Rousseau.

His "Social Compact," "New Eloisa," and "Emilius," had a powerful influence on the age. In his works of fiction we find no beings of creative fancy, no force of wit, and no power of sustaining character. Eloquent descriptions, scenes of tenderness and pathos, and the ebullitions of highly-excited passion supply their place, and indicate the peculiar character of his talent.—*Edinburgh Enc.*

His complete works, Paris, 37 vols. 8vo, $25 00.

Chatham.

In eloquence he was never surpassed by any of his countrymen. His speeches were bold and sublime, and his influence over the minds of his audience was irresistible. In 1804 appeared his "Letters" to his nephew, which contain much excellent advice, clothed in easy and familiar language, and reflect equal honour on the author's head and heart.—*Enc. Am.*

His Letters, New-York, 12mo, $0 50.

Sterne.

His works consist of "The Life and Opinions of Tristham Shandy," a sentimental romance, remarkable for its eccentricity, and for an interesting delineation of character, but not without occasional obscenity; "A Sentimental Journey;" Sermons and Letters, published since his death.

London, 8vo, $3 75.

Blair.

A pulpit orator and author. His sermons are distinguished by a polished style, and a clear, easy, and methodical exposition. He gained much reputation by his Lectures on Rhetoric and Belles-Lettres.—*Enc. Am.*

His Sermons, London, 1 vol. 8vo, $2 50.

His Lectures, London, 3 vols. 8vo, $5 00.

Gray.

His Letters are admirable specimens of the epistolary style. They are descriptive of a tour to the lakes of Westmoreland and Cumberland. "He that reads his Epistolary Narrative," says Dr. Johnson, "wishes that to travel, and to tell his travels, had been more of his employment."

London 8vo, $1 87.

Smollett.

His novels always enliven, and never tire us; we take them up with pleasure, and lay them down without any strong feeling of regret. We look on and laugh, as spectators of an amusing, though inelegant scene, without closing in with the combatants, or being made parties in the events.—*Enc. Am.*

London, 8vo, $4 75.

Walpole.

In his "Correspondence," the object was to say what meant little with the utmost novelty in the mode, and with the most ingenious compliment to the person addressed, so that he should admire himself, and admire the writer. They are, of course, very tiresome after a short time, yet their ingenuity is not without merit.—*Hallam.*

3 vols. 8vo, $7 50.

Lessing.

"In his best drama, 'Nathan the Wise,'" says Schlegel, "a remarkable tale of Boccacio is wrought up with a number of inventions which are wonderful, yet not improbable, when we consider the circumstances of the times; the fictitious persons are grouped round a celebrated historical character, the great Saladin, who is drawn with historic truth; the Crusades in the background, the scene at Jerusalem, all this gives to the work a romantic character; while the thought, foreign to the age in question, which the poet has interspersed for the sake of his philosophical views, form a contrast somewhat hazardous, but yet exceedingly attractive."

Whole works in German, Berlin, 3 vols. 8vo, $3 50.

Wieland.

A German writer, who rivals Voltaire in universality of talent and literary fertility. He himself declared his Letters and Commentaries on Horace those of his works on which he placed the greatest value, and from which his head, heart, taste, conceptions, and character could be best known.—*Enc. Am.*

Sheridan.

As a speaker he ranks among the most finished and varied of the rhetorical school, and his speech against Warren Hastings has been deemed one of the most striking of English eloquence upon record.—*Enc. Am.*

2 vols. 8vo, $3 50, London.

Thomas.

An ingenious French writer. His "Èloges" of distinguished men are in general characterized by vigorous eloquence, boldness of thought, and a warm zeal for the interests of humanity, virtue, and knowledge; but they are not always free from exaggeration of style and expression, and too great an effort after effect.—*Enc. Am.*

Tooke.

A celebrated English philologist. In his "Diversions of Purley" appeared his knowledge of language and logical acuteness, which raised him to a high rank as a philologist. —*Enc. Am.*

1 vol. 8vo, $3 75, London.

Burke.

His oratory was pre-eminently that of a full mind, which

makes excursions to a vast variety of subjects, connected by the slightest and most evanescent associations, and that in a diction as rich and varied as the matter.—*Enc. Am.*

4 vols. 8vo, $10 00, London.

La Harpe.

His reputation rests on his "Lycée," which is an invaluable work to the student of French literature, of which it gives a complete history from its commencement to the author's own time. The criticisms on the different writers are not founded on principles acknowledged by the English, but perhaps the value of the book is on that account greater, as it exhibits the object of the French authors, and the standard according to which they are to be judged when compared with each other.—*Penny Cyc.*

Hazlitt.

His chief title to fame is derived from essays on subjects of taste and literature, which are deservedly popular. His principal merits as a writer are force and ingenuity of illustration, strength, terseness, and vivacity. We hardly know, in the whole circle of English literature, a finer specimen of accumulative eloquence than the account of the intellectual life of Coleridge in the "Spirit of the Age."—*Penny Cyc.*

12mo, $1 62, London.

Patrick Henry.

He was a natural orator of the highest order, combining imagination, acuteness, dexterity, and ingenuity with the most forcible action, and extraordinary powers of face and utterance. His style of speaking was altogether more successful than that of his contemporaries.—*Enc. Am.*

Maury.

His "Principles of Eloquence" is decidedly the best work which has as yet appeared on the subject, and is, as it were, an excellent emblem of the oratory on which it chiefly dwells; admirable in its arrangement, full of good sense in much of its detail, with a felicitous and judicious application of the principles of Cicero and Quintilian to his subject, but at times flashy in style.—*Quart. Rev.*

1 vol. 12mo, with an Introduction by A. Potter, D.D., 50 cents, New-York.

Madame de Genlis.

Her works are distinguished by their pleasing style a

noble sentiments. Most of them belong to the class of historical novels.—*Enc. Am.*

Her Memoirs, 2 vols. 8vo, $3 50, New-York.

Goethe.

He has presented German literature with some novels which will always rank among the best. The clearness and simplicity of his prose style make it the best model for the imitation of his countrymen. His best productions are "The Sorrows of Werther" and "Wilhelm Meister's Apprenticeship."

His works, 1 vol. 8vo, $5 50, London.

La Fontaine.

A German novelist. His novels are entertaining, but not distinguished by merit of a high order.—*Enc. Am.*

Fisher Ames.

As a speaker and as a writer he had the power to enlighten and persuade, to move, to please, to charm, to astonish. He united those decorations that belong to fine talents to that penetration and judgment that designate an acute and solid mind. It was easy and delightful for him to illustrate by a picture, but painful and laborious to prove by a diagram.

8vo, $3 50, Boston.

Pitt.

His eloquence, if not more elevated or profound, was, upon the whole, more correct than that of any other orator of his time. Although neither illuminated by the flashes of genius which characterized his father's (Lord Chatham) oratory, nor by the imagination which distinguished the eloquence of Burke, it was more uniformly just than that of either, while the indignant severity and keenness of his sarcasm were unequalled.

Godwin.

Celebrated as the author of "Caleb Williams." There is not a moment's pause in the action or sentiments; the breath is suspended, the faculties are wound up to the highest pitch, as we read. Page after page is greedily devoured. There is no laying down the book till we come to the end, and even then the words still ring in our ears, nor do the mental apparitions ever pass away from the eye of memory. —*Edinb. Rev.*

Schiller and Goethe, their Correspondence from 1794 *to* 1805.

With many trivial circumstances are intermingled acute and profound observations on literature and life, free and eloquent speculation on philosophical opinions, many lights as to the origin and progress of their respective literary enterprises, their habits of study and composition, their hopes and fears as to the great and stormy events, the moral and political revolutions which were passing around them, their views on some points harmonizing, in others standing opposed to each other in strong contrast, both in their substance and in the manner in which they are advocated and illustrated.—*Edinb. Rev.*

6 vols. 8vo.

Pinkney.

A highly-distinguished American lawyer. Whoever has listened to him upon a dry and complicated question of mere technical law, where there seemed to be nothing on which the mind delighted to fasten, must recollect what a charm he diffused over the most intricate discussions by the clearness and purity of his language, and the calm flow of his graceful elocution.

Pinkney, Life and Writings of, 8vo, $2 00, New-York.

Fielding.

His chief merits as a novelist are wit, humour, correct delineation of character, and knowledge of the human heart. He is too fond of the manners and scenery of vulgar life, and too prone to excuse gross deviations from propriety and good conduct under the vague qualification of "goodness of heart."—*Enc. Am.*

3 vols. 8vo, $5 00, London.

Jean Paul F. Richter.

We defy the most careless or prejudiced reader to peruse his works without an impression of something splendid, wonderful, and daring; but they require to be studied as well as read if the reader, especially the foreign reader, wishes to comprehend rightly either their truth or their want of it.—*Edinb. Rev.*

W. E. Channing.

The late Dr. Channing has left some of the noblest prose of our language. Whenever he leaves controversial theology, and deals with the great principles of morality and humanity, he is alike forcible, generous, beautiful, and true.

Canning.

His eloquence was persuasive and impassioned; his reasoning clear and logical; his manner graceful; his expression winning, and his whole appearance prepossessing.

Speeches of G. Canning, with a Memoir by R. Thierry, London, 1828.

Dr. Mason.

He possessed uncommon power as a preacher and controversialist. It was impossible to listen to his preaching without feeling a great variety of emotions. His funeral discourse on General Alexander Hamilton is a specimen of his ability in that department of composition.—*Enc. Am.*

Madame de Staël.

In her works, whether we consider them as fragments or as systems, we do not hesitate to say that there are more original and profound observations, more new images, greater sagacity, combined with higher imagination, and more of the true philosophy of the passions, the politics, and the literature of her contemporaries, than in any other author we can remember.—*Edinburgh Rev.*

Sir Walter Scott.

His narrative is kept constantly full of life, variety, and colour; and it is so interspersed with glowing descriptions, lively allusions, and flying traits of sagacity and pathos, as not only to keep our attention continually awake, but to afford a pleasing exercise to most of our other faculties. The great charm of his works is derived from the kindness of heart, the capacity of generous emotions, and the lights of native taste, which he ascribes so lavishly, and, at the same time, with such an air of truth and familiarity, even to the humblest of his favourites.—*Edinburgh Rev.*

Coleridge.

All his prose writings have incidental merits sufficiently many and great to rescue them from oblivion, merits discernible either in scattered criticisms on our older writers both of poetry and prose, or in illustrations drawn from stores of knowledge which a very wide reading had amassed, or in passages of great acuteness and sound practical wisdom, whenever the author lowers his flight to subjects to which such qualities can be applied with any hope of profit. His works contain occasional passages of great beauty and power. —*Penny Cyc.*

Southey.

Though, in general, we prefer Mr. Southey's poetry to his prose, we must make one exception. The Life of Nelson is, beyond all doubt, the most perfect and most delightful of his works.—*Edinburgh Rev.*

William Wirt.

One of the most elegant writers, as well as one of the most finished orators and lawyers, of our country. His "British Spy," a series of essays written in early life, as well as his Life of Patrick Henry, will remain as monuments of his genius.

IX. THEOLOGY.

(A.) GREEK FATHERS.

Ignatius, first century.

A bishop of Antioch, whose writings are much appealed to in the Episcopal controversy.

Clement of Alexandria, second century.

His works are of great importance, as enabling us to judge of the state of science in his time, and because they contain fragments and accounts of lost works of antiquity. The most complete edition is that of John Potter, Oxon, "A Theatro Sheldon," 1715, reprinted Venice, 1757.

Origen, A.D. 185.

Of his works (represented as 6000), besides his book "De Principiis," directed against heretics, and in which he presents a system founded on Platonic Philosophy, there are extant only his exhortations to martyrdom, commentaries, homilies, and scholia on the Holy Scriptures, of which he may have intended to explain the whole. His work against Celsus is considered as the most complete and convincing defence of Christianity of which antiquity can boast.—*Enc. Am.*

His works, complete in 4 vols. folio, were published by De la Rue, Paris, 1733-59.

Eusebius, A.D. 272.

(See third part.)

Athanasius, 296.

"His life, his struggles, his genius," says Villemain, "did more for the advancement of Christianity than all the powers of Constantine. The writings of such a man are not the works of a mere theologian. If he often contended on points of deep obscurity, his aim was to establish that religious unity, of which he well understood the value and the power." —*Eschb.*

The best edition of his works is that of Montfaucon Greek and Latin, Paris, 1698, 2 vols. folio.

Chrysostom, 354.

His works include 300 discourses and orations, and above 600 homilies. His discourses show an inexhaustible richness of thought and illustration, of vivid conception and striking imagery. He is sometimes too florid; he uses some false ornaments; he accumulates metaphors, and carries both his views and his figures too far.—*Eschb.*

His works were published by Montfaucon, Greek and Latin, Paris, 1718–38, 13 vols. folio.

(B.) LATIN FATHERS.

Clement of Rome, first century.

He is counted among the apostolic fathers, because St. Paul, in his epistle to the Philippians, mentions a Clement as co-labourer with him, and St. Peter is said to have given him the spiritual consecration. He wrote two letters to the Corinthians, of which the first is extant almost entire, but disfigured with some corruptions and interpolations; of the second, only a fragment exists.—*Enc. Am.*

Irenæus, second century.

The errors of the various classes of heretics and schismatics were opposed by a great number of writers, whose books are lost; but the few books of Irenæus, in which he examines and refutes the doctrines of the whole body of them, are still extant, partly in Greek, partly in a Latin version.—*Eschb.*

The best edition is that of J. E. Grabe, Oxford, 1702, folio.

Tertullian, second century.

Of his writings, the most noted is his Apology for the Christian Religion, which contains much information on the manners and conduct of the early Christians, and asserts the falsehood of the calumnies by which they were assailed, and the injustice of persecuting them.—*Enc. Am.*

The best edition is by Havercamp, Leyden, 1718, 8 vols.

Justin the Martyr, second century.

He is spoken of in high terms of praise by the ancient Christian writers, and was certainly a zealous and able advocate of Christianity, but mixed up too much of his early Platonism with its doctrines.—*Enc. Am.*

The best edition of his works is that of Oberthur, Wurtzburg, 1777, 3 vols. 8vo.

Ambrose, 340.

He is famous for his zeal in the cause of Christianity, and for his learning.—*Enc. Am.*

The best edition of his works is by the Benedictines, 2 vols. folio, 1681–90.

Jerome, 340.

He is famous for his eloquence, his virtues, and his extensive learning. His works, which are on all theological subjects, were edited by Erasmus, 1526, and at Paris, 1693.—*Blake.*

Augustine, 354.

There have been fathers of the Church more learned, masters of a better language, and a purer taste; but none have ever more powerfully touched the human heart, and warmed it towards religion. "S. Augustini Confessionum libri xiii." were published by Augustus Neander, Berlin, 1823.—*Enc. Am.*

See *Philosophers* for notices of others.

MIDDLE AGES.

Averroes, 1160.

He regarded Aristotle as the greatest philosopher, and explained his writings with only a slight deviation from his views. Against the orthodox Arabians, he set himself up as a defender of philosophy on rational principles.—*Enc. Am.*

Best edition of his works is that of Venice, 1608.

Aquinas, 1224.

A celebrated scholastic divine. His principal work, "Summa Theologiæ," bears a high reputation in the Roman Catholic Church, and the second section on morals is universally esteemed.—*Enc. Am.*

Wickliff, 1324.

He was a bold speculator both in religion and politics; and the influence of his writings on the state of public opinion in England and Germany was very great.—*Enc. Am.*

Occam, fourteenth century.

He was well acquainted with the Scriptures, and with the philosophy of Aristotle, and possessed a subtile genius, and much eloquence. His works, which display both wit and subtilty, were published, 2 vols. folio, Paris, 1476.—*Blake.*

Duns Scotus, fourteenth century.

An eminent scholastic divine. He left behind him numerous works, which were collected by Lucas Waddingius in 12 vols. folio, Lyons, 1639.—*Enc. Am.*

Thomas à Kempis, 1388.

His "De Imitatione Christi libri iv.," the most celebrated of his works, has been translated into all modern languages, and has been republished more than one thousand times. It penetrates so deeply into the genuine spirit of Christianity that it has been received with equal favour by the most opposite sects.—*Enc. Am.*

Raimond de Sebonde, 1400.

He has been said, in a treatise, to have established the first regular system of natural theology; but, even if nothing of that kind could be found in the writings of schoolmen, which is certainly not the case, such an appellation seems hardly due to Sebonde's book, which is intended, not so much to erect a fabric of religion independent of revelation, as to demonstrate the latter by proofs derived from the order of nature.—*Hallam.*

Ficinus, 1433.

He developed in his "Theologica Platonica" a system chiefly borrowed from the later Platonists of the Alexandrian school, full of delight to the credulous imagination, though little appealing to the reason, which, as it seemed remarkably to coincide in some respects with the received tenets of the Church, was connived at in a few reveries which could not so well bear the test of an orthodox standard. The whole of his Platonic theology appears a beautiful, but too visionary and hypothetical, system of theism, the groundworks of which lay deep in the meditations of ancient Oriental sages. His writings were printed in Paris, 1641, in 2 vols. folio.—*Hallam.*

MODERN TIMES.

Erasmus, 1467.

He was the first conspicuous enemy of ignorance and superstition, the first restorer of Christian morality on a scriptural foundation; and, notwithstanding the ridiculous assertion of some modern, that he wanted theological learning, the first who possessed it in its proper sense and applied it to its proper end. His Epistles, which occupy two folio volumes in the best edition of his works, are a vast treasure for the ecclesiastical and literary history of his times.—*Hallam.*

The best edition is by Le Clerc, Leyden, 1703, 10 vols. folio.

Luther, 1483.

This great reformer was a man of high endowments of mind, and great virtues; he had a vast understanding, which raised him to a pitch of learning unknown in the age in which he lived.—*Enc. Am.*

His works were published at Erlangen, 1826, 60 vols.

Melancthon, 1497.

His "Logi Theologici," which appeared first in 1521, opened the path to an exposition of the Christian creed, at the same time scientific and intelligible, and became the model to all Protestant writers of dogmatics.—*Enc. Am.*

His works appeared together in 4 vols. folio, at Wittenberg, 1601.—*Blake.*

Cranmer, 1489.

Even in that age of comparative darkness, the penetrating mind of Cranmer, though still entangled with the bewildering dogmata of papal superstitions, had learned, from an intimate acquaintance with the Scriptures in their original language, not merely to despise as useless, but to detest as destructive of the beauty and the power of religion, all those distinctions without difference, all those technical phrases without meaning, which composed the lifeless body of school divinity, and which, in some degree, are blended with the systematic religion of the present day.—*Edinburgh Encyc.*

4 vols. 8vo, $15 00, Oxford.

Calvin, 1509.

As a theologian, he was equal to any of his contemporaries

in profound knowledge, acuteness of mind, and, as he himself boasts, in the art of making good a point in question. As an author he merits great praise.—*Enc. Am.*

His works were printed in 9 vols. folio, Amsterdam, 1667.

Ridley, 1500.

He distinguished himself by his tempered zeal in favour of the Protestant Church.—*Enc. Am.*

Hooper, 1500.

His writings, and especially his letters, preserved in Fox's Monuments of the Church, are excellent specimens of his learning, and of his mental abilities.—*Blake.*

Beza.

Among his many works, his exegetic writings, and an able and correct history of Calvinism in France, from 1521 to 1563, which is ascribed to him, are still much esteemed.—*Enc. Am.*

Jewell, 1522.

In his episcopal character he displayed that activity and vigilance so necessary in the establishment of order and regularity after emancipation from Catholic tyranny. His works were numerous and respectable.—*Blake.*

The finest Christian eloquence, sound wisdom, deep learning, and evangelical piety, mark the writings of this reformer. *Bickersteth.*

Bellarmin, 1542.

Bellarmin's great work, entitled "Body of Controversy," written to vindicate the Romish Church, shows him to have been deeply versed in Scriptural learning, and in the doctrine and practice of the Church in all ages.

(See third part.)

Hooker, 1553.

His fame rests upon that incomparable work, "The Ecclesiastical Polity," in eight books, a work greatly admired. His books will get reverence by age, for there is in them such seed of eternity that they will continue till the last fire shall devour all learning.

The most convenient edition is that of Oxford, 3 vols. 8vo.

Socinus, 1539.

The "Prælectiones Theologicæ," published in 1609, contain a systematic theology, according to his views, and are praised by Eichhorn for the acuteness and depth they display.—*Hallam.*

Perron, 1556.

As a theological disputant, he acquired much celebrity at Paris; but he soon after abjured the tenets of the Protestants, and laboured with great assiduity to convert others to the Catholic faith. His works have been collected in 3 vols. folio.—*Blake.*

Arminius, 1560.

In his public and private life he has been admired for his moderation; and though many gross intimations have been thrown against him, yet his memory has been fully vindicated by the ablest pens.—*Blake.*

His works, translated by James Nichols, 8vo, $8 50, London, 1825.

Laud, 1573.

Speaking of his morals and learning, Hume observes, "He was virtuous, if severity of manners and abstinence from pleasure could deserve that name. He was learned, if polemical knowledge could entitle him to that praise." Hume's judgment on the character of a theologian and controversialist is never too favourable. That Laud had great faults is not to be disguised. That he was honest, conscientious, and erudite, can hardly be questioned by a candid mind.

Episcopius, 1583.

The great chief of the Arminian Church in theological literature. His works form 2 vols. folio. The most distinguishing peculiarity of Episcopius was his reduction of the fundamental doctrines of Christianity far below the multitudinous articles of the churches, confining them to propositions which no Christian can avoid acknowledging without manifest blame; such, namely, wherein the subject, the predicate, and the connexion of the two are declared in Scripture by express or equivalent words. Justice has been done to this eminent person in a recent English work, "Nichols's Calvinism and Arminianism Displayed."—*Hallam.*

Grotius, 1583.

His religious opinions were very favourable to the Church of England, and it is no despicable testimony to the purity and authenticity of the doctrines of that communion that its tenets and discipline were commended and applauded by a man whose judgment was so discriminating, and whose opinions so respectable and so satisfactory, especially on the subject of religion, to which he devoted for a long time all the powers of a strong, vigorous, and unprejudiced mind.—*Blake.*

Usher, 1584.

He is justly celebrated for his "Annals of the Old Testament." No former annals of the world had been so exact in marking dates and collating sacred history with profane. It was, therefore, exceedingly convenient for those who possessed not sufficient leisure or learning for these inquiries; and they might very reasonably confide in such authority.—*Hallam.*

Petavius, 1584.

A French Jesuit. His great and extensive erudition was employed in the defence of the Catholic religion against the Protestants. He was the most consummate scholar the Jesuits ever had. As a chronologist he was particularly eminent, and his Latin is universally acknowledged as elegant and refined. His works were published at Leyden.—

Daille, 1594.

An eminent Protestant divine. In 1628 he wrote his celebrated book, "On the Use of the Fathers;" in 1633 he published his "Apology for the Reformed Churches." These books, from their importance and the masterly manner in which the subject was treated, excited a great interest.

Sir Matthew Hale, 1600.

This great man, eminent for his learning, piety, and private virtues, wrote several valuable works on subjects of divinity philosophy, and law. They were published with his Lif and Death by Bishop Burnet, and an Appendix by the Rev Mr. Thirlwall.

2 vols. 8vo, $4 50, London, 1805.

Chillingworth, 1602.

A converted Protestant divine. His book, called "The Religion of Protestants, a Safe Way to Salvation," was so universally admired, that it passed through several editions, and will remain a lasting monument of the author's superior abilities, and of sound reason and pure religion.—*Blake.*

His works, with a life by Birch, 8vo, London, 1840, $3 00.

Cocceius, 1609.

A German theologian, an advocate for the millennium, and deeply read in the Apocalypse. His works were published in 10 vols. folio.

Pearson, 1612.

(See third part.)

Jeremy Taylor, 1613.

(See third part.)

Leighton, 1613.

(See third part.)

Hammond, 1614.

His "Paraphrase and Annotations on the New Testament," published in 1653, is a work of great merit and general utility.—*Blake.*

Baxter, 1615.

(See third part.)

Bossuet, 1627.

His "History of the Variations of the Protestant Churches," and his Universal History, are well known, but his funeral orations, delivered in honour of the princes and great men of the time, possess peculiar sublimity.

His works, 4 vols. royal 8vo, $9 00, Paris, 1841.

Pascal, 1627.

(See third part.)

Barrow, 1630.

(See third part.)

South, 1633.

A celebrated English divine. His Sermons possess great merit, and unite with judgment and erudition art, and a strong vein of satirical moroseness.

They appeared in 7 vols. 8vo, $20 00, Oxford, 1823.

Burnet, 1635.

(See third part.)

Bull, 1636.

His learning, as his judicious editor, Nelson, observes, was tempered with that modest and humble opinion of it that made it shine with greater lustre.

His works were published by Nelson in 4 vols. 8vo.

Stillingfleet, 1635.

His greatest work, "Origines Sacræ," or, "A Rational Account of Natural and Revealed Religion," astonished every reader for its erudition, elegance, strength, and clearness of argument. All his works are the composition of an able scholar, deep divine, and a sound argumentative philosopher.—*Blake.*

His Origines, 2 vols. 8vo, Oxford, 1817, $3 50.

Simon, 1638.

A French critic, who owes much of his fame to his "Critical History of the Old Testament." Many paradoxes, as they then were called, in this famous work, are now received as truths, or, at least, pass without reproof. Simon may possibly be too prone to novelty, but a love of truth, as well as great acuteness, are visible throughout.—*Hallam.*

Dupin, 1657.

Author of the celebrated "Nouvelle Bibliothèque des Auteurs Ecclesiastiques," a complete history of theological literature, at least within the limits of the Church, which, in a long series of volumes, he finally brought down to the close of the seventeenth century. It is unquestionably the most standard work of that kind extant, whatever deficiencies may have been found in its execution. Integrity, love of truth, and moderation distinguish this ecclesiastical history, perhaps, beyond any others. He is often near the frontier of orthodoxy, but he is careful, even in the eyes of Catholics, not to overstep it.—*Hallam.*

20 vols. 4to, $21 00, Paris.

Basnage, 1655.

A French divine. His "History of the Jews since the Time of Christ," 15 vols. 12mo, is particularly valuable.—*Enc. Am.*

Beausobre.

An able French theologian. The most esteemed of his writings was his "History of the Manichæans," 2 vols., a work praised by Gibbon.—*Enc. Am.*

Henry, 1662.

An eminent dissenting divine. As a writer, his labours are highly valued, but especially his Expositions of the Bible, in 5 vols. folio, a valuable and most excellent performance.—*Blake.*

London, 1833, 1 vol. royal 8vo, $5 00.

Clarke (*Samuel*), 1675.

A profound metaphysician, who applied his powers to some of the most difficult questions in natural and revealed religion.

Butler (*Joseph*), 1692.

Author of the "Analogy," a work which needs no praise.

Kennicott, 1718.

A celebrated Hebrew scholar. His excellent Sermons recommend him, but more, the publication of the Hebrew text of the Bible, collated from the various MSS.—*Enc. Am.*

Rosenmüller, 1736.

His "The East in Ancient and Modern Times," 16 vols., "Manual of Bible Antiquities," and "Manual of Bible Criticism and Exegesis," 4 vols., in German, contain a great mass of valuable matter, critical, exegetical, geographical, historical.

Paley, 1743.

(See third part.)

Horsley.

A most cogent and learned controversialist, an acute critic, and an eloquent preacher.

Porteus, 1731.

An able, pious, and eminently useful prelate.

Hall, 1774.

A celebrated English divine. His fame as such was established by his sermon upon Modern Infidelity. The plainest and least laboured of all his discourses are not without delicate imagery and the most felicitous terms of expression. —*Enc. Am.*

12 vols. 8vo, $35 00.

PART III.

USEFUL BOOKS

FOR

POPULAR AND MISCELLANEOUS LIBRARIES.

The wholesom'st meats that are will breed satiety,
Except we should admit of some variety.
In music, notes must be some high, some base.
And this I say, these pages have intendment,
Still kept within the lists of good sobriety,
To work in men's ill manners good amendment.

SIR JOHN HARRINGTON.

PRINCIPLES.

The following have occurred to the author as principles which might, with propriety, regulate the choice of books for private or public libraries. They have been kept in view in the selections made throughout this part.

1. Works of mere fiction* should be excluded.

2. The greatest care should be taken to exclude works of a licentious cast.

3. Native should be preferred to foreign authors.

4. Works of established reputation should always be selected in preference to those of a more recent and ephemeral character. The popularity of many books is exceedingly short-lived.

5. Books calculated to seize upon the attention and quicken the mental activity of the young, should be multiplied. Hence the value of Travels, Voyages, Biography, &c., &c.

6. Books should be preferred which are calculated to cultivate vigour of thought, and purity and elegance of taste. Hence the value of standard classics of our own language, as compared with the ordinary publications of the day.

7. Whenever controversial works are admitted, both sides should be allowed to speak through their ablest representatives.

8. Until a library contains at least 500 volumes, no money should be expended in the purchase of books in any foreign language.

9. Where of two works, otherwise equal in merit, one only

* By works of mere fiction, those are more especially intended which only excite and amuse without improving taste, enlarging knowledge, or strengthening virtuous principle. It is believed that this is the case with a very large proportion of what are usually called novels.

can be purchased, preference should usually be given to that which has been republished in the United States, since that will be the cheapest.

10. Some regard should be paid to the mechanical execution of books; a volume printed on good paper, in open, fair type, and with substantial binding, being more likely to be read, less likely to be abused, and better calculated to cultivate a taste for neatness and elegance.

11. Where a work can be purchased in the form of one or several volumes, the latter should be preferred, as conducing to the circulation of it, by enabling several readers to be employed upon it at the same time.

USEFUL BOOKS, &c.

I. HISTORY.

Whether the collected wisdom of ages and nations be not found in books?
BERKELEY'S *Querist*.

1. *Bossuet's Universal History.*

THE discourse of Bossuet is, perhaps, the greatest effort of his wonderful genius. Every preceding abridgment of so immense a subject had been superficial and dry. He first irradiated the entire annals of antiquity, down to the age of Charlemagne, with flashes of light, that reveal a unity and coherence, which had been lost in their magnitude and obscurity.—*Hallam.*

8vo, old calf, $1 50, London, 1786.

2. *Tytler's Universal History.*

The plan and extent of Mr. T.'s history, and the advantage which he possesses in good taste, and a simple, manly, and intelligible strain of writing, enable him to adorn his pages with a great many light and important touches, which writers, being confined to the dry task of composing annals, are compelled to omit.—*Quart. Review.*

6 vols., Family Library, $2 70, New-York, Harper & Brothers.

In this work, Ancient History is delineated, by making our principal object of attention the predominant states of Greece and Rome, and incidentally touching on the most remarkable parts of the history of the subordinate nations of antiquity, when connected with, or relative to the principal object. For the delineation of *Modern History*, a similar plan is pursued; the leading objects are more various, and more frequently change their place; a nation, at one time the principal, may become for a while subordinate, and afterward resume its rank as principal, but uniformity of design still characterizes this moving picture; the attraction is always directed to the history of a predominant people, and other nations are incidentally noticed when there is a natural connexion with the principal object.—*The Author.*

3. *Von Müller's Universal History.*

(Translated from the German.)

The object of this eminent writer was not the bare chronicling of events or tracing the details of each particular story in the annals of mankind; it was rather to take a survey of the course or tide of human affairs; to observe the ebbings and flowings of national prosperity, of social culture, of public liberty and happiness; to furnish us with distinct, but rapid glances at those great influential causes which have contributed to stamp on every age its peculiar character. Accordingly, particular facts, and even the order and connexion of events, are only regarded as of secondary importance; yet the work is widely distinguished from that species of meager abstraction which has been termed the philosophy of history.—*Preface to Translation.*

4 vols., Stimpson & Clapp, Boston, 1831.

Universal histories must not be used as substitutes for more minute and regular histories, nor as short methods of acquiring knowledge; they are meant to give commanding views, comprehensive estimates, general impressions, but not to take the lead in the study of history.—*Smyth's Lectures.*

ANCIENT HISTORY.

The S. S. Histories of the Old Testament.

"I walk many times in the pleasant fields of the Holy Scriptures, where I pluck up the goodlisome herbs of sentences by pruning, eat them by reading, digest them by musing, and lay them up at length in the high seat of memory by gathering them together; so that, having tasted their sweetness, I may perceive the bitterness of life."—*Queen Elizabeth.*

Rollin's Ancient History.

From the useful moral reflections which Rollin's works contain, and the constant regard which he pays to the great interests of religion and morality, they have obtained a high degree of popularity.—*Edinburgh Encyclopædia.*

1 vol., $3 50, Harper & Brothers, New-York.

Turner's Sacred History.

Mr. Turner is often capable of affording his reader valuable topics of reflection; but, though apparently a most patient antiquary, his imagination is so active, that his style is unexpectedly loaded with metaphors, to a degree that is not only inconsistent with historical composition, but with *all* composition. Very extensive reading is displayed, and many curious particulars may be collected, and much instruction may be derived from his work.—*Smyth's Lectures.*

Family Library, 1 vol. 18mo, 50 cents.

Josephus's Works.

Josephus has been admired for his lively and animated style, the bold propriety of his expression, the exactness of his descriptions, and the persuasive eloquence of his orations.—*Anthon's Class. Dictionary.*

His writings are of great value in illustrating the Bible and the History of Religion.—*Moss's Bibliography.*

Translation by Whiston, 1 vol. royal 8vo, $3 25, London, 1839.

Prideaux's Connections.

The Old and New Testaments connected with the History of the Jews and Neighbouring Nations. By Humphrey Prideaux, D.D.

There are few works in Theology of more value to the student than this; and the popularity which it enjoys is equal to its merit. It contains a large mass of erudition and accurate information on every topic of Jewish history and antiquities, and on all the links which connected that peculiar people with the surrounding nations. It is indispensable to the biblical, and interesting to the general scholar.

2 vols. 8vo, $3 75.

A. H. L. Heeren's Ancient History.

We never remember to have seen a work in which so much useful knowledge was condensed into so small a compass.—*North American Review.*

Heeren's researches have been various and accurate; his style is clear, his judgment profound, his freedom from prejudice exemplary. No one has surpassed him in the kind of historic writing to which he has devoted himself.—*American Quarterly Review.*

1 vol. 8vo, $2 00, D. Appleton & Co., New-York.

Greppo on Hieroglyphics and the Ancient Egyptians.

The overthrow of a distinguished Egyptian king was connected with the departure of the Hebrews from the land of Egypt. Are there any notices of them, or of their oppressors, on the monuments of this country, or among the numerous manuscripts which are every day discovered amid the tombs and ruins? Is there any confirmation of the Scripture account, derived from these accidental and hitherto inaccessible sources of knowledge? On these questions some light is thrown in this work.—*Moses Stewart.*

Gliddon's Ancient Egypt—her Monuments, Hieroglyphics, and History.

This work is from the hands of an intelligent American, long resident as consul in Egypt, and deeply interested in antiquarian researches. It is rich in information, but not distinguished for scientific accuracy.

J. G. Wilkinson.

The Manners and Customs of the Ancient Egyptians, including their Private Life, Government, Laws, Arts, Manufactures, Religion, and Early History.

A most interesting and instructive work: not the result, entirely, of the author's own investigations, but confessedly authentic.

4 vols. 8vo, $15 00.

Robertson's Ancient India.

As an historian, Dr. Robertson is admired for skilful and luminous arrangement, distinctness of narrative, and highly graphical description. His style is dignified and perspicuous.—*Encyclopædia Americana.*

Goldsmith's Greece.

This work, although elegantly written, and highly calculated to attract and interest young readers, enters into no critical discussion of disputed points, and is superficial and inaccurate.—*Life of Goldsmith.*

1 vol. 18mo, 50 cents, Harper & Brothers, New-York.

Mitford's Greece.

Mr. Mitford has brought to his task acuteness and patient

investigation, and by the aid of these valuable qualities he has generally been successful in unravelling the intricate web of Grecian politics; yet in the higher faculties and accomplishments of an historian, and particularly an historian of Greece, he is singularly deficient. He confines himself entirely to a narration of the actions of men, but never informs us how they thought. Statements unfavourable to Democracy are made with unhesitating confidence, and with the utmost bitterness of language. Every charge brought against a monarch or an aristocracy are sifted with the utmost care. —*Edinburgh, Quarterly, and North American Reviews.*

This, I think, is the merit of Mitford, and it is a great one. His very anti-Jacobin partialities, much as they have interfered with the fairness of his history, have yet completely saved it from being dull. He took an interest in the parties of Greece, because he was alive to the parties of his own time. He described the popular party in Athens just as he would have described the Whigs of England. He was unjust to Demosthenes, because he would have been unjust to Mr. Fox.—*Dr. Arnold.*

8 vols. 12mo, $7 50, D. Appleton & Co., New-York.

Gillies' Ancient Greece, its Colonies and Conquests from the earliest Period.

This work enters less into critical and recondite details than that of Mr. Mitford, though sufficiently accurate and comprehensive for all historical purposes; and is, in style of composition, decidedly superior to it. It has been translated into the German and French languages.—*Warren's Law Studies.*

Herodotus.

The contents of his works are highly instructive and useful, although some things in them have no sufficient evidence to support them. His style is characterized by dignity and simplicity united, and presents a striking resemblance to the poetical drapery of Homer.—*Eschenburg's Classical Manual.*

A very valuable and elaborate performance is the translation by William Beloe. The language is smooth and elegant, yet literal. The work is enriched with a variety of learned and amusing notes.—*Moss's Bibliography.*

3 vols., $1 35, Harper & Brothers, New-York.

Thucydides.

Thucydides is impartial in his writings, and given to a noble, flowery, but frequently, on account of copiousness of thought, obscure style. He was eyewitness of many of the events he narrates; the rest he collected with accuracy and care.—*Eschenburg's Classical Manual.*

The merit of the translation by William Smith is superior to any praises we can bestow.—*Moss's Bibliography.*

2 vols., 90 cents, Harper & Brothers, New-York.

Xenophon.

Xenophon excels among historical writers through his simplicity, taste, and decorum.—*Eschenburg's Classical Manual.*

The best translation yet published is by Edward Spellman, a very faithful and useful version.—*Moss's Bibliography.*

2 vols., 85 cents, Harper & Brothers, New-York.

Polybius.

Polybius may be considered as the originator and model of narration, and most valuable for his minute descriptions of martial institutions: a result of his own military experience. His style is not entirely correct and classical, yet that of a man of business, reading, and thought.—*Eschenburg's Classical Manual.*

The translation by Mr. Hampton bears a high reputation, and the many succeeding editions prove the extensiveness of its circulation.—*Moss's Bibliography.*

8vo, $2 75, London.

Bishop Thirlwall's History of Greece.

Although the author's fancy is everywhere subject to his correct historical taste, the student will not fail to detect traces of that scholar-like delight in the graceful and lovely fictions of antiquity, which is so peculiarly attractive to minds of congenial temper. It animates the reader through the toilsome intricacy of some parts of his progress, like a brook by the wayside, which, though it only sparkles occasionally in the traveller's eye, yet enlivens him by the sense of its constant companionship.—*Edinb. Rev.*

7 vols. 12mo, $12 25, London.

Wordsworth's Greece, Pictorial, Descriptive, and Historical.

Of all the illustrated works which have been lately submitted to public notice, none is more likely to be a favourite than that under notice. It is truly a splendid publication. The name of Dr. Wordsworth is a guarantee that the literary department is conducted in a manner worthy of so interesting a subject.—*Literary Gazette.*

Royal 8vo, $8 50, London, 1840.

Heeren's Researches into the Politics, Intercourse, and Trade of the Principal Nations of Antiquity.

A work of the very highest rank among those with which modern Germany has enriched the literature of Europe.—*Quart. Rev.*

6 vols. 8vo, $24 00, London.

Heeren's Ancient Greece.

Few writers have better succeeded than Mr. Heeren in treating questions of antiquity with the spirit of modern philosophical criticism. He is a prudent mediator between the bold speculations of some of his countrymen and the credulous learning of the last century.—*N. Am. Rev.*

8vo, $1 50.

Boeckh—Public Economy of Athens.

The author has displayed immense erudition and care in this elaborate treatise on the Athenian finances. There is not a word of vague declamation from beginning to end. No subject is avoided because it is difficult, none neglected because minute. A vast deal of information is collected from numerous sources, illustrating the ordinary concerns of business in the best days of Athens.—*N. Am. Rev.*

The study of such a work is essential to correct the schoolboy notion that refers all events and revolutions to the arms of the soldier or the rhetoric of the orator, overlooking the vulgar causes that lay as much at the bottom of ancient as of modern transactions.—*London Athenæum.*

Translated from the German, 2 vols. 8vo, $4 00, London.

Potter's Grecian Antiquities.

This work has gone through many editions, and is almost indispensable to the classical student.—*Enc. Am.*

1 vol. 12mo, $2 25, London, 1841.

Goldsmith's Rome.

A work intended for the perusal of the young, and certainly written in an interesting manner, but almost always superficial, and frequently inaccurate.—*N. Am. Rev.*

18mo, 50 cents, H. & B., New-York.

G. B. Niebuhr's History of Rome.

(Translated by J. C. Hare and C. Thirlwall.)

This work exhibits a far more complete and satisfactory view of the government and political institutions of Rome than can anywhere else be found.—*N. Am. Rev.*

Mr. Niebuhr has been very successful in showing that the foundation of the earlier portions of history is not to be sought in documents, but in traditionary poems, which have been deprived of their beauty of imagery and force of expression without being, for that reason, rendered more consistent with the truth.—*Am. Quart. Rev.*

2 vols. 8vo, $3 25.

Adam Ferguson—History of the Progress and Termination of the Roman Republic.

Authentic and dignified; and the latter volumes, on the struggles and termination of the Republic, are full of interesting reflections.—*Chancellor Kent.*

18mo, 50 cents, H. & B., New-York.

Vertot's Roman Revolution.

This work, though a favourite with its author, is without great critical value, yet when it appeared in 1719, it was received with much applause, which will be seen from the fact that Lord Stanhope, one of the ministers of George I., applied to Vertot for information respecting the formation of the Roman Senate, &c., &c.—*Enc. Am.*

J. C. L. Sismondi's Roman Empire.

As an historian, Sismondi is distinguished for his full and accurate narrative, drawn with great scrupulousness from original sources; and his works are replete with instruction in regard to facts, and in pictures of the changes in the social condition. But he is sometimes prolix, and we often miss the profound views and large conclusions of the philosophical historian.—*Enc. Am.*

History of Rome (Lardner's Cabinet Cyclopædia).

The authors from whom more important points have been

abstracted are, in the first book, Niebuhr (in his third, untranslated, volume), Wachsmuth, and Heeren (in his chapters on Carthage); but the largest contributions have been drawn, throughout the volume, from the great work of Professor Schlosser, of Heidelberg, and the views of manners and literature will be recognised by the German student as selections from that author. A neglected book, the "Scienza Nuova" of Vico, has deserved acknowledgment long before the date of this notice, as throwing a strong original light on the early portions of Roman history, and the primitive relations between patricians and plebeians.—*Advertisement.*

1 vol., Carey, Lea, & Blanchard, Philadelphia, $2 00.

Gibbon's Decline and Fall of the Roman Empire.

If this work be not always history, it is often something more than history, and above it: it is philosophy, it is theology, it is wit and eloquence, it is criticism the most masterly on every subject with which literature can be connected. If the style be so constantly elevated as to be often obscure, to be often monotonous, to be sometimes even ludicrously disproportioned to the subject, it must, at the same time, be allowed, that whenever an opportunity presents itself, it is the striking and adequate representative of comprehensive thought and weighty remark.

Yet how much is there, both in the matter and manner of the whole and of every part of this work, which we cannot approve. In the earlier part of it, the author respected the public, and was more diffident of himself; hence these faults are not at first so glaring. But as he advanced and gained confidence in his own powers, he indulged himself in liberties which are equally shameful and gratuitous. With what surprise and disgust are we to see in such a writer as Gibbon the most vulgar relish for obscenity! With what pain are we to find him exercising his raillery and sarcasm on such a subject as Christianity! How dearly shall we purchase the pleasure and instruction to be derived from his work, if modesty is to be sneered away from our minds, and piety from our feelings.—*Smyth.*

New edition, with notes by Rev. H. H. Milman and Guizot, 4 vols. 8vo, $6 00.

Livy.

In Livy are combined all the qualities of a dignified and a

practical historian, viz., fidelity, accuracy, observation, and a masterly style.—*Eschenburg's Classical Manual.*

The translation by Mr. Baker is a respectable one on the whole; and, as an auxiliary to the right understanding of the original, perhaps the best that has been yet published in English.—*Moss's Bibliography.*

5 vols., $2 25.

Cæsar.

The works of Cæsar are uncommonly valuable, both from the circumstance that Cæsar himself was both an eyewitness and the principal sharer in the events detailed, and also from the elegant, appropriate style and historic beauty, which prevail in them without sinking into dryness.—*Eschb.*

The translation by William Duncan, if our judgment does not mislead us, is the best that has yet been made. The translator has in a great measure caught the spirit of his author, and, as far as the genius of our language would permit, has preserved Cæsar's turn of phrase and expression.—*Moss's Bibliography.*

2 vols., 90 cents.

Sallust.

Adopting Thucydides as his model, he was successful in a happy conciseness of style, and an animated representation of events.—*Eschenburg's Classical Manual.*

The translation by William Rose is a very faithful, accurate, and excellent version.—*Moss's Bibliography.*

1 vol., 40 cents.

Tacitus.

The History of Tacitus is a model of acumen, of the most judicious arrangement and order of the events, and of the most condensed beauty in the expression of thought.—*Eschb.*

Tacitus, translated by Arthur Murphy. On the whole, we think that Mr. Murphy has deposited a very valuable offering on the altar of public instruction, the produce, no doubt, of many years of industry.—*Moss's Bibliography.*

Evangelists and Acts of the Apostles.

The two parts of which the Scriptures consist are connected by a chain of compositions, which bears no resemblance, in form or style, to any that can be produced from the stores of Grecian, Indian, Persian, or even Arabian learning. The antiquity of those compositions no man doubts; and the unstrained application of them to events long subsequent to their publication is a solid ground of belief that they were genuine predictions, and consequently inspired.—*Sir William Jones.*

Eusebius's Ecclesiastical History to the Year 324 of the Christian Era, and the 20th of the Reign of Constantine.

It is a most important production, as furnishing the principal information which we possess concerning the first ages of Christianity, and the books of Scripture then received as inspired writings.—*Edinburgh Cyc.*

The translation by Rev. C. F. Cruse is executed with fidelity, and brings the great work within the reach of every reader.

8vo, $2 50, D. Appleton & Co., New-York.

Dr. W. Cave's Primitive Christianity.

This work is very interesting and valuable as a picture of usages, opinions, &c., in the Christian Church during the first four centuries. Its author is rather an undistinguishing admirer, so much so as to be called by Jortin "the white-washer of the ancients." He is evidently honest, however; and the questionable character of some things which he commends or fails to censure is sufficiently obvious to every reader.

2 vols. 12mo, $2 25, D. Appleton & Co., New-York.

Rev. H. H. Milman's History of Christianity.

Milman should not be cited as a grave authority, but as a popular and entertaining writer. A rationalistic spirit is the greatest fault of his historical writings. His narratives are often brilliant and impressive, and his researches are, in many instances, marked by acuteness and originality.

1 vol. 8vo, $1 90.

J. L. Von Mosheim's Ecclesiastical History.

(Translated by James Murdock or Archibald Maclaine.)

The author's ingenious illustrations of the sacred writings, his successful labours in the defence of Christianity, and the light he has cast upon the history of religion and philosophy by his uninterrupted researches, appear in these volumes, which are deservedly placed among the most valuable treasures of sacred and profane literature; and the learned and judicious work that is here presented to the public will undoubtedly render his name illustrious in the records of religion and letters.—*Translator's Preface.*

3 vols. 8vo, $7 50.

Milner's Ecclesiastical History, from the Days of the Apostles till the famous Disputation between Luther and Miltitz in 1520.

We need scarcely say how earnestly we recommend the whole work to our readers, especially the younger class, from whom it well merits close and impartial attention.—*Christian Observer.*

Milner is able, learned, and conscientious, but he is not always impartial.

8vo, $3 00.

Adam's Roman Antiquities.

Few books in so small a compass contain so large a mass of useful information, and the matter, multifarious as it is, is in general well digested and arranged. The chief defect, perhaps, and it is one which pervades many parts of the work, is an inattention to the effects of time in changing the customs of the Romans. Thus, though Dr. Adam has collected a large mass of facts connected with the political institutions of Rome, yet, not perceiving how the meaning of terms varied in the different ages, he has often so arranged the passages extracted by him from Latin authors on this subject as entirely to mislead both himself and his reader.—*Penny Cyc.*

8vo, $1 75, London, 1839.

Smith's Dictionary of Greek and Roman Antiquities.

(Edited by Professor Anthon.)

This is the joint production of several distinguished scholars in England. It imbodies the researches of the latest travels, and is regarded as a very complete and accurate work, embracing in a moderate compass the matter previously scattered through several volumes, and superseding, in a considerable degree, the compilations of Potter and Adam.

8vo, $5 00.

MODERN HISTORY.

William Smyth's Lectures on Modern History.

The object of these Lectures, effected in so finished a manner, is to teach students and readers generally how to read history for themselves; to show them the path, and furnish them the best lights for pursuing it; to enable them to form a just estimate of the principal authors, and to bring forward in bold relief those prominent parts of history to which their attention should chiefly be directed.—*Jared Sparks.*

2 vols. 8vo, $4 50, Little and Brown, Boston.

Arnold's Lectures on the Study of Modern History.

Dr. Arnold acquaints his hearers with the nature and value of the treasure for which they are searching, and this he does with a perspicuity, simplicity, and beauty of language, and a strength and originality of thought, that shows him to have possessed both the art and the power of the finished historian.—*J. G. Cogswell.*

25 cents.

Dr. Priestley's Lectures on History and General Policy.

These Lectures are very useful, as they give an account of all books and sources of information belonging to English history.—*Smyth's Lectures.*

4to, $3 00, London.

Guizot's History of Civilization in Europe, from the Fall of the Roman Emvire to the French Revolution.

The Lectures of Professor Guizot, now *premier* of France, are calculated, in their whole scope and tenour, to exalt, establish, and render more beautiful the whole framework of the social system to which we belong, and which has secured to us so many of the rights and privileges of citizens, so many of the blessings of Christianity.—*Translator's Preface.*

8vo, $1 00, D. Appleton & Co., New-York.

Russell's Modern Europe.

History of Modern Europe, with a view of the Progress of Society, from the Rise of the Modern Kingdoms to the Peace of Paris in 1763, by William Russell, LL.D with a continuation by William Jones, Esq.

Perhaps the student cannot do better than proceed from Robertson's Charles V. to Letter LXVI. of "Russell's Modern Europe"—a very meager work, it is true—taking care to substitute Hume, and even Smollett, for the corresponding portions of English history.—*Warren's Law Studies.*

3 vols. 8vo, $5 00.

Hallam's Middle Ages.

The object of this work is to exhibit, in a series of historical dissertations, a comprehensive survey of the chief circumstances that can interest a philosophical inquirer during the period usually denominated the Middle Ages.—*Preface.*

Mr. Hallam thinks for himself, and he is a critic and examiner of the labours of those who have gone before him.—*Smyth.*

8vo, $2 00.

James's History of Chivalry.

I wished to write upon Chivalry and the Crusades, because I fancied that in the hypotheses of many other authors I had discovered various errors and misstatements, which gave a false impression of both the institution and the enterprise; and I have endeavoured, in putting forth my own view of the subject, to advance no one point, however minute, which cannot be justified by indisputable authority.—*Advertisement.*

1 vol. 18mo, 50 cents.

Sharon Turner's Anglo-Saxons.

The volumes of Mr. Turner contain many particulars which the student will not readily find elsewhere: he will, from the text and from the notes, sufficiently comprehend what is the knowledge which the study of the Saxon language and Saxon antiquities would furnish him with.—*Smyth.*

Philadelphia, 1841, 3 vols. 8vo, $5 00.

Churton's Early English Church.

The fruit of much research, and though pervaded by a reverence rather too profound for the "dark ages," which the author thinks were dark only "through excess of brightness," this volume is still worthy of study.

1 vol. 16mo, $1 00.

Michelet's Elements of the Modern History of Europe.

(Translated, with an Introduction, by A. Potter, D.D.)

Michelet is one of the most learned and eloquent of the living historians of France, and in such historians no country is so rich. No one since Bossuet has sketched Universal History with so bold and graphic a pen.

1 vol. 18mo, 50 cents.

Hume's History of England.

As an historian, Mr. Hume is most generally popular. The beauty of his diction, the interest which his elegant turn of thought imparts to the course of events described, render it, on the whole, the most pleasing book of English history in our language.—*Edinburgh Enc.*

Yet there are two great lines of objection to Mr. Hume's history: first, his inaccurate representation of the very authorities he quotes; secondly, he ascribes to the personages of history, as they pass before him, the views and opinions of later ages; those sentiments and reasonings, for instance, which his own mind was enabled to form, not those which were or could be formed by men thinking and acting many centuries back.—*Smyth.*

London, 1760, 4 vols. 4to, $8 00.

Lingard's History of England from the first Invasion of the Romans.

The merits of Dr. Lingard are of a high class. He generally discusses controverted facts with candour, acuteness, and perspicuity. He selects, in general, judiciously, arranges naturally, relates without prolixity and confusion.—*Edinburgh Review.*

He is the advocate of the Roman Catholic Church.

Paris, 1840, 8 vols. 8vo, $18 00.

Mackintosh's History of England.

These volumes are full of weighty matter, and are everywhere marked by paragraphs of comprehensive thought and sound philosophy, political and moral: they are well worthy their distinguished author.—*Smyth.*

8vo, $2 25, H. & B., New-York.

M'Culloch's Statistics of the British Empire, with Historical Notices.

The editor has endeavoured to make this work generallv interesting and useful, and it is eminently so.

London, 2 vols. 8vo, $8 00.

A. H. L. Heeren's Political System of Europe.

This historian has investigated the most important periods

of the political existence of the ancient and modern nations with great sagacity, and has portrayed them with great perspicuity.—*Enc. Am.*

2 vols. 8vo, $2 25, New-York, Bartlett & Welford, 1829.

James's Naval History of England.

Robertson's History of Charles V.

The talents of Dr. Robertson as an historian were for some time reckoned superior to those of any rival author. Mr. Stewart is of opinion that his Charles V. unites the various requisites of good writing in the greatest degree.

8vo, $1 75, H. & B., New-York.

Robertson's History of Scotland.

8vo, $1 75, H. & B., New-York.

Robertson's History of the Discovery and Settlement of America.

The style of this work is regarded as less uniformly polished than that of his other works, and as less simple and concise, though it contains many passages equal, if not superior, to anything else in his writings.—*Edinburgh Enc.*

8vo, $1 75, H. & B., New-York.

Blunt's History of the Reformation.

Like everything from the same source, interesting and able.

D'Aubigney's History of the Reformation.

This work is a lively picture of passing events, feats of war, and intrigues of court, in which the characters of the personages concerned are sketched by a satiric but lively pen.—*Penny Cyc.*

3 vols. 12mo, $1 00, New-York, Robert Carter.

Burnet's History of the Reformation.

A production of labour and authority, to which the state of the times in which he published the first volume (1679) added so much of incidental value, that a vote of thanks to the author passed both houses of Parliament, accompanied with a request that he would complete the design.—*Edinburgh Enc.*

Scarcely any other book of equal importance, perhaps, stands so much in need of preliminary explanations as this great work of the celebrated writer whose name it bears.

And it must often have been a matter of just surprise to the readers of this history, that in the editions hitherto published, the errors in the first and second volumes have been reprinted, which the author himself noticed at the end of the third volume. In the present edition, the text will be found corrected as it should be, and many explanatory notes added throughout the work.—*Editor's Preface.*

Burnet's History of the Reformation, revised and corrected, with additional notes and a preface by Rev. E. Nares, D.D., 4 vols. 8vo, $8 00, D. Appleton & Co., New-York.

Smedley's Reformation in France.

Alison's History of Europe.

An elaborate and able work, but grievously disfigured by political prejudices. The gross blunders which the author perpetrates in regard to our own country show how much his antipathy to republican institutions has interfered with his researches as an historian, and contribute seriously to shake that confidence which would otherwise be inspired by his apparent conscientiousness.

$4 00.

Florian's History of the Moors.

Facility, grace, harmony, and a sensibility rare in the French character, are the most striking characteristics of his works. His descriptions of manners are striking and faithful.—*Enc. Am.*

18mo, 50 cents.

Clarendon's History of the Rebellion and Civil Wars in England.

You ask me about reading history. You are quite right to read Clarendon; his style is a little long-winded, but, on the other hand, his characters may match those of the ancient historians, and one thinks they would know the very men if you were to meet them in society. Few English writers have the same precision either in describing the actors in great scenes, or the deeds which they performed. He was, you are aware, himself deeply engaged in the scenes which he depicts, and therefore colours them with the individual feeling, and sometimes, doubtless, with the partiality of a partisan.—*Sir W. Scott's Letter to his Son.*

6 vols. 8vo, $7 50, Little & Brown, Boston, 1829.

Neal's History of the Puritans.

This work is of considerable authority, and very honourable to the talents of the author.—*Blake's Biog. Dict.*

2 vols. 8vo, $2 00.

Miss Aikin's Courts of Queen Elizabeth and King James.

Both these works are valuable contributions to history. They give us vivid pictures of the British court during two of the most memorable reigns.

Fox's History of James II.

This work, left unfinished, and published after the death of Mr. Fox, remains as a monument of his distinguished talents, and a testimony of his relish for the pleasures of taste. —*Edinburgh Encyc.*

8vo, $1 00, Philadelphia, 1808.

Prescott's Ferdinand and Isabella.

Mr. Prescott's merit chiefly consists, in the skilful arrangement of his materials, in the spirit of philosophy which animates the work, and in a clear and elegant style that charms and interests the reader. His book is one of the most successful historical productions of our time. The inhabitant of another world, he seems to have shaken off all the prejudices of ours. In a word, he has in every respect made a most valuable addition to our historical literature.—*Edinburgh Rev.*

3 vols. 8vo, $7 50, Little & Brown, Boston, 1841.

Irving's Conquest of Grenada.

Mr. Irving has seldom selected a subject better suited to his peculiar powers than the Conquest of Grenada. Indeed, it would hardly have been possible for one of his warm sensibility to have lingered so long among the remains of Moorish magnificence, with which Spain is covered, without being interested in the fortunes of a people whose memory has almost passed into oblivion, but who once preserved the sacred flame when it had become extinct in every corner of Christendom, and whose influence is still visible on the intellectual culture of Europe.—*North American Rev.*

Mrs. Calcott's History of Spain.

Everything is done by Mrs. Calcott that can be done by good sense and good principles of civil and religious liberty, and by commendable diligence in the collection and display of the materials which her subject supplied; and the student will see the main points presented to his view, and reasonable observations made, and, on the whole, feel his mind left in a state of sufficient repose and satisfaction with respect to this portion of his course of historical reading. But it is impossible that his original expectations from this part of history can be gratified, more particularly if he is a person of poetical temperament, and has got his imagination excited by all the enchanting dreams that, by means of ballads, romances, histories, and dramas, are forever associated with this renowned land of magnificence, chivalry, and love.—*Smyth.*

D'Anquetil's History of France.

He is the author of several works on history, of which, however, only this is held in much esteem.—*Penny Cyc.*

Immense learning, acquaintance with almost all the European languages, and a restless activity were united in it, with the purest love of truth, with sound philosophy, rare disinterestedness, and an excellent heart.—*Enc. Am.*

Dumas—Progress of Democracy.

(Translated by an American.)

The title of this book in the original is simply "Gaul and France," without one additional or explanatory word; but on presenting it to the public in English, the translator has ventured to adopt a different title, which, though not that of the author, is, nevertheless, descriptive of his work, and of the purpose with which he wrote it.

12mo, $1 00, New-York.

History of Denmark, Sweden, and Norway, by Crichton and Wheaton.

This is the joint production of two of the ripest scholars of the present day, who have made the subject of Runic literature and antiquities, as well as of Northern history generally, their particular study. The volumes are distinguished not less by erudite research than by the charms of style, and the general ability with which they are written.—*Advertisement.*

2 vols. 18mo, 50 cents.

History of Venice, by Smedley.

2 vols. 18mo, 90 cents.

History of Poland, by Fletcher.

18mo, 45 cents.

History of Palestine, by Russell.

In this volume the author has presented at once a topographical description of the Holy Land as it exists at present, and also a history of the wonderful people by whom it was anciently possessed; accomplishing thereby an object which has not been attempted by any former writer. It contains, besides, a view of the political constitution, the antiquities, literature, and religion of the Hebrews, with an account of their principal festivals, and the manner in which they were observed. It concludes with an outline of the natural history of Palestine, applied to the illustration of the sacred writings, and more especially of the Mosaic laws.—*Preface.*
1 vol. 18mo, 50 cents.

History of Egypt, by Russell.

The object of this volume is to present to the reader, in a condensed form, an account of all that is known respecting Egypt, both in its ancient and in its modern state.—*Preface.*
1 vol. 18mo, 50 cents.

History of the Barbary States.

This work has for its object an historical outline of those remarkable provinces which stretch along the southern shores of the Mediterranean, during the successive periods when they were occupied by the Phœnicians, the Romans, the Vandals, the Arabs, and the Moors, as well as a delineation of their condition since they acknowledged the dominion of the Porte.—*Preface.*
1 vol. 18mo, 50 cents.

Sismondi's History of the Italian Republics.

As an historian, Sismondi is distinguished for his full and accurate narrative, drawn with great scrupulousness from original sources; and his works are replete with instruction in regard to facts, and in their pictures of the changes in their social condition.—*Enc. Am.*
Abridged edition, 1 vol. 18mo, 50 cents.
This abridgment of a large work is, of course, much less interesting than the original, but it may be read with profit.

Crichton's History of Arabia.

These volumes contain a description of the country, an account of its inhabitants, antiquities, political condition, and early commerce, the life and religion of Mohammed, the conquests, arts, and literature of the Saracens, the caliphs of Damascus, Bagdad, Africa, and Spain, the civil government and religious ceremonies of the modern Arabs, origin and suppression of the Wahabees, the institutions, character, manners, and customs of the Bedouins, and a comprehensive view of its natural history. They belong to a series of publications (Edinburgh Cabinet Library), of which the following notice is given in the Spectator: "Among the various serial publications of the day, the Edinburgh Cabinet Library is one of the best, the most instructive, and the most popular."

2 vols., 90 cents.

Frazer's History of Persia.

It has been the study of the author, by adopting a distinct arrangement, and by consulting the best authorities, to present his readers with a correct and complete picture of that interesting portion of Western Asia. His personal acquaintance with many parts of the country has afforded him material assistance in describing its aspect, productions, and inhabitants; and he has availed himself of the observations of the greater number of modern travellers, both to correct his own opinions and to supply additional facts.—*Preface.*

1 vol. 18mo, 45 cents.

Southey's History of Brazil.

Mr. Southey's prose works are remarkable for the purity and beauty of the style. The History of Brazil is thus characterized in a letter of Walter Scott to the author: "Twenty times twenty thanks for the History of Brazil, which has been my amusement, and solace, and spring of instruction for this month past. It is most singularly entertaining, and throws new light upon a subject which we have hitherto understood very imperfectly. Your labour must have been immense, to judge from the number of curious facts quoted, and unheard-of authorities which you have collected."

Malcolm's History of British India.

This work has become a manual of modern Indian diplomacy; and although we differ, in some important particulars, from the opinions of Sir John Malcolm, we must always do justice to the liberal spirit in which they are conceived, and the manliness with which they are expressed. The work, as a whole, is well worthy of its author's reputation.—*Quart. Rev.*

2 vols. 8vo, $5 50.

Davis's History and Description of China.

The pages of this volume being intended wholly for the use of the general reader, so much only of each subject has been touched upon as seemed calculated to convey a summary, though at the same time accurate species of information, in an easy and popular way. More detailed knowledge on each separate point must be sought for by the few who are likely to require it, in one or other of the numerous works given in the catalogue contained in this work.—*Introduction*

2 vols. 18mo, 90 cents.

Sforzozi—History of Italy.

(Translated by Green.)

Murray's History of British America.

The author, deeply impressed with the importance of his task, has anxiously sought every means of rendering its performance complete and satisfactory. In tracing the condition and history of the aboriginal tribes, he has had access to extensive works in the French language, to which former writers appear to have been strangers. He has devoted much attention to the statistics and present state of the colonies; an undertaking attended with considerable difficulty, on account of the recent changes which have rendered all previous information in a great measure useless.

2 vols. 18mo, 90 cents.

Sismondi's History of Literature of the South of Europe.

This work forms an epoch in literary history, and proves that the author raised his views above the narrow conventional rules, during his days, predominant in France.—*Enc. Am.*

It is a work written in that flowing and graceful style which distinguishes the author, and succeeding in all that it seeks to give, a pleasing and popular, yet not superficial or unsatisfactory, account of the best authors in the Southern languages.—*Hallam.*

4 vols. 12mo, $5 00, I ittle & Brown, Boston.

Hallam's History of Literature.

The advantages of such a synoptical view of literature as displays its various departments, in their simultaneous condition through an extensive period and in their mutual dependancy, seem too manifest to be disputed.—*Preface.*

Mr. Hallam has great industry and acuteness; his knowledge is extensive, various, and profound; his mind is equally distinguished by the amplitude of its grasp, and by the delicacy of its tact.—*Edinb. Review.*

2 vols. 8vo, $3 75, Harper & Brothers, New-York.

Taylor's Natural History of Society.

The design of this work is to determine, from an examination of the various forms in which society has been found, what was the origin of civilization; and under what circumstances those attributes of humanity, which in one country become the foundation of social happiness, are in another perverted to the production of general misery. That much may be effected towards improving the condition of mankind by a close investigation into the moral elements which form the basis of the various modifications society has assumed throughout different ages, in the barbarous, as well as more civilized nations, cannot be doubted; and it affords us sincere gratification to find this subject, so fraught with important objects for reflection, considered, and laid before the public by so able a writer.—*Scottish Journal.*

2 vols. 12mo, $2 25, D. Appleton & Co., New-York.

Schlegel's Philosophy of History.

2 vols. 12mo, $2 50, D. Appleton & Co., New-York.

Schlegel's History of Literature.

The influence which the brothers Schlegel have exerted on belles-lettres in general, especially in promoting a more correct understanding of the literature of the Middle Ages, is very great, and extends far beyond their native country. They will be remembered in the history of literature as two minds of uncommon vigour.—*Enc. Am.*

8vo, $2 00 D. Appleton & Co., New-York.

AMERICAN HISTORY.

Hale's History of the United States.

A valuable compendium, and useful as an introduction to the study of larger and more complete works.

Bradford's American Antiquities and Researches into the Origin and History of the Red Race.

In this work the author investigates some interesting problems, and it is well worthy of perusal.—*Lond. Athen.*

$1 50, New-York, 1841.

Morton's New-England's Memorial.

(Edited by Judge Davis.)

This history is a curiosity in several respects. It was the earliest history of New-England, and confined principally to the Plymouth Colony. It was compiled upon the recommendation of the commissioners of the four united colonies of New-England, in 1656, and the object was "to collect the special and remarkable passages of God's providence towards them."—*Chancellor Kent.*

Chronicles of the Pilgrims.

(Edited by the Rev. Alexander Young.)

Full of interest and instruction.

Winthrop's Journal.

(Edited by Savage.)

This work relates to the first settlement of Massachusetts and the other New-England colonies. The notes of the learned editor add greatly to its interest and value.—*Chancellor Kent.*

2 vols. 8vo, $4 00, Boston.

Drake's Book of the Indians.

The author submits his work with some confidence, from a consciousness of having used great exertions to make it useful, and of having treated his subject with the strictest impartiality. All verbiage has been avoided, and plain matters of fact have been arrived at by the shortest and most direct course.—*Preface.*

It is a work of high authority for facts.

8vo, $3 00, Boston.

Mather's Magnalia.

Credulity, pedantry, quaintness, eccentricity, are blended, in most of his works, with marvellous erudition and instructive details of history and opinion. His largest and most celebrated work is his "Magnalia Christi Americana," or the Ecclesiastical History of New-England from 1625–1698. —*Enc. Am.*

2 vols., $6 50, Hartford.

Hutchinson's History of Massachusetts.

A colonial publication, and one very respectable. Mr. Hutchinson laboured hard in the field of our colonial antiquities, producing for a result two volumes of early history, which will ever be considered a mine of wealth by all future historians and antiquarians.—*North American Review.*

3 vols. 8vo, $7 00, Salem.

Collections of the Massachusetts Historical Society.

Very rich in valuable materials for history.

27 vols. 8vo, $27 00, Boston, 1806–38.

Collections of the New-York Historical Society.

They deserve a conspicuous place among the historical productions of the State of New-York.—*Natural History of New-York.*

3 vols. 8vo, $5 00, New-York.

Pitkin's History of the United States from 1763–1797.

Those who have read little of the history of their country will find in this work much new and useful information; and those who are more conversant with our annals will not disdain a collection of facts extracted from contemporary writers, and from public documents, which it would be laborious to trace, and difficult to find. His style is not always pure, his manner not elevated; he seldom attempts delineation of character, but his principles are sound, and his narrative impartial.—*American Quarterly Review.*

2 vols. 8vo, $4 50, New-Haven, 1828.

Irving's Life of Columbus.

This is one of the works which are at the same time the

delight of the readers, and the despair of critics; it is as nearly perfect as any work well can be. Its attraction lies in the charm of finished elegance, which it never loses. The most harmonious and poetical words are carefully selected. Every period is measured and harmonized with nice precision. —*North American Review.*

2 vols. 8vo, $2 75.

Bancroft's History of the United States.

Readers may rest assured, that from beginning to end, they will find this History full of interest, and the best-instructed student of our history may read it with profit.—*North American Review.*

3 vols. 8vo, $6 00. Abridged, 2 vols. 12mo, $2 00, Boston.

Graham's History of North America.

This is a European production, and is written with great gravity and dignity, moderation and justice. — *Chancellor Kent.*

4 vols. 8vo, $8 00, London, 1836.

Botta's History of the American Revolution.

Mr. Jay was reading this History when I visited him in 1820, and he told me that its general accuracy was undoubted.—*Chancellor Kent.*

2 vols. 8vo, $2 50, New-Haven.

Lyman's Diplomacy of the United States.

It is an admirable treatise, which we recommend to the youth of our country.—*Edinb. Encyc., Am. ed.*

Hammond's Political History of New-York, from the Adoption of the Constitution to 1840.

The work is written with candour and studied accuracy.—*Gov. Seward.*

Smith's History of New-York.

The style is plain, and the narrative perspicuous. The author, in its preface, calls it a *narrative*, and adds, "It deserves not the name of history, though, for brevity's sake, I have given it that title; it presents only a regular thread of simple facts." This is a just description of its character.—*North American Review.*

It is sensibly written, and with perfect authenticity.—*Chancellor Kent.*
2 vols. 8vo, $3 50, New-York.

Yates and Moulton's History of New-York.

The excellence of the only volume published has caused a very general regret that the purpose of the authors was relinquished.—*North American Review.*
1 vol. 8vo, $1 50, New-York.

Dunlap's History of New-York.

Mr. Dunlap attempted to execute a history of this state, and he collected very valuable materials, but neither his habits nor the time which he allowed himself were adequate to the proper execution of the task.
2 vols. 8vo, $4 50.

W. W. Campbell's Annals of Tryon County.

This work is a valuable contribution to the history of the state, and especially instructive concerning the trials and sufferings of our frontier population, exposed to Indian barbarities during the war of the Revolution.—*Natural History of New-York.*
8vo, $1 00, New-York.

M. Greenleaf's Survey of Maine,

with reference to its geological features, statistics, and political economy.
8vo, $1 25, Portland, 1829.

Belknap's History of New-Hampshire.

The first volume appeared in Philadelphia in 1784. This work was reprinted in England, and mentioned in the periodical literature of the day in very respectful terms. Being one of our earliest domestic histories, it was received in this country with peculiar respect.—*Chancellor Kent.*
1 vol. 8vo, $3 00, Dover, 1831.

Williams's History of Vermont.

2 vols. 8vo, $3 50, Burlington, 1809.

Baylies's Historical Memoir of the Colony of New-Plymouth from 1644 *to* 1686.

A very respectable work.—*Chancellor Kent.*
2 vols. 8vo, $5 00, Boston, 1830.

Trumbull's History of Connecticut.

This history commences with the first settlement of the colony, and it is brought down to 1764. It is a work of substantial merit and uncommon interest. As the first settlers were intelligent, learned, pious, and discreet pilgrims, they established a republic of the most simple and perfect kind, and furnished it with a code of popular instruction, and of civil and religious discipline, and of social institutions, and of order and decorum, unparalleled in the history of mankind. The colonial republic of Connecticut, as represented in this work, is a phenomenon in the history of civil society.—*Chancellor Kent.*

Thomas T. Gordon's History of New-Jersey.

8vo, $3 00, Trenton, 1834.

Proud's History of Pennsylvania from 1681 *to* 1742.

This work is of great research, and abounds with valuable matter; but it is the most confused and tedious composition that ever tormented human patience.—*Chancellor Kent.*
2 vols. 8vo, $4 50, Philadelphia, 1797.

Beverley's History of Virginia.

Williamson's History of North Carolina.

This work is a valuable addition to the annals of the American Continent.
2 vols. 8vo, $4 00, Philadelphia, 1812.

Ramsay's History of South Carolina.

This work is characterized by vigorous thought, neatness of style, judiciousness, and fidelity.

M'Call's History of Georgia.

Butler's History of the Commonwealth of Kentucky.

1 vol. 8vo, $1 50, Louisville, 1834.

Haywood's History of Tennessee.

A. Stoddard's Sketches of Louisiana.

8vo, $1 50, Philadelphia, 1812.

B. Marbois's History of Louisiana.

The History of Louisiana and of its cession makes the citizen of the United States acquainted with the origin of his country's title to a territory, the importance of which, before the lapse of many ages, will be scarcely inferior to that of all the states of the original confederacy combined; and it unfolds to the statesman a diplomatic transaction, little noticed at the time, which must hereafter exercise the greatest influence on the general balance of power among the nations of Christendom. The translator merits high praise, not more for his patriotism in making this work accessible to American readers than for the ability with which he has executed his task.—*N. Am. Rev.*

8vo, $2 00, Philadelphia, 1830.

Lee's Memoirs of the Southern War.

A work which, if not remarkable for great polish of style, is entitled, from its bold, manly, and sincere tone, as well as the power of the descriptions and the interest of the information, to rank with the best works relating to the Revolutionary war.—*Enc. Am.*

2 vols. 8vo, $4 00.

II. BIOGRAPHY.

The night before the celebrated battle at Pharsalia, that was to decide the fate of the known world, Brutus was in his tent reading, and making notes from his author with a pen.

Life of Christ.

This volume contains the Life of Christ in the words of the Evangelists, forming a complete harmony of the Gospel History of our Saviour. Several other Lives of our Saviour have been written, among which, that by Jeremy Taylor may be mentioned as one of the most interesting.

New-York, 16mo, $1 00

Cave's Lives of the Apostles.

This is justly esteemed the best book upon the subject.—*Penny Cyc.*

London, 2 vols. 12mo, $2 00.

Plutarch's Lives.

They have been universally considered as a rich treasure for the antiquarian, the statesman, and the scholar.—*Heeren.*

New-York, Harper & Brothers, 8vo, $2 00.

Le Bas—Life of Wickliff.

The object of this work is to produce within a reasonable compass the substance of the information which has been preserved to us relative to a very extraordinary man; a man whose strength of character doubtless made an impression on the mind of his country which has never been effaced.—*Preface.*

New-York, 1 vol. 18mo, 45 cents.

Le Bas—Life of Cranmer.

The object of this attempt has been to collect into a compendious narrative the substance of more voluminous compilations, and to present it to the public in a manner which may enable them duly to estimate their obligations to the great master builder of the Protestant Church of England.—*Preface.*

New-York, 2 vols. 18mo, 90 cents.

Le Bas—Life of Laud.

This work, written in a candid style, has not been republished, we believe, in this country.

Bishop Burnet's Lives.

Burnet merits the praise of vigour, depth, and variety of knowledge, but was hasty and rough in his composition—*Enc. Am.*

1 vol. 12mo, $2 00.

Izaak Walton's Lives.

Though possessed of much general information, Walton made no pretensions to learning, and the charm of his writings depends on the air of verisimilitude and unaffected benevolence which they exhibit.—*Enc. Am.*

New-York, 16mo, $1 00.

Mrs. Dobson's Life of Petrarch.

The Life of Petrarch is a striking lesson for youth! What an awful lesson for all human beings! to engage them to seize with ardour those fair and unruffled moments that may fix the most pure and sacred principles in their hearts, and lay the foundation of that solid peace through life which, once lost, is never perfectly regained; not even under the influence and direction of the brightest understanding and the most fervent piety.—*Mrs. Dobson.*

1 vol. 8vo, $1 00.

Roscoe's Lorenzo de Medicis.

The numerous historical events and interesting circumstances, collateral with the main subject, the attractive form in which the literature and associations of Italy were brought into view in the course of the work, and the important epoch in the world's history embraced in the period to which it referred, all tend to enhance its practical worth, and the gratification to be derived from its perusal.—*N. Am. Rev.*

Philadelphia, 2 vols. 8vo, $4 50.

Roscoe's Leo X.

Though the Life of Leo X. is not equal to Roscoe's Lorenzo, it is a composition which displays talent and extensive research.—*Enc. Am.*

Philadelphia, 4 vols. 8vo, $6 00.

Memoirs of Sully.

They are made valuable by principles of excellent morality, by civil and political maxims derived from truth, by an infinite number of views, schemes, and regulations of almost every kind, with which they are filled. Yet there is a great want of method, and defect of style in the whole; and as to the diction, it has every fault which diction can admit.—*Preface to Translation.*

London, 3 vols. 4to, $6 00.

De Retz—Memoirs.

Their animated style, their excellent portraiture of character, their acute and brilliant remarks, distinguish their pages as much as the similar qualities did the author. "They are written," says Voltaire, "with an air of greatness, an impetuosity and an inequality which are the image of his life; his expression, sometimes incorrect, often negligent, but almost always original, recalls continually to his readers what has been so frequently said of Cæsar's Commentaries, that he wrote with the same spirit as he carried on his wars."—*Hallam.*

London, 4 vols. 12mo, $4 00. Philadelphia, 1817, 3 vols. 8vo.

Rev. M. Russell's Life of Cromwell.

It has been the study of the author to give an unbiased view of Cromwell's conduct in his early life, at his first entrance upon public business, in his achievements as a soldier, in his rise to political power, and, finally, in his government of the three kingdoms which he was the first to conquer.—*Preface.*

2 vols. 18mo, 90 cents.

Wilde's Love and Madness of Tasso.

In this work Mr. Wilde has given us some new matter, and has awakened high expectations in regard to his contemplated Life of Dante.

Mrs. Lee's Old Painters.

This is a delightful book, especially for the young. It is full of taste and right feeling, and contains instruction for the heart as well as the head.

Cunningham's Lives of Painters and Sculptors.

Everything from the pen of Allan Cunningham has some charm. On such a subject he could not but write instructively and with feeling.

5 vols. 18mo, $2 10.

Luther's Life and Times, by Mrs. Lee.

Graphic, picturesque, and, with a few exceptions, just.

Scott's Life of Luther.

2 vols. 18mo, 90 cents.

Jortin's Life of Erasmus

is a valuable work.—*Enc. Am.*

2 vols. 4to, $8 00, London.

M'Crie's Life of Knox.

The materials for this work are derived from a diligent

collection of the different writers on that part of ecclesiastical history of which he treats, and from a considerable number of manuscript letters of the reformer.—*Christ. Obs.*
8vo, $2 00, Edinburgh.

Thiebault's Memoirs of Frederic the Great.

A very entertaining picture of the most extraordinary man of his time.
2 vols. 8vo, $2 50, London, 1806.

Barrow's Life of Peter the Great.

This work is a compilation from the scattered fragments of histories, lives, anecdotes, and notices in manuscript or in print of one of the most extraordinary characters that ever appeared on the great theatre of the world in any age or country.—*Preface.*
1 vol. 18mo, 45 cents.

Agnes Strickland's Queens of England, comprising the Lives of Queen Catharine Parr and Queen Mary.

This agreeable book may be considered a valuable contribution to historical knowledge. It contains a mass of every kind of matter of interest.—*Athenæum.*

Forster's Statesmen of the Commonwealth.

Fox's Book of Martyrs.

This work has preserved many facts, some of greater, some of less importance, that are nowhere else to be found. The veracity and honesty of the venerable author may be affirmed to be quite unimpeached.—*Penny Cyc.*
Folio, $3 00, London.

Madden's United Irishmen.

To the readers disposed to study the policy of the Irish government of those days, this work possesses the additional advantage of a clear and succinct narrative of a vast many particulars, necessary to be thoroughly understood in order to form a correct notion of the character of the events.—*London Athenæum.*

Phillips's Recollections of Curran and some of his Contemporaries.

One of the most extraordinary pieces of biography ever produced. No library should be without such a piece.—*Lord Brougham.*
8vo, $1 25.

Sir D. Brewster's Martyrs of Science.

1 vol. 18mo, 45 cents.

Brewster's Life of Newton.

Anything from the pen of Dr. Brewster deserves reading. In these books he has found a theme that has warmed his heart and given new energy to his pen.
1 vol. 18mo, 45 cents.

Arago's Life of Watt.

This *éloge* is a brief sketch of Watt's life, but it is from the hand of a master. All should read and study it. It contains the best condensed history of the steam-engine extant.
8vo, $3 00, London.

Boswell's Life of Johnson.

One of the most amusing, and, in some respects, one of the most perfect of all biographical works.—*Penny Cyc.*
5 vols. 12mo, $3 50, London.

Johnson's Lives of British Poets.

This work, with an occasional exhibition of political bias and strong prejudices, forms a valuable addition to British biography and criticism.—*Enc. Am.*
1 vol. 12mo, $2 00, London.

Life of Schwartz.

An interesting record of the life and labours of one of the most remarkable and useful men of his time.

Life of Henry Martyn, by Sargent.

Mr. Martyn was one of the most gifted men who ever devoted himself to the cause of Christian missions; and Mr. Sargent has given us a faithful and vivid portrait of the man and of his life.

Life of Bishop Heber, by his Widow.

We may, without scruple, recommend a narrative which could not be but interesting, as containing the chief memoranda of the bishop's life, with extracts from his letters and publications.—*Christian Observer.*

2 vols. 8vo, $2 50, New-York.

Life of Wilberforce, by his Sons.

Wilberforce is made to tell the story of his own life in his own words, and nothing is introduced except where it was necessary by way of explanation, or to preserve the connexion.—*Preface.*

2 vols. 8vo, $2 50, Philadelphia.

Lockhart's Life of Scott.

This book must rank as one of the most valuable of the age. It is just such a life as we wanted of so great a man.—*New-York Review.*

7 vols. 12mo, $6 00, Philadelphia.

Lockhart's Life of Burns.

Among the accounts of the life of this distinguished author, this is the latest and most complete.—*Penny Cyc.*

Life of Sir James Mackintosh, by his Son.

A delightful book—full of matter, and exciting to profitable thought.

2 vols. 12mo, Lea and Blanchard, Philadelphia.

Romilly's Memoirs, written by himself, with his Letters, Correspondence, and Political Diary, edited by his Sons.

Alike instructive and interesting.

3 vols. 8vo, $7 50, London.

Life, Character, and Literary Labours of Samuel Drew.

It is interesting, as containing the life of an humble shoemaker of London, whose work on the Soul is remarkable for depth, clearness, and intensity of reasoning.

75 cents, New-York.

Life of Cuvier.

This volume contains the life of one of the first zoologists of Europe, whose profound knowledge was not less remarkable than his elevated views.—*Enc. Am.*

Baxter's Life and Times, by the Rev. William Orme.

Mr. Orme always writes with zeal and ability.
2 vols. 8vo, $1 87, Boston, 1831.

Roberts's Life of Hannah More.

Peculiarly valuable on account of the correspondence which is interwoven with the memoir. It embraces letters from many of the most remarkable of Miss More's contemporaries, male and female.
2 vols. 12mo, $1 50, Harper & Brothers, New-York.

Lockhart's Napoleon.

A spirited and accurate review of a most wonderful life.
2 vols. 18mo, 90 cents.

History of Napoleon by M. Laurent de l'Ardeche, Member of the Institute of France, with 500 Illustrations after Designs by Horace Vernet, and 20 Original Portraits.

The literary merits and the illustrations of this work invest it with much interest. It is afforded at a very reasonable price.
1 vol., $2 50, Appleton & Co., New-York.

Mrs. Jameson's Female Sovereigns.

The intention of this work is to present in a small compass, and at one view, an idea of the influence which a female government has had *generally* on men and nations, and of the influence which the possession of power has had *individually* on the female character.—*Preface.*
2 vols. 18mo, 90 cents.

Lives of Early Navigators.

This work contains, from the very nature of the subject, much curious and valuable information, gleaned from many sources, and, in every instance, verified by scrupulous examination, and reference to the fountain head.—*Preface.*
1 vol. 18mo, 45 cents.

Lives of Eminent Men.

These Lives are selected from the Entertaining Library, published by the British Society for the Diffusion of Useful Knowledge. They are brief, but not meager, and contain many entertaining notices of some of the most remarkable men of modern times.

2 vols. 18mo, 90 cents.

Blake's Biographical Dictionary.

A valuable compilation. As far as we have had occasion to consult it, we have found it accurate, and it is certainly the most cheap and convenient manual of the kind that we have.

Gorton's Biographical Dictionary.

This work is executed with superior ability.—*Penny Cyc.*

2 vols. 12mo, $3 00, London.

Irving's Life of Goldsmith.

Executed with Mr. Irving's characteristic skill and taste.

2 vols. 18mo, 90 cents.

Mrs. Heman's Life, by her Sister.

A touching and beautiful record of the life of one of the most gifted female poets of our time.

Memoirs of Silvio Pellico.

A story of suffering and oppression endured, for the sake of principle, with the most heroic constancy. It cannot be read without intense interest and sympathy.

50 cents.

Life and Remains of E. D. Clarke.

Intensely interesting.

8vo, $1 00.

Hunter's Sacred Biography.

This has long been a standard work. It is written by Mr. Hunter, who translated one or more volumes of Saurin's Sermons.

8vo, Harper & Brothers, New-York.

Williams's Alexander the Great.

This work is chiefly intended for youthful readers who may feel a wish to trace the extraordinary progress of Alexander with due attention to geography and chronology. The study of history unconnected with these two branches of knowledge is mere trifling, and may be beneficially superseded by the historical romance.—*Preface.*

18mo, 45 cents.

Life of Mohammed, by Rev. George Bush.

Mr. Bush is able and conscientious, and the subject of this volume can never lose its interest.

18mo, 45 cents.

Napoleon's Court and Camp.

A lively sketch.

18mo, 45 cents.

Distinguished Females, by an American Lady.

18mo, 45 cents.

Memoirs of Duchess d'Abrantes.

8vo, $1 38.

Lord Brougham's Historical Sketches of Statesmen who flourished in the time of George III.

It would be a very great mistake to suppose that there is no higher object in submitting these sketches to the world than the gratification of curiosity respecting eminent statesmen, or even a more important purpose, the maintenance of a severe standard of taste respecting oratorical excellence. The main object in view has been the maintenance of a severe standard of public virtue, by constantly painting political profligacy in those hateful colours which are natural to it, though sometimes obscured by the lustre of talents.—*Introduction.*

2 vols. 8vo, $1 75.

AMERICAN BIOGRAPHY

Belknap's American Biography.

Dr. Belknap wrote with ease and correctness, though not with elegance; he was more remarkable for research and extensive information than for brilliancy or originality. This work is often consulted.—*Enc. Am.*

3 vols. 18mo, $1 35.

Sparks's Series of American Biography.

These volumes supply a very important deficiency in our literature, and give proof of the industry and perseverance of Mr. Sparks.—*N. Am. Rev.*

10 vols. 12mo, $7 50.

Life of David Brainard.

His narrative of his labours at Kaunameck, and his journal, or account of the rise and progress of a remarkable work of grace among a number of Indians in New-Jersey and Pennsylvania in 1746, are highly interesting.—*Enc. Am.*

Life of Josiah Quincy, Jr.

This Memoir, written by his son, Josiah Quincy, the present President of Harvard College, in 1825, is highly interesting.—*Enc. Am.*

Tudor's Life of James Otis.

A worthy tribute to the character and services of a patriot and a man of genius. It is written with taste, feeling, and candour.

Sparks's Life of Washington.

The latest and most accurate.

1 vol. 8vo, $2 00.

Marshall's Life of Washington.

The style of this work is in perfect keeping with the character of the author. It is perspicuous, simple, and forcible. It possesses no studied ornaments, no select phrases, no elegant turns, and no ambitious floridness. It is plain, pure, and unpretending.—*N. Am. Rev.*

5 vols. 8vo. $9 00.

Life of John Jay, by William Jay.

In these pages an attempt is made to delineate the character of one who was not the least among those who devoted themselves to the service of their country, and acquired a title to its gratitude. Many of the papers and letters appended to the Life are important, and all will be found interesting, as throwing light either upon individual character, or upon the circumstances of the times to which they relate. *Preface.*

2 vols. 8vo, $5 00.

Life of Alexander Hamilton, by his Son.

These volumes exhibit much valuable matter relative to the Revolution, the establishment of the Federal Constitution, and other important events in the annals of our country.—*N. Y. Rev.*

2 vols. 8vo, $5 00, D. Appleton & Co., New-York.

Life of Gouverneur Morris.

The author, Mr. Sparks, has brought to his task so much of intelligent research, so much historical anecdote, and rich and various illustration, that his work is of real, as it will be of lasting value.—*N. Am. Rev.*

3 vols. 8vo, $3 50, New-York.

Life of De Witt Clinton.

This memoir, by Dr. Hosack, is written in a very candid, liberal spirit. The work does great credit to his industry and good judgment; he has shown an indefatigable activity in collecting materials, by a wide range of inquiry and correspondence.—*N. A. Rev.*

Life of Peter Van Schaack.

As the biography of an eminent American of elevated character, of high integrity, and of honourable association, who, in sentiment, was opposed to taking up arms in the American Revolution, this work, composed, as it mainly is, of original contemporaneous materials, which may help to guide the future historian, will not be without value.-*Preface.*

Life of Jefferson, by Thomas Tucker.

This is the memoir of an eminent man by a warm admirer. It cannot but be interesting.

2 vols. 8vo, $4 00, Philadelphia, 1837.

Autobiography, Reminiscences, and Letters of John Trumbull.

Though, both in subject and handling, somewhat unimaginative, the memoir is not without interest as a memorial of talents unremunerated, and of hopes withered; while it affords subject for many reflections on the antecedents and prospects of American independence.—*London Athenæum.*

Life of William Livingston, by Theodore Sedgwick, Jun.

Governor Livingston was among the most revered of our Revolutionary fathers. His life, by his grandson, is written with ability and discrimination.

8vo, $2 00.

Life of Rev. John H. Livingston, D.D.

This volume contains, it is believed, a faithful picture of the revered individual whose eventful life it portrays, and at the same time exhibits all the most prominent features of the history of the Reformed Dutch Church in this country.—*Committee of General Synod.*

1 vol. 8vo, New-York.

Letters of Mrs. John Adams.

It will naturally be presumed that this correspondence of an uncommonly sensible woman like Mrs. Adams, who lived in an eventful period of our history, and was personally, and for the most part intimately acquainted with the great men of her times, must be full of interest and instruction; and so, in fact, it will be found by every reader.—*N. Y. Rev.*

2 vols. 16mo, $1 75, Boston.

Letters of John Adams to his Wife.

It is unnecessary to give the character of letters written by such a man under such circumstances.

2 vols. 16mo, $1 75, Boston.

Mrs. Grant's Memoirs of an American Lady.

A delightful picture of life in America, and especially in Northern New-York, one hundred years ago.

Life of Brant, by William L. Stone.

2 vols. 8vo, $3 00, New-York, 1841.

Life of Red Jacket, by William L. Stone.

1 vol. 8vo, $2 00, New-York, 1841.

Mr. Stone is a zealous and successful student of our early, and especially of our aboriginal history. His Life of Brant might be called with propriety a History of the Border War.

Life of Lemuel Haynes.

All biographies of men who have forced their way to use-

fulness and respectability, in spite of appalling obstacles, are deeply interesting. This of Mr. Haynes is particularly so.
12mo, 90 cents.

B. B. Thatcher's Indian Biography.

Nothing of the same character is before the public. In these pages the author has intended to bestow on the more eminent individuals the notice they deserve, and to pass over the vast multitude distinguished only by detached anecdotes, or described only in general terms.
2 vols. 18mo, 90 cents.

Mackenzie's Life of Commodore Perry.

A worthy sketch of the brief, but brilliant career of one of our naval heroes.
2 vols. 18mo, 90 cents.

Life of Franklin.

The Life of Franklin affords a striking proof of the influence in society of sound understanding, united with steady industry, and supported by candid integrity. It should be read and pondered by all young men.
2 vols. 18mo, 90 cents.
A larger and more complete Life of Franklin has been written by Mr. Sparks, and forms the first vol. of his excellent edition of Franklin's Works.

Life of Fulton, by C. D. Colden.

In this sketch Mr. Colden has done justice to a noble theme.

Memoirs of American Missionaries, viz:

Munson and Lyman, Indian Archipelago, 12mo, New-York, 1839, $1 00.
Mrs. S. L. Smith, Mission in Syria, 12mo, Philadelphia, 1839, $1 00.
Mrs. E. B. Dwight and Mrs. Grant, Turkish and Persian Mission, 12mo, 1841, $1 00.
Mrs. H. L. Winslow, Missionary at Ceylon, 12mo, 1841, $1 00.
Rev. Gordon Hall, Missionary at Bombay, 12mo, Andover, $1 00.
G. D. Boardman, Missionary to Burmah, 12mo, Boston, 1835, $1 00.
Mrs. Judson, Missionary to Burmah, 18mo, 75 cents.

Wirt's Life of Patrick Henry.

This distinguished biographer gives an accurate account of a most eminent man.

Philadelphia, 1836, $1 25.

III. GEOGRAPHY, VOYAGES, TRAVELS, &c.

"Employ your time in improving yourself by other men's documents; so shall you come easily by what others have laboured hard for; prefer knowledge to wealth, for the one is transitory, the other perpetual."—*Isocrates to his friend Democritus.*

M'Culloch's Universal Gazetteer.

"If extensive and accurate information with respect to the present condition of the world is desired, it is believed that this great work, with its improvements, will afford the opportunity of obtaining it, with least pessible expense of time, trouble, and means."—*Editor's Preface.*

2 vols. 8vo, $5 00, Harper & Brothers, New-York.

Encyclopædia of Geography, by Hugh Murray.

It is now publishing from the English original, an able and valuable work. The author has studiously collected the most recent, authentic, and accurate accounts of the extent, nature, features, population, productions, industry, political constitution, literature, religion, and social state of the various regions of the globe, with the leading details as to their districts and cities.

Malte Brun's Universal Geography.

This system of universal geography is the most complete of all the geographical systems. An English translation has been made from the original Danish, and it has passed through several editions in the United States, one of which contains many corrections by J. G. Percival.—*Enc. Am.*

10 vols., $36 00, Boston.

Butler's Classical Geography.

A very complete work, indispensable to the classical student.

Cook's Voyages.

As a navigator Cook was of the highest order, whether we

contemplate the discoveries he made or the means by which they were accomplished.—*Edinb. Enc.*

2 vols. 4to, $22 00, London.

Dampier's Voyages.

They are written by himself in a strongly-descriptive style, bearing all the marks of fidelity, and the nautical remarks display much professional, and even philosophical, knowl edge.—*Enc. Am.*

3 vols. 8vo, $4 00, London.

Hawkins's Voyages.

They took place about 1562. He is branded, on the page of history, as the first Englishman, after the discovery of America, who made a merchandise of the human species. —*Enc. Am.*

Parry's Voyages.

In the arduous situations in which Mr. Parry was placed, he displayed not merely the skill of an officer, but the qualities of a man of talent.—*Enc. Am.*

2 vols. 18mo, 90 cents.

Ross's Voyages.

The whole enterprise is a monument of perseverance, hardiness, and courage, as well as of intelligence and skill, highly honourable to the English nation.—*Enc. Am.*

2 vols. 8vo, $4 50, London, 1819.

Wrangel's Expedition to the Russian Polar Sea.

A delightful book.

Lord Macartney's Embassy to China, 1792, 1793, 1794.

2 vols.

Barrow's Travels in China, as attached to the same Embassy.

2 vols. 4to, $8 00, London.

Lord Amherst's Embassy to China, by Ellis, 1816.

These three productions give us the best account, by intelligent and sagacious observers, of the manners and customs, and arts, and learning, of a mean and semi-barbarous race, without any due sense of the obligations of humanity, justice, or truth.—*Chancellor Kent.*

Anson's Voyage.

This work is elegantly written, and was, during the last generation, the most popular nautical production.—*Chancellor Kent.*

8vo, $2 00, London.

La Perouse's Voyage round the World.

(Translated from the French.)

This was one of the most unfortunate of all the efforts at nautical discovery, and awakens the deepest sympathy.

2 vols. 8vo, $5 00, London, 1798.

Vancouver's Voyage of Discovery in the North Pacific.

This great voyage was performed with admirable skill, discipline, perseverance, and success.—*Chancellor Kent.*

3 vols. 4to, $15 00, London.

Waddell's Voyage towards the South Pole.

Captain Waddell penetrated the Antarctic Sea to lat. 74, which was three degrees farther south than Cook or any preceding navigator had penetrated.—*Chancellor Kent.*

Morrell's Voyages in the Southern Hemisphere, in America, Africa, and Asia.

They were performed with admirable skill, and with enthusiastic spirit and enterprise.—*Chancellor Kent.*

8vo, $1 50.

Two Years before the Mast.

This voice from the forecastle has been listened to wherever ships sail and our language is spoken. It is truly a spirit-stirring voice.

18mo, 45 cents.

C. S. Stewart's Visit to the South Sea.

The work does great credit to the talent, literary taste, intelligence, philanthropy, and piety of the author.—*North American Review.*

2 vols., $1 75.

Moore's Views of Society in France, Switzerland, and Germany.

Few travellers were better qualified to observe and record the state of society than Dr. Moore.
2 vols. 8vo, $2 50, London, 1783.

Count Ségur's Russian Expedition, or the Invasion of Russia by Napoleon Bonaparte.

We could not indicate a man who, from the nature of his literary habits and tastes, and the vivacity of his character, would be deemed more able to describe all that he had observed.—*American Quarterly Review.*
2 vols. 18mo, 90 cents, New-York.

Chateaubriand's Travels.

Chateaubriand travelled through Greece and Rhodes to Jerusalem, from whence he went to Alexandria, Cairo, and Carthage, and returned, by way of Spain, to France in 1807. He is distinguished for his talents for description.—*Enc. Am.*
8vo, $1 50, New-York, 1814.

Journal of the Landers.

This work is one of the most interesting in its kind which has appeared in modern times. Independently of the very spirited, running style of travellers, quite as good-humoured as they are energetic, and of the novelty attached to the descriptions, it is sufficient to immortalize the journal and its author alike, that it records the discovery of the termination of the Niger.—*North American Review.*
2 vols. 18mo, 90 cents.

Bruce's Travels in Egypt, Nubia, and Abyssinia, to discover the Sources of the Nile, 1768–73.

The first and last are very interesting. He was an intrepid and faithful traveller, and modern writers bear testimony to his general accuracy.—*Chancellor Kent.*
18mo, 45 cents.

Travels of Anacharsis, by Barthelemie.

Under the form of an ingenious fiction, Barthelemie has contrived to produce a most instructive commentary on his favourite subject, the Antiquities of Greece; and by the elegance of his style, the liveliness of his narrative, and the justness of his reflections, he has rendered his work attractive to the unlearned as well as to the learned reader.—*Edinb. Enc.*

5 vols. 4to, $10 00, Paris.

Lewis and Clark's Travels.

Mr. Jefferson gives Lewis the following character: "Of courage undaunted, possessing a firmness and perseverance of purpose which nothing but impossibilities could divert from its direction; intimate with the Indian character, customs, and principles; guarded, by exact observation of the vegetables and animals of his own country, against losing time in the description of objects already possessed," &c., &c. —*Enc. Am.*

2 vols. 18mo, 90 cents, New-York.

Humboldt's Narrative.

This work has justly been called by a competent judge "a work of gigantic extent and richness to which the modern literature of Europe can hardly offer a parallel."—*Enc. Am.*

An abridgment was published, 18mo, 45 cents, H. & B., New-York.

Fisk's Travels in Europe.

This instructive volume has had a wide circulation, and has well deserved it.

8vo, $3 25.

Miss Sedgwick's Letters from Abroad.

Miss Sedgwick has far exceeded her predecessors: for they only described characters and scenes; while she, to continue the metaphor, has carried her researches into the parlours, nay, into the very pantries of private individuals. Miss Sedgwick occupies a high position in America, not merely as an ornament of its world of light literature, but as a moral teacher.—*London Athenæum.*

2 vols. 12mo, $1 90.

J. S. Forsyth's Italy.

There are countries of the globe which possess a permanent and peculiar interest in human estimation. They are those where the most momentous historical events occurred and civilization first dawned. Foremost among them stands

Italy; thus, so accurate a work as the one mentioned will be perused with great interest and pleasure.—*N. Am. Rev.*
12mo, $1 50, London.

Laing's Tour in Sweden—Residence in Norway —and Visit to Holland.

Mr. Laing is among the very ablest and most judicious travellers of our time. He is not without some prejudices, but he is diligent, observing, and conscientious.

Prescott's Conquest of Mexico.

This work is founded on original documents, chiefly supplied by the Royal Academy of History at Madrid. These documents are the fruits of more than fifty years' laborious researches by Navarrete, the venerable president of the Academy, by Vargas Ponce, his predecessor, and by the celebrated historian Muñoz. They were obtained under sanction of government, from the various public offices and repositories in Spain and her colonies; and consist of the correspondence of the parties, instructions of the court, contemporary memoirs, military journals and official documents, in manuscript, most of them unknown or inaccessible to preceding historians. Besides this, additional materials have been drawn from Mexico, London, and Paris.—*Pub. Adv.*
3 vols. 8vo, New-York.

Latrobe's Mexico.

12mo, 65 cents, New-York.

Poinsett's Notes.

Life in Mexico, by a Lady.

These works should be read. Together they furnish quite a complete picture of an interesting country.

Stephens's Central America.

Mr. Stephens's book is of great interest, as giving a copious description of those mysterious relics of the early possessors of the American Continent, which have never hitherto excited their due share of interest.—*London Athenæum.*
2 vols. 8vo, $5 00.

Stephens's Travels in Yucatan.

2 vols. 8vo, $5 00.

Stephens's Egypt, Arabia Petræa, and the Holy Land.

2 vols. 12mo, $1 75.

Stephens's Greece, Turkey, Russia, and Poland.

We hold Mr. Stephens in high esteem as a recorder of travelling experiences. Cheerful, manly, observant, graphic. —*London Athenæum.*

Dr. Olin's Travels in Egypt, Arabia Petræa, and the Holy Land.

This work, from the pen of the distinguished President of the Wesleyan University, is the latest on the subject. It is rich in information, pervaded by a lofty spirit, and entitled to entire confidence.

2 vols. royal 12mo, $2 50.

Tanner's Canals and Railroads of the United States.

This work is full of valuable statistics in regard to the canals and railroads of the United States; indeed, the whole work is to be regarded much more in the light of a statistical than an engineering treatise.—*London Athenæum.*

Public Works in the United States,

(Edited by Strickland, Gill, and Campbell).

The book is creditable to the artists, the publishers, and the engineers.—*London Athenæum.*

Barrow's Austria, Lombardy, &c., &c.

Sir R. Bonnycastle's Canadas.

To the settler in search of a location, or the traveller following in the author's track, this will be invaluable as a guide. book.—*London Athenæum.*

Bonnycastle's Newfoundland in 1842.

These volumes are of the largest pretensions, and the mass of information they afford is most varied and extensive.—*London Athenæum.*

Catlin's Indians.

This book contains a pleasant narrative of adventure, and

X 2

a circumstantial and detailed history of the manners and customs of an interesting people, whose fate is sealed, whose days are numbered, whose extinction is certain.—*London Athenæum.*

2 vols. 8vo, $8 00, New-York.

Moffat's Missionary Labours and Scenes in Southern Africa.

The indefatigable and cheerful spirit, the lively humour, the keen observation, and natural eloquence, albeit not of the most correct or classic kind, which breathe in every page, together with the obvious goodness of heart and manly feeling of the author, render the volume as agreeable as it is instructive.—*London Athenæum.*

Williams's Missionary Enterprises.

This work is, throughout, highly attractive for the variety of its matter, for the light it throws on the social condition of different tribes of savages, and for the continuity of the whole story.—*Evangelist.*

1 vol. 12mo, $1 50, Appleton & Co., New-York.

Schoolcraft's Travels to the Sources of the Mississippi.

Schoolcraft's Mississippi Valley.

Schoolcraft's Expedition to Itasca Lake.

Mr. Schoolcraft is advantageously known to the literary community as an accurate and judicious observer, and an enterprising traveller.—*N. Am. Rev.*

8vo, $2 00, New-York.

Sepulchres of Etruria, by Mrs. Gray.

The researches which have recently been made in regard to Etruscan remains are of the deepest interest to the antiquarian and student of history. The work of Mrs. Gray is full of information, conveyed in the most agreeable manner.

Madame de Staël's Germany.

This work is rich in acute and ingenious ideas, but has been justly criticised as containing many erroneous views. Her taste is not altogether correct; her style is irregular, and has too much pretension; but in all her works we find original and profound thought, great acuteness, a lively imagination, a philosophical insight into the human heart, and into the truths of politics and literature.—*Enc. Am.*

2 vols. 12mo, $1 25.

Howitt's Rural and Domestic Life in Germany.

So far as this book contains the results of Mr. Howitt's experiences, gained during a residence at Heidelberg, it is pleasant and welcome; but the sketches of cities, made in "a general tour," are somewhat commonplace and superficial. Neither can we recommend the reader to place much reliance on his judgment in art, or his sweeping sketches of literature and opinion.—*London Athenæum.*

2 vols. 8vo, 50 cents, Philadelphia.

Howitt's Rural Life in England.

This is the best of Mr. Howitt's works in this department of literature. He always writes with spirit, and in a kindly tone, but his opinions are of less value than his descriptions.

8vo, $2 87, Philadelphia, 1841.

Forrey's Climate of the United States, and its Endemic Influences.

A volume of highly interesting facts, condensed into the smallest compass.—*London Athenæum.*

Russia and the Russians, by Köhl.

A very pleasing and interesting volume, which gives samples of that "infinite variety" which characterizes social life in St. Petersburgh.—*London Athenæum.*

J. Cleveland's Voyages from China to the North-west Coast of America.

This voyage was one of extraordinary character, both in its prosecution and results, and evinced a degree of enterprise and perseverance worthy of imitation.—*North American Rev.*

2 vols. 8vo, $1 75.

Norman's Ruined Cities of Yucatan.

This work comprises a detailed account of Mr. Norman's researches, illustrated by numerous drawings of the most important ruins from sketches made on the spot, and including a collection of idols, &c., &c., the first ever discovered, and which are extremely curious and unique.—*London Athenæum.*

2 vols. 8vo, $1 00, J. & H G. Langley, New-York, 1843.

Southgate's Tour in Persia, Armenia, Kurdistan, and Mesopotamia.

This work, from the pen of one of the missionaries of the American Episcopal Church, is marked by great intelligence and candour, and contains much useful information.
2 vols. 12mo, $1 00, New-York.

Laborde's Journey to Mount Sinai.

Robertson's Researches in Palestine, Mount Sinai, and Arabia Petræa.

This is a most important contribution to Biblical Geography. The author deserves the gratitude of all who are interested in the study of sacred literature.—*London Athenæum.*
3 vols. 8vo, $8 00.

Rockwell's Sketches of Foreign Travel and Life at Sea,

including a cruise on board a man-of-war; as also a visit to Spain, Portugal, the South of France, Italy, Sicily, Malta, the Ionian Islands, &c., &c., &c., and a treatise on the Navy of the United States.
2 vols. 8vo, $1 50, Boston, 1842.

Smith and Dwight's Researches in Armenia.

Exceedingly interesting.—*Chancellor Kent.*
2 vols. 8vo, $3 50, London.

Grant's Nestorians.

This volume contains sketches of travels in ancient Assyria, Armenia, Media, and Mesopotamia, and illustrations of Scripture prophecy. Well worth reading.
12mo, $1 00, New-York.

Heber's India.

These travels of Bishop Heber through his vast diocese are written in the best spirit, and contain much information in regard to the religious, social, and industrial condition of the Hindus.

Sir John Malcolm's Memoir on Central India.

2 vols. 8vo, $5 25, London.

Miss Sinclair's Scotland and the Scotch.

1 vol. 12mo, 75 cents.

Miss Sinclair's Shetland and the Shetlanders.

Miss Sinclair has proved herself to be a lady of high talent and rich-cultivated mind. Her style is characteristic of her mind, transparent, piquant, and lively, yet sustained by pure moral and religious feeling.—*N. Y. American.*

1 vol. 12mo, 87½ cents.

Washington Irving's Astoria.

These volumes are full of exciting incident, and by reason of Mr. Irving's fine taste and attractive style, they possess the power and charms of romance.—*Chancellor Kent.*

2 vols. 8vo, Philadelphia, 1836.

Reynolds's Voyage around the World.

This was a voyage round the world in the United States frigate Potomac, 1831–34.

8vo, $3 25

Mutiny of the Bounty.

A Description of Pitcairn's Island and its Inhabitants, with an Account of the Mutiny, and of the subsequent Fortunes of the Mutineers.

1 vol. 18mo, 45 cents.

Combe's Travels in the United States.

These volumes, by the phrenologist who lately visited our country, are well worth reading. They point with force and candour to some of our prevailing faults, and do justice, generally, to our merits.

J. S. Buckingham's America, Historical, Statistic, and Descriptive.

Pronounced by Lord Morpeth (who says that he travelled with it over the country) to be an impartial and accurate work.

2 vols. 8vo, $3 50.

Sir E. L. Bulwer's England and the English.

This work inquires into the existent character of the English people, and the construction and bearings of their social system; it examines the present state of their religion, their morals, their education, and their literature, and from them it proceeds to a brief survey of the political position in which they are now placed.—*Introduction.*

H. L. Bulwer's France.

The object of this work is, in describing the present, to connect it with the past, which, in speaking of what is daily and accidental, would separate it from what ages have sanctioned, and distant ages are likely to see; a work which, in showing the effect which time, and laws, and accident produce upon the character of the people, would also show the manner in which the character of a people traverses time, enters into laws, and dominates over accident.—*Introduction.*

Lockhart's Valerius.

This work, with those of Mr. Ware, and the Julia of Baiæ of Mr. Brown, are fictions; but being intended as faithful delineations of the ancient world at certain periods in respect to manners, morals, and opinions, they may well be studied as a substitute for actual travels.

Ware's Zenobia; or, The Fall of Palmyra. In Letters of Lucius M. Piso, from Palmyra, to his friend, M. Curtius, at Rome.

This work is, in general, beautifully written, with a fine perception of classical elegance exhibited in the cast of thought and in the turns of expression, while, at the same time, it is in a style of pure and choice English.—*N. Y. Rev.*
2 vols. 12mo, $2 50.

Ware's Probus; or, Rome in the Third Century.

2 vols. 12mo, $2 00.

Ware's Julian; or, Scenes in Judea.

2 vols. 12mo, $2 00.

Rev. J. W. Brown's Julia of Baiæ.

This is a fine picture of Rome under Nero, and especially of the character and sufferings of the disciples of Christ.

IV. POLITICS, LAW, &c., &c.

"The fortunes of nations are determined, under Providence, by their practical leaders, and men are formed by their education."—WHEWELL.

Constitutions of the United States, and of the several States, at large.

12mo, $1 25, Philadelphia.

Adams's Defence of the American Constitutions.

This is a defence of the state constitutions. Many speculative writers and theoretical politicians, says Chancellor Kent, about the time of the commencement of the French Revolution, were struck with the simplicity of a legislature with a single assembly, and concluded that more than one house was useless and expensive. This led the elder President Adams to write and publish his great work, entitled "A Defence of the Constitutions of Government of the United States," in which he vindicates with much learning and ability the value and necessity of the division of the Legislature into two branches, and of the distribution of the different powers of the government into distinct departments.

3 vols. 8vo, Philadelphia, 1797.

Duer's Lectures on the Constitutional Jurisprudence of the United States.

I have passed rapidly through it, and that rapid glance has satisfied me of the value of the work, and the correctness of its principles and statements.—*Chief-justice Marshall.*

It is a work of great use.—*Edw. Livingston.*

1 vol. 18mo, 50 cents, New-York.

The Federalist on the New Constitution, written in 1788, by Hamilton, Madison, and Jay.

A work which this nation to its latest posterity will regard as a legacy next in value to the instrument itself, of whose principles it affords so beautiful an elucidation, and so masterly a defence.—*North Am. Rev.* 8vo, $2 00.

Madison Papers.

An invaluable contribution to the constitutional history of our country, and a sure guide to the proper understanding of the national compact. 3 vols. 8vo, $10 00.

Debates in the Convention of New-York in 1822, on the amending of the State Constitution.

Debates in the Massachusetts Convention in 1820, for framing a New Constitution.

Debates in the Convention of Virginia, 1829.

Story's Commentaries on the Constitution of the United States.

Just and true.—*Chancellor Kent.*
3 vols. 8vo, $10 00.

Kent's Commentaries on American Law.

We cannot but recommend this book to the attention of the profession, and particularly to the students of our jurisprudence.—*Am. Quart. Rev.*
4 vols. 8vo, $12 00.

Wheaton's Elements of International Law.

Clear and comprehensive; illustrated by many important examples, and brought down to our own time.

Messages of the Presidents of the United States.

This work may be considered as a history, or the materials for a history, of the great North American Republic, from the Declaration of Independence to the present hour. It commences with the Inaugural Address of Washington, and comes down to that of President Tyler.—*London Athenæum.*

De Tocqueville's Democracy in America.

It is a work of profound observation, and contains most wholesome admonition.—*Chancellor Kent.*
2 vols. 8vo, $4 00, New-York.

Adam Smith's Wealth of Nations.

The inquirer will find in this great work the great and simple principles which constitute the basis of political economy distinctly stated in the most elegant language, proved and illustrated by curious and instructive details of facts, and followed out into the most important, and generally most correct practical conclusions.—*N. Am. Rev.*
1 vol. 8vo, $2 25, London.

Say's Political Economy.

Say was a distinguished political economist, and his works are highly esteemed.—*Enc. Am.*

8vo, $2 25, Philadelphia.

Wayland's Political Economy.

A careful perusal of this work will render one well acquainted with the principles of the science. Those who are not desirous of becoming acquainted with its history need refer to no other volume. They will here meet with nothing that is not eminently plain and practical.—*New-York Rev.*

Philips's Political Economy.

The literary execution of this work is highly creditable to the author. The style is correct, perspicuous, and elegant; and we have no hesitation in recommending this work to be read and consulted as a manual.—*N. Am. Rev.*

It is an able vindication of the protective policy.

Carey's Political Economy.

Mr. Carey has brought together in these volumes a great amount of useful and curious information.

3 vols. 8vo, $6 00, Philadelphia.

Potter's Political Economy.

Two objects have been kept in view in preparing this work: first, to provide a treatise for general readers adapted to the times, and especially to the wants of our country, which should not be encumbered unnecessarily with controversial matters, or with abstract discussions; secondly, to furnish a cheap and convenient *manual* for seminaries, in which larger and more expensive text-books could not well be used.—*Adv.*

1 vol. 18mo, 45 cents, New-York.

Sedgwick's Public and Private Economy.

Full of useful and timely thoughts, conveyed in a rambling, but agreeable manner.

The Washington Papers,

(Edited by Jared Sparks).

The valuable matter published in these volumes is accompanied by notes and illustrations from the editor; these carry with them internal evidence of the care, industry, and judgment with which they have been prepared.—*N. Am. Rev.*

12 vols. royal 8vo, $30 00, Boston, 1832.

Franklin's Writings,

(Edited by Jared Sparks).

The known ability of Mr. Sparks is a sufficient guarantee that the work is executed in a manner worthy its great subject
10 vols. 8vo, $25 00, 1839.

Jefferson's Writings.

In the four volumes of his posthumous works, edited by his grandson, Thomas Jefferson Randolph, there are abundant materials to guide the literary or historical critic in forming an estimate of his powers, acquirements, feelings, and opinions.—*Enc. Am.*
4 vols., $6 00, Charlottesville, 1829.

Principles of Morals and Legislation, by Jeremy Bentham, with a Sketch of his Life, &c., &c., by John Neal.

This is the work of one of the most powerful thinkers of our time. Though unsatisfactory in many of its principles, it furnishes rich materials for reflection to thoughtful and inquiring minds.

Montesquieu's Spirit of Laws.

This work may be termed a code of national law, and its author the legislator of the human family; we feel that it emanates from a liberal heart, regarding the whole human race with affection. No one has ever reflected more profoundly on the nature, foundation, manner, climate, extent, power, and peculiar character of states; on the effects of rewards and punishments, on religion, education, and commerce.—*Enc. Am.*
2 vols. 12mo, $2 50, Edinburgh, 1793.

Ferguson on the History of Civil Society.

An able work.
4to, $2 00, London.

Russell's Principles of Statistical Inquiry.

"For the object of showing the advantages which would accrue from a full exposition of the various resources of the country," says the author, "I have given short statements of the information existing regarding them. It has been my object to propose no subject for inquiry without accompanying it with some observations for the purpose of directing the attention of the reader, which, I hope, may be deemed sufficient reason for the trivial nature of the notices sometimes introduced."—*Preface.*

Delolme on the Constitution of England.

It is not a complete system of the political laws of England, and has been reproached as being superficial; but it contains much ingenious reflection on the English Constitution.—*Enc. Am.*

8vo, $2 50, London.

Pitkin's Statistics of the United States.

This work, published in 1816, was received with much approbation. The mind of Mr. Pitkin is fond of occupying itself in collection, and labours such as his form the useful foundation of enlarged and liberal history.—*Am. Quart. Rev.*

8vo, $2 00, Hartford, 1835.

Harrington's Oceana.

The Oceana, which is a political romance, and the Utopian image of a republic, is a work of genius, thought, and invention, and is characterized by an enthusiastic love of liberty. —*Enc. Am.*

1 vol. folio, $3 50, London.

Sir Philip Sidney's Discourses on Government.

They contain much historical information, and are composed with clearness, acuteness, and force.—*Enc. Am.*

3 vols. 8vo, $3 50, New-York, 1805.

F. Lieber's Political Ethics.

It is a work full of deep reflection, solid principle, and sound and apposite illustrations.—*Chancellor Kent.*

2 vols. 8vo, $4 50, Boston.

Lieber's Legal and Political Hermeneutics.

I regard this as a work eminently useful to our profession; not merely useful to students, but to men of long experience at the bar, as a most lucid exposition of the principles, and admirable illustration of the science of interpretation and construction.—*Professor Greenleaf.*

12mo, $1 00, Boston.

Lieber's Property and Labour.

Lessons like those contained in this volume are always seasonable. In this age, pre-eminently devoted to industrious

enterprise, they are especially needed, and it is much to be desired that they may be widely circulated.—*Introd. by A. P.*
18mo, 45 cents, New-York.

Course of Legal Study.

In this volume, the author, David Hoffman Esq., has rendered to students essential service by indicating with a just selection the most instructive works, but especially by displaying the order in which the multitudinous parts of a various science may most usefully be considered.—*N. Am. Rev.*

Science of Government.

This is a useful compilation.

V. ETHICS, MENTAL PHILOSOPHY, &c., &c.

"Studies serve for delight, for ornament, and for utility; read not to contradict and confute, nor to believe and take for granted, nor to find talk and discourse, but to weigh and consider."—BACON.

Stewart's Works.

In these works may be found some notice of almost everything of importance which has been elicited by genius and talent on the subject of the human mind, enriched with the author's own candid and comprehensive views and original remarks, enabling the reader to understand all that has been effected in this interesting field of inquiry, and all that remains to be done.—*N. Am. Rev.*
7 vols. 8vo, $8 50, Cambridge, 1831.

Reid's Essays.

Mr. Reid was a patient, modest, and deep thinker, whose observations on suggestion, on natural signs, on the connexion of what he calls sensation and perception, are marked by the genuine spirit of observation.—*Sir J. Mackintosh.*

Locke's Essay on the Understanding.

In the estimation of Sir James Mackintosh, Locke's Essay still stands the most conspicuous landmark in the progress of metaphysical philosophy for the last two centuries.
8vo, $3 00, Philadelphia, 1838.

Cousin's Psychology.

The science is deeply indebted to Cousin for the new light

bestowed by his genius, and the attraction with which he has clothed a subject often unjustly and ignorantly depreciated. *N. Am. Rev.*

Brown's Mental Philosophy.

The work of a bold and brilliant mind, containing many valuable suggestions, but sometimes crude and unsatisfactory. Mr. Brown belongs to the school who refer the phenomena of mind to association.

Rauch's Psychology.

Schmucker's Psychology, or Elements of a New System of Mental Philosophy, on the Basis of Consciousness and Common Sense.

12mo, $1 00, New-York.

Upham's Elements of Mental Philosophy,

embracing the two departments of the Intellect and the Sensibilities.

2 vols. 12mo, $2 50, New-York.

All these are works which ought to be in the hands of the student of mental philosophy.

Abercrombie on the Intellectual Powers.

On the whole, this work must be considered as containing much useful information. If some of his arguments are formed with little attention to vigour, we must remember that he wrote for many who cannot appreciate a course of reasoning that is not conducted in a popular manner.—*N. Am. Rev.*

1 vol. 18mo, 45 cents, New-York.

Payne's Elements of Mental and Moral Philosophy.

In his Mental Philosophy, Mr. Payne follows Dr. Brown, and may be conveniently used as a popular expounder of his doctrines. In his Moral Philosophy, he finds in Scripture and in our own consciousness safer guides.

Whately's Logic.

Mr. Whately states in his preface that he has taken, without scruple, whatever appeared most valuable from the works of former authors. Thus, by combining the excellence of so many other works on the subject, this is one of the best treatises in the English language.—*Enc. Am.*

Coleridge's Aids to Reflection.

The objects of this work are, to direct the reader's attention to the value of the science of words, their use and abuse; to establish the distinct characters of prudence, morality, and religion; to substantiate and set forth at large the momentous distinction between reason and understanding; to exhibit a full and consistent scheme of the Christian dispensation, and, more largely, of all the peculiar doctrines of the Christian faith.—*Preface.*

12mo, $2 00, London.

Abercrombie—The Philosophy of the Moral Feelings.

1 vol. 18mo, 40 cents, New-York.

Zimmerman on Solitude.

The author employed his leisure time in the publication of pieces both in prose and verse, and, among others, his popular work on Solitude.—*Enc. Am.*

1 vol. 12mo, $2 75.

Coleridge's Table-Talk.

This volume will show the conversations of Mr. Coleridge, and its contents may be taken as pretty strong presumptive evidence that his ordinary manner was plain and direct; and even when, as sometimes happened, he seemed to ramble from the road, and to lose himself in a wilderness of digressions, he was at that very time working out his foreknown conclusion through an almost miraculous logic.—*Preface.*

1 vol. 12mo, 70 cents.

Coleridge's Friend.

This work is a friend indeed; venerable, yet familiar; thoughtful, and of kindest, noblest feelings, teaching wisdom for meditation, and alluring to meditation by presenting to the mind not amusement merely, but

"Flowers
Of sober tints, and herbs of medicinal powers."

N. Am. Rev.

3 vols. 12mo, $4 50, London.

Paley's Moral Philosophy.

A work of much simplicity and pertinence of illustration, and in some parts of much wisdom, but exceptionable in many of its definitions and principles, both in politics and morals.—*Enc. Am.*

Hale's Contemplations.

Sir Matthew Hale wrote them with the same simplicity that he formed them in his mind. In them there appears a generous and true spirit of religion, mixed with most serious and fervent devotion.—*Burnet.*

2 vols. 8vo, $1 50, London, 1711.

Wayland's Elements of Moral Science.

The aim of this work, being designed for the purpose of instruction, is to be simple, clear, and purely didactic. The author has rarely gone into extended discussion, but has contented himself with the attempt to state the moral law, and the reason of it, in as few and as comprehensive terms as possible.—*Preface.*

It is conceived in a lofty spirit, and parts of it are executed with surpassing ability.

Aristotle's Ethics and Politics.

(Translated by J. Gillies.)

This work abounds with the most solid maxims, and inculcates with peculiar force the most important duties of social life; and it is admirably calculated to unite practice with knowledge, and to form the enlightened statesman, while it encourages the patient student in the pursuit of polite literature.—*Moss.*

2 vols. 4to, $5 00, London, 1813.

Pascal's Thoughts.

They burn with an intense light; condensed in expression, sublime, energetic, rapid, they hurry away the reader till he is scarcely able or willing to distinguish the sophisms from the truth they contain.—*Hallam.*

12mo, $1 00, London.

Pilgrim's Progress.

"Yet e'en in transitory life's late day,
That mingles all my brown with sober gray,
Revere the man, whose *Pilgrim* marks the road,
And guides the *Progress* of the soul to God."—COWPER.

Bishop Butler's Analogy.

There is in the writings of Mr. Butler a vastness of ideas, a reach and generalization of reasoning, a native simplicity and grandeur of thought, which command and fill the mind. At the same time, his illustrations are so striking and familiar, as to instruct as well as persuade.—*Wilson's Preface.*
18mo, 50 cents, New-York, 1843.

Milton's Prose Writings.

In them his spirit and vigour are striking, and his style, although sometimes harsh and uncouth, is pregnant with energy and imagination.—*Enc. Am.*
7 vols. 8vo, $38 00.

Locke and Bacon's Essays, in one volume, with an Introductory Essay by A. Potter, D.D.

To cultivate an acquaintance with these great masters must be an object of cherished interest, not merely with the scholar, but with all who would improve their minds. Among their works are some not only free from the language of the schools and level to the general understanding, but which, to use Bacon's own phrase, "come home to men's business and bosoms." Such are those included in the present volume. —*Introduction.*
1 vol. 18mo, 45 cents, New-York.

Bacon's Advancement of Learning.

In the Advancement of Learning, Bacon aspired to fill up, or, at least, to indicate the deficiencies in every department of knowledge.—*Hallam.*
8vo, $1 50, London, 1838.

Mackintosh's Progress of Ethical Philosophy.

This noble sketch fills us with regret that the author did not leave behind him some work on philosophy commensurate with his learning and great ability, and proportioned to the wants of our age.

Nott's Counsels to Young Men.

The fruit of experience and deep reflection. These *counsels*, originally addressed to the author's pupils as they were about

to leave his parental care, will be found pertinent to the wants of all young persons, and especially of all young men.
1 vol. 18mo, 50 cents, New-York.

Chalmers's Moral and Intellectual Constitution of Man.

The admirers of Chalmers are to be found among all classes of readers, for there are in his works marks of genius enough to command the respect of men of intellect, and expansion and repetition enough to render their perusal easy to undisciplined minds. A warm glow of imagination is thrown over the whole, and is by no means one of the least efficient causes of his popularity.—*New-York Review.*
1 vol. 12mo, 60 cents, New-York.

Sir H. Davy's Consolation in Travel.

Apart from the scientific value of the labours and researches of Sir H. Davy, they are pervaded by a tone and temper, and an enthusiastic love of nature, which are as admirably expressed as their influence is excellent.—*Penny Cyc.*
1 vol. 12mo, 50 cents.

Sir H. Davy's Salmonia.

The work was written during a slow recovery from sickness, and the tone of the dialogue reflects throughout what a good and great man's mind might be expected to exhibit under such circumstances. A very great number of curious facts concerning the natural history of fishes are here recorded, and the high scientific character of the author is an ample pledge for accuracy.—*Quart. Rev.*

Walton's Angler.

This has long been a standard work of our language, and has passed through so many editions as to ascertain its undiminished attractions, in spite of the fashion of all things that pass away.—*Quart. Rev.*
12mo, $1 00, London.

Combe on the Constitution of Man.

A treatise which has served more than all his other works to render the author's name favourably known in the United States. It has been stereotyped, and published as a reading book for schools.—*N. Y. Rev.*
1 vol. 18mo, 50 cents, New-York.

Combe's Elements of Phrenology.

A popular treatise, which has gone through several editions. —*Enc. Am.*

Spurzheim on Education.

Well worth consulting, especially on the subject of physical education.

Fenelon's Ancient Philosophers.

Fenelon's works in the departments of philosophy, theology, and the belles-lettres have immortalized his name. His style is fluent and pleasing, pure and harmonious.—*Enc. Am.*

De Gerando on Self-Education.

The leading idea of De Gerando is, that all the course of man's life should be a continued self-education, embracing all his faculties, and directing all his actions; and he has developed these principles in his works.—*Penny Cyc.*

Smith's History of Education.

A good compilation from the learned works of the Germans on pedagogics, and a most timely contribution to our literature.
1 vol. 18mo, 45 cents, New-York.

The School and the Schoolmaster, by A. Potter, D.D., and G. B. Emerson, A.M.

This volume was prepared at the request of a friend of common schools (Hon. James Wadsworth), and published through his instrumentality. Twelve thousand copies have been circulated gratuitously in the State of New-York, and four thousand copies in Massachusetts. Though prepared with special reference to the condition and wants of common schools in the State of New-York, its general principles and most of its details will be found applicable to similar schools in other parts of the country, and, indeed, to all seminaries employed in giving elementary instruction.---*Advertiscment.*
1 vol. 12mo, $1 00.

Todd's Student's Manual.

This work is very simple; it is, in many respects, exceedingly well adapted to the purpose for which it is intended. It has been received with much approbation.
50 cents.

Burton's Anatomy of Melancholy.

Burton's learning, which was various and extensive, is copiously displayed in this work, first published in 1621, and repeatedly reprinted.—*Enc. Am.*

1 vol. 8vo, $2 25, London, 1821.

Philosophical Miscellanies.

(Translated from the French of Jouffroy, Cousin, and B. Constant, by George Ripley.)

Valuable, as affording an insight into the present state of pnilosophical speculation in France.

2 vols. 8vo, $1 50, Boston.

Taylor's Natural History of Enthusiasm.

While it has been the writer's principal aim to present before the Christian reader, in as distinct a manner as possible, the characters of that perilous illusion which too often supplants genuine piety, he has also endeavoured so to fix the sense of the term enthusiasm as to wrest it from those who misuse it to their own infinite damage.—*Advertisement.*

Taylor's Natural History of Fanaticism.

Taylor's Spiritual Despotism.

The writings of Mr. Taylor are distinguished for vigour and originality, and for the play of a very fertile imagination Their greatest defect is a certain indistinctness or incompleteness of thought, the result of haste, and of crowding ideas upon each other not always very closely related. He is useful rather as a suggestive writer than as a teacher.

Saturday Evening, by the same.

Home Education, by the same.

Theory of Another Life, by the same.

1 vol. 8vo, $1 00, D. Appleton & Co., New-York, 1836.

Translation of Cicero's Offices.

This is, to this day, the finest treatise on virtue, inspired by pure human wisdom.—*Enc. Am.*

Mr. Melmoth's translation is an elegant one.—*Monthly Rev.*

Melmoth's translation of Cicero on Old Age.

This translation is executed with a masterly hand; the language is pure and classical, and expresses the sense of the original with fidelity and spirit.—*Critical Rev.*

Melmoth's translation of Cicero on Friendship.

This is an elegant translation of this admired treatise.—*Monthly Rev.*

Mrs. H. More's Works.

"If, as the revered authoress has asserted, there be between him who writes and him who reads a kind of coalition of interests, a partnership of mental property, a joint stock of tastes and ideas, how great must be her satisfaction, who, over so wide a field, has sown, from life's dawn till its late decline, only seeds of virtue, and germes of that wisdom which turneth many to righteousness."—*Mrs. Sigourney.*

8vo, $3 50, New-York.

Lowell Offering.

This work deserves special attention, being the joint production of young women employed as operatives in the cotton mills of Lowell. It is delightful to find so much talent and cultivation, and so lofty a moral spirit coupled with factory life.

Miss Edgeworth's Moral and Popular Tales.

They are the mature and seasonable fruits of those faculties that work the surest and continue the longest in vigour, of powerful sense and nice moral perception, joined to a rare and invaluable talent for the observation and display of human character.—*Edinb. Rev.*

10 vols. 12mo, 75 cents per volume, New-York.

Miss Sedgwick's Home.

An excellent little book, though inferior in spirit and interest to the author's later productions.—*N. Y. Rev.*

Miss Sedgwick's Live and Let Live.

It is designed to expose and correct the faults of masters and mistresses in their relation to servants. We recommend it to all mistresses who have not read it.—*N. Y. Rev.*

18mo, 45 cents, New-York.

Miss Sedgwick's Poor Rich Man and Rich Poor Man.

This volume is full of interesting incident, nice and accurate observation of life and human nature, fine traits of delineation of character, rich humour, and occasional touches of exquisite pathos.—*N. Y. Rev.*

18mo, 45 cents, New-York.

Miss Sedgwick's Means and Ends.

This volume, as a manual of self-education for American young women, is above praise.

18mo, 45 cents, New- York.

Wealth and Worth.

The Lawyer—his Character and Rule of Holy Life, by Edward O'Brien, Esq.

The model of this well-conceived little volume is the Country Parson, by George Herbert. The author, now no more, affirms in the introduction "that it is a sincere book," and it bears the marks of it visibly. It is well to have the thoughts of men of all professions and callings occasionally lifted from the earth by works of this enthusiastic order.—*London Athenæum.*

Mary Howitt's Tales.

Full of talent, and as salutary in their tendency as they are rich in incident and interest.

Mrs. Ellis's Wives of England.

1 vol. 12mo, 12½ cents, D. Appleton & Co., New-York.

Mrs. Ellis's Daughters of England.

Mrs. Ellis's Mothers of England.

All rich in useful hints and heart-improving reflections.

The Listener, by Caroline Fry.

Nothing proceeded from Miss Fry's pen that was not forcible and instructive. This is, perhaps, her best work, and it is truly admirable.

Duncan's Sacred Philosophy of the Seasons; illustrating the Perfections of God in the Phenomena of the Year.
4 vols.

Old Humphrey's Addresses.

Old Humphrey's Thoughts.

These volumes are among the happiest of the many efforts made in our time to communicate moral and religious instruction in a kind, cheerful, and yet impressive manner. Old Humphrey is a quaint humorist, full of wise hints and consoling or admonitory thoughts, overflowing with love to God and good-will to men.

Xenophon's Memorabilia of Socrates.

(Translated.)

This is one of the most remarkable and instructive books which has come to us from the literature of ancient Greece.

Herbert's Country Parson.

A quaint, but beautiful sketch of a faithful Christian pastor.

Cecil's Remains.

Full of weighty and sagacious reflection. Its matter is so miscellaneous, that it is peculiarly fitted as a table-book to fill up leisure moments.

VI. CRITICISM AND BELLES-LETTRES.

> "There's no want of meat, sir;
> Portly and curious viands are prepared
> To please all kinds of appetites."—MASSINGER.

Kames's Criticism.

In this elaborate work, it was the object of the author to subject the impressions made on the mind by the productions of the fine arts to the standard of reason, by showing that what is generally called taste is by no means arbitrary, but depends on certain principles or laws of the human constitution.—*Edinburgh Enc.*
8vo, $2 00, 11th edition, London, 1839.

Blair's Lectures on Rhetoric and Belles-Lettres.

With a view of teaching to others that art which had contributed so materially to the advancement of his reputation, Mr. Blair prepared these Lectures, which do honour to the taste and judgment of the author.—*Edinburgh Enc.*

They contain, in addition to a system of elementary rhetoric, a fund of useful information in regard to the literature of preceding times.

Campbell's Philosophy of Rhetoric.

This work affords a display of grammatical skill, critical acumen, discriminating taste, and philosophical talent, of which there are but few examples in the republic of letters. The style is simple, perspicuous, and precise.—*Edinburgh Enc.*

8vo, $1 50, New-York.

Whately's Rhetoric.

This able work of the present Archbishop of Dublin is confined, for the most part, to that part of rhetoric which treats of the *selection* and *management* of arguments.

8vo, $1 50, New-York.

Crabb's Synonymes.

We find in this work a patient examination of words in all their bearings, and a collection of remarks on the peculiar uses of each that are highly valuable.—*Quart. Rev.*

8vo, $2 38, Harper & Brothers, New-York.

Horne Tooke's Diversions of Purley.

This celebrated work contains ideas concerning grammar and the formation of words. The knowledge of language and logical acuteness which he displayed in this performance raised the author to a high rank as a philologist.—*Enc. Am.*

8vo, $3 75, London.

Eschenburg's Manual of Classical Literature.

The general design of this work is to exhibit in a condensed but comprehensive summary, what is most essential on all the topics belonging to the department of classical literature and antiquities, and, at the same time, to give refer ences to various sources of information, to which the scholar may go when he wishes to pursue any of the subjects by farther investigation.—*Preface.*

It is a work of the highest authority, and the American editor has made many useful additions to the original.

Mrs. Jameson's Female Characters of Shakspeare.

Mrs. Jameson says in her introduction, "I have endeavoured to illustrate the various modifications of which the female character is susceptible, with their causes and results. I have illustrated certain positions by examples, and leave my readers to deduce the *moral* themselves, and draw their own inferences."

William Hazlitt's Essays, collected by his Son.

These Essays on subjects of taste and literature are deservedly popular. He is a writer of force and ingenuity, of illustration, strength, tenderness, and vivacity.—*Penny Cyc.*

16mo, $1 62, London, 1839.

J. Montgomery's Lectures on Literature.

Containing much interesting matter in an agreeable dress, and recommended by the pure moral feelings which characterize Mr. Montgomery's poetry.

Abbé Maury's Principles of Eloquence, with an Introduction and Notes, by A. Potter, D.D.

This work is decidedly the best which has yet appeared upon the subject, and is, as it were, an excellent emblem of the oratory on which it chiefly dwells: admirable in its arrangements, full of good sense in much of its detail, with a felicitous and judicious application of Cicero and Quintilian to his subject, but at times flashy in style.—*Quart. Rev.*

1 vol. 18mo, 45 cents, New-York.

Newman's Rhetoric.

A useful text-book in seminaries of learning.

Sir Joshua Reynolds's Discourses on the Theory and Practice of Painting.

They are written in an easy, agreeable manner, and contain many just observations, much excellent criticism and valuable advice; but being undertaken before he had profoundly considered the subject, they are frequently vague and unintelligible, and sometimes contradictory.—*Fuseli.*

Translation of Cicero's Orations, by Duncan.

As the merit of Mr. Duncan's translation of Cicero's select orations is well known, we need to add nothing to recommend this work to public notice—*Monthly Rev.*
3 vols. 18mo, $1 25, New-York.

Translation of Cicero on Oratory, by E. Jones.

This translation appears to be executed with great fidelity. The language is clear and perspicuous, smooth, nervous, and elegant.—*Critical Rev.*

Translation of Quintilian's Institutes of Eloquence, by Patsall.

This is the best version known to us; it is distinguished by a superior degree of spirit and energy.—*Critical Rev.*
2 vols. 8vo, $5 00, London, 1774.

Rollin's Belles-Lettres.

Rollin's writings are distinguished for purity and elegance of style, but they are diffuse and prolix.—*Enc. Am.*
3 vols. 8vo, $6 00, London.

Pliny's Letters, translated by Melmoth.

The letters of Pliny are valuable to us, as all original letters of other times must be, because they necessarily throw much light on the period in which they were written.—*Anthon.*
2 vols. 8vo, $2 50, London, 1757.

Demosthenes's Orations, translated by Leland.

In energy and power of persuasion, in penetration and power of reasoning, in the adaptation of the parts to the whole, in beauty and vigour of expression, in strong and melodious language, he surpassed all his predecessors.—*Enc. Am.*
2 vols. 18mo, 85 cents, New-York.

Cicero's Letters, translated by Melmoth.

They give a more exact and lively idea of the state of the

republic than any of Cicero's other works, and display most strongly the characteristic traits of the author.—*Enc. Am.*
2 vols. 18mo, 85 cents, New-York.

Longinus, translated by Smith.

The only remaining work of this Platonic philosopher is a Treatise on the Sublime. It illustrates with great acuteness the nature of the sublime in thought and style, by rules and examples.—*Enc. Am.*
8vo, $1 00, London.

Fuseli's Lectures.

They contain (if we except some of his remarks on contemporaries, which were sometimes all but unavoidably modified by personal feelings) some of the best criticisms on the fine arts in the language.—*Penny Cyc.*
4to, $5 00, London.

Flaxman's Lectures on Sculpture.

Although of no extraordinary merit as literary compositions, they are full of good sense and good feeling, and may be studied, not by those alone of his profession, but by artists and men of taste generally.—*Penny Cyc.*
8vo, $5 50, London.

Sir Philip Sidney's Arcadia and Progress of Poesy.

The work by which Sir Philip is principally known is his *Arcadia*, which is one of the earliest specimens of the grave or heroic romance. It is a mixture of prose and verse, the latter exhibiting various attempts to naturalize the measures of Roman poetry.—*Enc. Am.*
$7 00, London.

John Selden's Table-Talk.

It is full of vigour, raciness, and a kind of scorn of the half learned. His style is often laboured and uncouth, although his speeches and conversations are luminous and clear.—*Hallam.*

Sir Thomas Browne's Religio Medici, &c., &c.

A book replete with sound sense and great information.

He published, besides, a treatise on "Vulgar Errors," a work of great and acknowledged merit.—*Blake.*

His works, folio, $6 00, London.

Feltham's Resolves.

This work somewhat resembles Lord Bacon's Essays, and exhibits an exuberance of wit and fancy that is perfectly astonishing. Metaphor follows metaphor; and they are not merely introduced as an idle and unmeaning sport, but are exponents in themselves, acute and profound.—*Penny Cyc.*

Mr. Hallam rates this book more humbly. The moral reflections, says he, of a serious and thoughtful mind are generally pleasing, and to this, perhaps, is partly owing the kind of popularity which the Resolves of Feltham have obtained; but they may be had more agreeably and profitably in other books.

8vo, $1 75, London.

Basil Montagu's Selections from the Works of Taylor, Hooker, Barrow, South, Latimer, Browne, Milton, and Bacon.

12mo, $1 50, London, 1839.

The Spectator and Tattler.

These earliest of the regular essays were written by Steele and Addison, and their merits were transcendent in contributing to reform the taste, purify the pleasures, and elevate the morals and literature of the nation.—*Chancellor Kent.*

8vo, $3 00, London.

Rambler and Idler.

Most of the papers in these two works were written by Dr. Johnson, and are characterized by great force of expression and depth of thought.

Guardian—Adventurer—Observer—and Mirror.

The first of these "British Classics" is adorned with papers from Pope and Berkeley, as well as from Steele; the second, intended as a sequel to the Rambler, is from the pen of Hawkesworth and Dr. Johnson; the papers in the Observer were all written by Cumberland; and those in the Mirror principally by Mackenzie, author of the "Man of Feeling."

D'Israeli's Amenities of Literature.

Though at first sight the work appears to be a series of essays, yet it will be found, on examination, that the subject of each essay is a salient point of our vernacular literature.—*Lond. Athen.*

D'Israeli's Curiosities of Literature.

This is a selection made with taste and judgment. The work has passed through several editions.—*Enc. Am.*

8vo, $5 00, London.

Charles Lamb's Works.

His delicious "Essays" are full of wisdom, pregnant with genuine wit, abound in true pathos, and have a rich vein of humour running through them all.—*Hall.*

His works, 8vo, $3 75.

Macauley's Miscellany.

Brilliant and instructive, laden with the fruits of much reading, but not always very profound or accurate.

3 vols. 8vo, $4 00, Philadelphia.

Recreations of Christopher North.

These papers of Professor Wilson appeared originally in Blackwood. They are various in character and degree of merit. Some of them are exquisite.

Verplanck's Discourses.

Mr. Verplanck's mind is deeply imbued with much reading in the best authors; his argument is never weak, and he evinces a judgment in a remarkable degree calm and unprejudiced. His style is pure, perspicuous, and beautifully elaborate; not always, perhaps, sufficiently spirited and flowing, and sometimes cumbersome and heavy.—*N. Y. Rev.*

Dr. W. E. Channing's Prose Works.

Among the present or recent philosophical writers in our own language, few have exhibited the same originality, depth, and power of thought so happily combined with the vigour and beauty of language, which are necessary to give them effect.—*N. A. Rev.*

5 vols. 12mo, $5 00, Boston, 1841.

Edward Everett's Works.

Judicious, eloquent, and instructive.

Hillhouse's Works.

These elegant volumes are the ripe production of a mind of high powers and high culture.—*N. Am. Rev.*

Dennie's Works.

Mr. Dennie possessed a brilliant genius and delicate taste, a beautiful style, a ready pen, a rich fund of elegant literature, and an excellent heart.—*Enc. Am.*

Goldsmith's Prose Works.

His prose, often entwined with humour, and always adorned with graces of a pure style, is among the best in our language. —*Blake.*

Dana's Poems and Prose Works.

Equally honourable to the author and to the literature of his country.

1 vol. 8vo, $1 25.

Burke's Works.

As a writer, whether we consider the splendour of his diction, the richness and variety of his imagery, or the boundless store of knowledge which he displays, it must be acknowledged that there are few who equal, and none who transcend him.

3 vols. 8vo, $5 00, London.

Pitt's Speeches.

His eloquence, if not more elevated or profound, was, upon the whole, more correct than that of any other orator of his time, and remarkably copious and well arranged.—*Enc. Am.*

Fox's Speeches.

His speeches were bold and sublime, and his influence over the minds of his audience was irresistible. In eloquence he was never surpassed by any of his countrymen.—*Enc. Am.*

Canning's Speeches.

His eloquence was persuasive and impassioned, his reasoning clear and logical, his manner graceful, his expression winning.—*Enc. Am.*

Brougham's Speeches.

As an orator, he is neither finished nor accurate in style, but his characteristics are ingenuity and force of argument, quickness and strength of sarcasm, and a prompt, vigorous, impassioned style of reasoning.—*Enc. Am.*

Webster's Speeches.

No man can ever cast his eye over the tables of contents of these volumes of speeches without being struck with their great variety, the versatility of talent they imply, and with the severe requisitions made upon the mind of the statesman. —*N. Am. Rev.*

2 vols. 8vo, $3 50, New-York.

Selections from the Edinburgh Review.

The object of the author was to imbody in these selections the best papers in the Review, particularly those of permanent interest, or likely to attract the greatest number of readers.—*Preface.*

6 vols. 8vo, $8 50, Paris.

Selections from Foreign Literature, by George Ripley and others.

We owe to these gentlemen many valuable pieces, which, without their aid, would not have been accessible to the merely English reader.

VII. POETRY.

"They say it is an ill mason that refuseth any stone; and there is no knowledge but in a skilful hand serves, either positively as it is, or else to illustrate some other knowledge."—HERBERT'S *Remains.*

Pope's translation of Homer.

3 vols. 18mo, $1 35, New-York.

Æschylus, translated by Potter.

The merit of Æschylus was very great in the department of tragedy.—*Eschb.*

1 vol. 18mo, 40 cents, New-York.

Euripides, translated by Potter.

The talent of Euripides for philosophy and eloquence appears in his tragedies, which are strikingly marked by sententious passages and pathetic scenes.—*Eschb.*

3 vols. 18mo, $1 30, New-York.

Sophocles, translated by Francklin.

His tragedies have the merit of a regular and judicious plan, a striking truth in characters, a masterly and energetic expression and play of the passions.—*Eschb.*

1 vol. 18mo, 45 cents, New-York.

Pindar, translated by Wheelwright.

Pindar is marked by his lofty sublimity, his bold energy of thought, his vivid and poetic imagination, and the flowing fulness of his diction.—*Eschb.*

1 vol. 18mo, 45 cents, New-York.

Aristophanes, translated by Mitchell.

His plays furnish valuable means for learning the state of manners and morals of the Greeks in his age.—*Eschb.*

2 vols. 18mo, $2 00, Philadelphia, 1822.

Dryden's Virgil.

Dryden's translation of this great poet cannot be considered, without a comparison with the original, more unfavourable to the English poet. His manner always assumes an eloquence in which the judgment is manly and the imagination profuse, and the force and fidelity of language at once preserved and heightened by the noblest structure of English rhyme.—*Edinb. Enc.*

2 vols. 18mo, 90 cents, New-York.

Horace, translated by Francis.

This version by Mr. Francis, particularly of the Odes, is highly Horatian. It is moral without dulness, gay and spirited with propriety, tender without winning.—*Monthly Rev.*

This praise is overcharged.

2 vols. 18mo, 90 cents, New-York.

Chaucer.

Chaucer's merits as a poet are great and various, but they are all inferior to his power of delineating living character. His men and women are not inferior even to Shakspeare's in comic spirit and resemblance to nature.—*Edinburgh Enc.*

Spenser's "Faery Queen."

It is by this work that Spenser will chiefly be judged. With all its defects, it furnishes admirable examples of the noblest graces of poetry, sublimity, pathos, unrivalled fertility of conception, and exquisite vividness of description.—*Edinburgh Enc.*

8vo, $2 25, London.

Milton.

Of the sublimity of the genius, and the depth and variety of the learning of Milton, there can be no difference of opinion; and in respect to the first, his own countrymen, at least, will scarcely admit that he has ever been equalled.—*Enc. Am.*

2 vols. 8vo, $3 00, Boston, 1838.

Young.

The fame of Dr. Young rests on his satires, tragedies, and Night Thoughts. The first are built on the supposition of fame being the universal passion of mankind. They abound more in flashes of wit and in caricature than in grave exposure of vice and folly; but they are lively and epigrammatic. The Night Thoughts exhibit great force of language, and occasional sublimity of imagination.—*Enc. Am.*

2 vols. 8vo, $2 50, London, 1840.

Pope.

As a poet, admitting that he was deficient in invention, it may be said of him that no English writer has carried farther correctness of versification, strength and splendour of diction, and the truly poetical quality of adorning every subject that he touched.—*Edinb. Enc.*

2 vols. 12mo, $2 25, London, 1828.

Dryden.

His poems prove him one of the greatest poets of his country; and, as Congrève says, "No man has written in any language so much and so various matter, and in so various manner, so well."—*Blake.*

5 vols. 16mo, $6 25.

Goldsmith.

His poetry, natural, melodious, affecting, and beautifully descriptive, finds an echo in every bosom.

8vo, $2 50, London.

Shakspeare.

Shakspeare is above all writers, at least above all modern writers, the poet of nature, the poet that holds up to his readers a faithful mirror of manners and of life. His characters are the genuine progeny of common humanity, such as the world will always supply, and observation will always find. —*Edinb. Enc.*

1 vol. 8vo, $3 50, New-York.

Burns.

As a poet, without accomplishing any work of extensive or complicated design, Burns has exhibited all the variety of poetical powers which can enter into the greatest works, the conduct of a plan only excepted.—*Edinb. Enc.*

2 vols. 12mo, $3 00.

Rogers.

His poems are not remarkable for passion or vigour, but they are surpassingly sweet, touching, and correct. The "Pleasures of Memory" has stood the test of time. His descriptions are marvellously accurate.—*Mrs. Hall.*

12mo, $5 00, London.

Wordsworth.

Wordsworth is ever true to nature. Passages from his poems have become familiar as household words, and are perpetually called into use to give strong and apt expression to the thoughts and feelings of others. His poems are full of beauties peculiarly their own—of original thoughts, of fine sympathies, and of grave, yet cheerful wisdom.—*Mrs. Hall.*

8vo, $3 50, Philadelphia, 1839.

Scott.

Whatever may be the merits of Sir Walter's other works, it is on his poetical ones, of course, including his historical romances, that his fame will chiefly rest.—*North Am. Rev.*

1 vol. 8vo, $5 50, Paris, 1838.

Southey.

Others have more excelled in *delineating* what they found before them in life, but none have given such proofs of extraordinary powers in *creating*. He excels in unity of design and congruity of character, and never did poet more adequately express heroic fortitude and generous affections.—*Mrs. Hall.*

1 vol. 8vo, $3 50, New-York, 1842.

Campbell.

The poetry of Campbell is universally felt, and, therefore, universally appreciated. His subjects have all been skilfully chosen: he has sought for themes only where a pure mind seeks them, and turned from the grosser passions, the meaner desires, and the vulgar sentiments of man, as things unfitted for verse.—*Mrs. Hall.*

18mo, $2 50, London, 1840.

Moore.

His poetry is deficient in those higher and more enduring materials which form the groundwork of imperishable fame. Its leading attribute is grace; he is always brilliant, but seldom powerful; his fancy is perpetually at play, and his poetry is exquisitely finished. We think that the "Irish Melodies" must be considered as the most valuable and enduring of all his works, and as a writer of song he stands without a rival.—*Mrs. Hall.*

1 vol. 8vo, $4 00, Paris, 1842.

Mrs. Hemans.

In our opinion, the poems of Mrs. Hemans are elegant and pure in thought and language; her later poems are vigorous, pathetic, and picturesque.—*Quarterly Rev.*

There was yet a stage to which they attained—they became sublime and religious.—*N. Y. Rev.*

1 vol. 8vo, $2 50, Philadelphia, 1841.

John Keats.

If you want a thorough enjoyment of the beautiful for beauty's sake (like a walk on a summer's noon in a land of woods and meadows), you must imbower yourselves in the luxuries of Keats.—*Mrs. Hall.*

1 vol. 12mo.

Pollok's Course of Time.

Allowing some grave faults in this great work, where shall we find another modern poem so sublime, so thrilling, or so splendid in imagination, or where an equal measure of poetical genius under a stronger control of conscious responsibility and Christian duty?—*Christian Observer.*

Letitia E. Landon.

Her poems have obtained a popularity scarcely second to that of any British writer.—*Mrs. Hall.*

Remains of Miss L. Davidson.

A tender heart, a warm sensibility, an ardent and vivid imagination, an eager desire for knowledge, characterize her earlier effusions; the later are marked with the melancholy traces of a wasting frame, and a dejected spirit feeling the fatal approach of death.—*Enc. Am.*

The same remarks may be applied to her younger sister, Margaret Miller Davidson—doomed, like herself, to an early grave; and whose writings have been published under the auspices of Mr. Washington Irving.

1 vol. 8vo, $1 50, Philadelphia.

Aikin's British Poets.

The object of this work is to comprise within a single volume a chronological series of the English classical poets from Ben Jonson to Beattie, without mutilation or abridgment, with biographical and critical notices.—*Advertisement.*

1 vol. 8vo, $1 00, Philadelphia.

Southey's British Poets.

This collection embraces the earlier poets, bringing the series down to the time when Dr. Aikin's begins. The two works together form a pretty complete library of English poets down to A.D. 1800.

Halleck's Selections from the British Poets.

This small volume, published by the Messrs. Harper, and edited by Fitz-Greene Halleck, is a seasonable and tasteful present to the youth of our country. It was originally published for the School District Library.

Bryant's Selections from American Poets.

Prepared for the same Library, and a worthy companion tc Mr. Halleck's Selections.

R. W. Griswold's American Poets.

This volume contains judicious selections from the most considerable of our poets, commencing with Philip Freneau of Revolutionary memory, and coming down to the present time. The critical and biographical notices are brief, but discriminating and elegant, and the mechanical execution worthy of all praise.

Bryant's Poems.

See part II.; also for notices of other American poets.

Translation of Dante.

Dante's works are important chiefly in three respects: as the productions of one of the greatest men that ever lived, as one of the keys of the history of his time, and as exhibiting the state of learning, theology, and politics in that age.—*Enc. Am.*

Translation by H. F. Carey, 3 vols. 12mo, $4 75, London, 1831.

Translation of Petrarch.

In tenderness, delicacy, and beauty, Petrarch equalled, but never surpassed, his great predecessors. His true glory consisted in his enthusiasm for all that is great and beautiful in antiquity: a taste which he communicated, not to Italy alone, but to Europe.—*N. Am. Rev.*

Rose's translation of Ariosto's "Orlando Furioso."

This poetical romance is a complete wilderness, in which there is no continued path; but in which are to be seen, at every step, the most magnificent scenes, the most picturesque prospects, the richest fruits, and the most brilliant flowers. Ariosto excels in narrative and description, and is distinguished by a nervous, expressive, and unaffected style.—*N. Am. Rev.*

Mr. Rose catches and portrays the humour of his author with a feeling the most kindred and congenial.—*Quart. Rev.*

8 vols. 12mo, $9 00, London.

Hunt's translation of Tasso's "Jerusalem Delivered."

This elegant poem abounds with all the pleasing description of tender scenes, the animated representation of battles, and the majestic flow of language which so much captivate and overpower the reader in the pages of Homer and Virgil.—*Blake.*

Mr. Hunt, in many respects, ranks far above the greater number of those who have aspired to make the readers of our language familiar with the poetry of other lands.—*Quart. Rev.*

2 vols. 18mo, $2 00, London.

La Fontaine's Fables.

They belong to that small class of works, the reputation of which never fades, and which are just as well known at present as they were in the 17th century.—*Penny Cyc.*

The translation of Mr. Wright is excellent.

3 vols. 8vo, $10 50, Paris, 1840.

VIII. PHYSICAL SCIENCE AND NATURAL HISTORY.

"It was an apt observation of the excellent Plutarch, that we ought to regard books as we do sweetmeats, not wholly to aim at the pleasantest, but chiefly to respect the wholesomest; not forbidding either, but approving the latter most."—FELTHAM.

Playfair's Discourse on the Progress of the Physical and Mathematical Sciences.

It combines the utmost clearness with the greatest brevity, and his examples are chosen from the most striking and splendid discoveries of modern science.—*Edinburgh Rev.*

Thomson's History of Chemical Philosophy.

This sketch, by one of the first chemists of the time, must be able, accurate, and interesting.

Arnott's Physics,

with additions by Dr. Hayes, is a good popular treatise.—*Enc. Am.*

It would seem a hopeless task to enter upon works on physical science generally, but *one* may be named, "The Elements of Physics," by Dr. Arnott, as one of the most extraordinary and valuable books of the age; one calculated to entice the student into the very recesses of natural philosophy, and well worthy of a very frequent perusal.—*Warren's Law Studies.*

2 vols. 8vo, $1 50, Philadelphia, 1838.

Good's Book of Nature.

This volume is designed to take a systematic, but popular survey of the most interesting features of the general *science of nature*, for the purpose of elucidating what has been found obscure, controverting and correcting what has been felt erroneous, and developing, by means of original views and hypotheses, much of what yet remains to be more satisfactorily explained.—*Preface.*

1 vol. 8vo, $1 25, New-York.

Fisher's Physics.

This work displays great accuracy of judgment, caution and originality in investigation, and shows a genius of high order in this department.

Ferguson's Lectures on Subjects in Mechanics, Hydrostatics, Pneumatics, and Optics.

Perspicuity in the selection and arrangement of his facts, and in the display of the truths deduced from them, are the characteristics of these lectures.—*Penny Cyc.*

8vo, $2 00, London, 1839.

Smellie's Philosophy of Natural History.

This work, taken in connexion with Dr. Ware's Introduction, is an admirable guide to the study of Zoology.

4to, $2 25.

White's Natural History of Selborne.

Many curious facts on the subject of Natural History may be found in that delightful work.—*School and Schoolmaster.*

1 vol. 18mo, 45 cents, New-York.

Huber on Bees.

This work contains some curious observations on Bees.—*Enc. Am.*

Euler's Letters.

They have, with the exception of the metaphysical part, been much esteemed, particularly for the singular perspicuity with which their author has explained some of the most profound truths in physics.—*Edinb. Enc.*

2 vols. 18mo, 90 cents, New-York.

Sir J. Herschel's Discourses on the Study of Natural Philosophy.

These discourses are admirable, proving in a clear and distinct manner the use of the study of Natural Philosophy. —*Enc. Am.*

1 vol. 12mo, 60 cents, New-York.

Herschel's Astronomy.

It is written in a popular and generally intelligible style, entirely free from mathematical symbols, and disencumbered, as far as possible, of technical phrases.

Daniell's Physics,

Being an Introduction to the Study of Chemical Philosophy, containing Optics, Electricity, Electro-magnetism, &c.

1 vol. 18mo, 69 cents, New-York.

Olmstead's Astronomy.

This work is a popular treatise on that science: it enters fully into its history, and considers the subject of Natural Theology so far as it is related to Astronomy.

Lardner's Mechanics.

A work which contains an uncommon amount of useful information, exhibited in a plain and very intelligible form. —*Olmstead.*

Renwick's Practical Mechanics.

This volume is alike creditable to the writer, and to the state of science in this country.—*Am. Quarterly Rev.*
1 vol. 18mo, 90 cents, New-York.

Mantell's Wonders of Geology.

From a very competent hand, and calculated to awaken interest in this delightful study.

Hitchcock's Geology.

We have not read a line in Mr. Hitchcock's work which has not inspired us with confidence in him as an accurate observer, governed by a liberal and philosophic spirit.—*North Am. Rev.*

De la Beche's Geological Manual.

A work of great importance in the science to which it relates, and which must henceforth take its place in the library of every student in Geology.

Lyell's Principles of Geology.

This work is exclusively confined to the consideration of the changes now going on upon the earth in the animate and inanimate creation, and the bearing of such changes on the interpretation of geological monuments.—*Preface.*
A very learned and able work.
3 vols. 12mo, $5 50.

Lyell's Elements of Geology.

12mo, $2 00.

Lee's Elements of Geology.

In this volume will be found, perhaps, the fullest description of the geological formations and mineral resources of

the United States, hitherto published in any systematic treatise.—*Preface.*
18mo, 50 cents, New-York.

Davy's Elements of Chemical Philosophy.

This work, although it bears marks of haste, contains much interesting matter, and is from one of the great masters.—*Penny Cyc.*

Beck's Chemistry.

A very good elementary treatise.

Kane's Chemistry.

This volume includes the most recent discoveries and applications of the science to medicine and pharmacy, and to the arts.
1 vol. 8vo, $2 00, New-York.

Chaptal's Chemistry applied to Agriculture.

There is nothing so indispensable to the interests of agriculture as that the knowledge of the physical laws should be more widely diffused; to contribute to this important object is the design of this work.—*Preface.*
1 vol. 18mo, 50 cents, New-York.

Liebig's Animal Chemistry; or, Organic Chemistry in its Application to Physiology and Pathology.

A great work, presenting some startling views, but entitled to deep consideration.
25 cents.

Cleaveland's Mineralogy.

The most copious and valuable work now in use.

Sheppard's Mineralogy.

A useful and entertaining work.

Kirby's Entomology of North America.

The descriptions given in this work are laboured and accurate. It is certainly the most scientific work which has appeared in any branch of Natural History in this country.—*Edinburgh Enc.*

Rennie's Insect Architecture.

This is certainly a very interesting work, and does credit to the author as a naturalist and a writer.—*North Am. Rev.*

Wyatt's Conchology.

This manual is prepared according to the system laid down by Lamarck, with the late improvements by De Blainville. The whole is exemplified and arranged for the use of students.

8vo, $1 75, New-York.

Yarrell's Fishes.

Audubon's Synopsis of the Birds of North America.

Above praise.

8vo, $3 75, Edinburgh, 1839.

Gray's Botanical Text-Book.

This work comprises an introduction to Structural and Physiological Botany, and the Principles of Systematic Botany, with an account of the chief natural families of the vegetable kingdom, and notices of the principal officinal or otherwise useful plants.

1 vol. 8vo, $1 50

Buffon's Natural History.

The mass of authenticated facts which is contained in his works, and the rank to which he has raised the science of natural history, entitle him to that fame which he now enjoys, and to that immortality which he himself anticipated.—*Edinburgh Enc.*

16 vols. 12mo, $28 50, London, 1779.

Goldsmith's Animated Nature.

Goldsmith composed this work out of Buffon and others, in a manner both amusing and instructive, although the scientific acquirements of the author were not sufficient to guard him against numerous errors.—*Enc. Am.*

6 vols. 8vo, $15 00, London.

Cuvier's Animal Kingdom.

In this work, the whole subject matter of Zoology is arranged according to the principles of organization, and beginning with man.—*Penny Cyc.*

1 vol. 8vo, $5 00, London, 1840.

Selby's Illustrations of British Ornithology.

This is the most complete scientific ornithology yet published. Every known British bird is enumerated, with an ample description of its plumage, habits, &c., &c.—*Advertisement.*

2 vols. 8vo, $7 50, Edinburgh, 1833.

Hayward's or Coates's Physiology for Schools.

Either of these is well adapted to the purpose.

Griscom's Animal Mechanism.

This is a plain and familiar exposition of the structure and functions of the human system.—*Advertisement.*

1 vol. 18mo, 45 cents, New-York.

Beck's Medical Jurisprudence.

This great work has passed through several editions, and is now regarded as a standard on both sides of the Atlantic.

Combe's Principles of Physiology applied to the Preservation of Health.

An admirable book, which is already introduced into many of our schools, and which we earnestly wish *every* young person would read and study.—*Miss Sedgwick.*

1 vol. 18mo, 45 cents, New-York.

Pritchard's Physical History of Mankind.

This is an able and instructive work; the fruit of laborious research, and possessing high authority.

Bridgewater Treatises.

There are eight in number, and those of Dr. Buckland on "Geology and Mineralogy," and Rev. Mr. Whewell on "Astronomy and General Physics," are most admirable, and take the first rank.—*Chancellor Kent.*

Dick's Celestial Scenery.

The author displays in this volume the wonders of the planetary system, illustrating the perfections of the Deity and a plurality of worlds.—*Advertisement.*

1 vol. 18mo, 45 cents, New-York.

Dick's Sidereal Heavens.

In this volume, the sidereal heavens, and other subjects con-

nected with astronomy, are depicted, as illustrative of the character of the Deity, and of an infinity of worlds.—*Advertisement.*
1 vol. 18mo, 45 cents, New-York.

Publications of the British Society for the Diffusion of Useful Knowledge.

Most of these are on branches of physical science or the useful arts. They are generally instructive, and some of them are very able.

Dean's Philosophy of Life.

From the pen of an able and estimable man; and though rather too much tinged with phrenology for our taste, it is still a useful and creditable work.

IX. THE USEFUL AND ORNAMENTAL ARTS, ENGINEERING, &c., &c.

"Whether it is possible a state should not thrive, whereof the lower parts are industrious and the upper wise."—BERKELEY'S *Querist.*

Loudon's Encyclopædia of Agriculture.

This work professes to embrace every part of the subject, and, what has hitherto never been attempted, to give a general history of agriculture in all countries.
1 vol. 8vo, $10 00, London, 1835.

Buel's Farmer's Instructer.

Of this work Professor Dean speaks thus: "This is the most perfect of Judge Buel's works, containing within a small compass the imbodied results of his agricultural experience; a rich legacy, to which our farming interest cannot remain insensible."
2 vols. 18mo, $1 00, New-York.

Fessenden's Agriculture.

A standard work.

Armstrong's Treatise on Agriculture.

This volume from the terse and polished pen of the late

General Armstrong, comprises a concise history of the origin and progress of agriculture, the present condition of the art at home and abroad, and the theory and practice of husbandry. —*Advertisement.*

1 vol. 18mo, 45 cents.

Lowe's Elements of Agriculture.

This work of a distinguished Scotch writer is regarded as the ablest elementary work on this subject which has issued from the British press.

The Agricultural Series of the British Society for the Diffusion of Useful Knowledge.

Full, and illustrated by good drawings and cuts.

Lindley's Theory of Horticulture.

This is an attempt to explain the principal operations of gardening upon physiological principles.

1 vol. 12mo, $1 25, Wiley & Putnam, New-York.

Liebig's Agricultural Chemistry.

Admirable. The publication of this work forms an important era in the history of agriculture and of chemistry. It has gone far towards settling some of the most difficult questions in regard to the proper food of plants, and laying thereby the foundation for a rational system of manuring and cultivation.

Downing's Landscape Gardening.

1 vol. 8vo. $3 50, Wiley & Putnam, New-York.

Downing's Designs for Cottage Residences.

Mr. Downing has practical knowledge and true taste, and evidently loves his pursuits. These qualities give freshness, charm, and value to whatever he writes on his favourite topic.—*Am. Quart. Rev.*

1 vol. 8vo, $2 50, Wiley & Putnam, New-York.

Loudon's Encyclopædia of Gardening.

The object of this work is to present in one systematic view the history and present state of gardening in all countries, embracing horticulture, floriculture, arboriculture, and landscape gardening.

$10 00, Wiley & Putnam, New-York.

Ure's Dictionary of Arts, Manufactures, and Mines,

containing a clear exposition of their principles and practice.
1 vol. 8vo, $14 00, London.

Ure's Philosophy of Manufactures.

This is an exposition of the scientific, moral, and commercial economy of the factory system of Great Britain.
8vo, $2 00, D. Appleton & Co., New-York.

Bigelow's Elements of Technology.

In this work Dr. Bigelow has given a very instructive account of the *materials* and *processes* employed in the arts, and has entered somewhat into the *rationale* of processes. It has won a high and well-merited reputation.

Potter's Science and the Arts.

The design of this work is to call attention to the fact that the arts are the result of intelligence; that they have each one its principles or theory; that these principles are furnished by science; and that he, therefore, who would understand the arts, must know something of science; while, on the other hand, he who would see the true power and worth of science, ought to study it in its applications. The work is made up of facts illustrating and enforcing these views, so arranged as to exhibit the invariable connexion between processes in art and laws in nature. It also explains the *rationale* of the leading arts.
1 vol. 8vo, 75 cents, Boston, Marsh, Capen, Lyon, & Webb.

Ewbank's Hydraulic Machinery.

It is an acceptable contribution to the literature of mechanical science and practical engineering; a valuable work of reference to those who have not access to the original sources, and a useful epitome to those who have.—*London Athenæum.*
D. Appleton & Co., New-York.

Pambour on the Steam-Engine. Also on Locomotion.

Both these works are much esteemed.

Mahan's Civil Engineering.

This work gives such a condensed view of most of the

branches of elementary engineering as may serve for a good introduction to the larger works, to which it everywhere refers the student.—*London Athenæum.*

1 vol. 8vo, $1 75.

Cressy's Practical Treatise on Bridge-building, and on the Equilibrium of Arches and Vaults

2 vols. folio, $9 00, Wiley & Putnam, New-York.

Town on Bridges, Railroads, Aqueducts, &c.

Roberts on the Manufacture of Iron.

J. W. Alexander on the Manufacture of Iron.

Quill's American Mechanic.

Millington on Civil Engineering, &c.

Evans's Millwright's and Miller's Guide

Benjamin's Practical Architect.

Bowditch's Practical Navigator.

Strickland's Canals and Railroads.

Blunt's American Coast Pilot.

All valuable works.

M'Culloch's Dictionary, Practical, Theoretical, and Historical, of Commerce and Commercial Navigation.

Different readers may resort to this work for different purposes, and every one will be able to find in it clear and accurate information, whether his object be to make himself familiar with details, to acquire a knowledge of principles, or to learn the revolutions that have taken place in the various departments of trade.

2 vols. 8vo, $10 00, London.

X. THEOLOGY.

"The first creature of God in the works of the days was the light of the sense; the last was the light of reason; and his Sabbath-work ever since is the illumination of his Spirit. First he breatheth light on the face of the matter, or chaos; then he breatheth light on the face of man; and still he breatheth and inspireth light into the face of his chosen."—BACON.

The Sacred Scriptures of the Old and New Testaments.

The Scriptures contain, independently of a Divine origin, more true sublimity, more exquisite beauty, pure morality, more important history, and finer strains both of poetry and eloquence, than could be collected within the same compass from all other books that were ever composed in any age or in any idiom.—*Sir William Jones.*

Horne's Introduction.

This work is designed as a comprehensive manual of sacred literature, selected from the labours of the most eminent biblical critics, both British and foreign.—*Preface.*

Alexander on the Canon of Scriptures.

Paley's Evidences.

This work contains a popular view of the arguments for the truth of the Christian religion, drawn up with the author's usual perspicuity and dialectic skill.—*Enc. Am.*

Paley's Horæ Paulinæ.

The chief object of this work was to bring together from the Acts of the Apostles and the Epistles such passages as furnish examples of undesigned coincidence, and thus prove the authenticity of the Scriptural writings.—*Enc. Am.*

Paley's Natural Theology.

This work will open the heart, that it may understand, or at least receive the Scriptures, if anything can. It is philosophy in its highest and noblest sense; scientific without the jargon of science; profound, but so clear that its depth is disguised.—*Quart. Rev.*

2 vols. 18mo, 90 cents, New-York.

Marsh's Lectures.

Their object is to teach the student how to study divinity, and then, as he gradually proceeds, to inform him of the distinguished writers on the several subjects.—*Preface.*

Campbell's Lectures on the Study of Theology.

In these lectures, with a great deal of sound and judicious remarks, there appears to be a portion of unreasonable prejudice against systems of divinity.—*Edinb. Enc.*

Campbell's Four Gospels.

This production must be considered, as it is actually considered by all who are capable of forming a judgment, as a most important acquisition to the library of the Biblical student.—*Edinb. Enc.*

Stewart's Translation of Romans.

Stewart's Translation of Hebrews.

No one can read these translations, with the accompanying notes, introduction, &c., without feeling that to great learning, industry, and ability, the author adds an humble, candid, and charitable spirit.

Turner's Edition of Planck's Introduction.

An able and excellent work.

Hengstenberg's Christology.

This work, translated by the late Dr. Keith, deserves a place in the library of every divine and theological student.

Knapp's Theology.

(Translated by Leonard Woods, Jr.)

One of the best systems of dogmatic theology which have been given to the world by the learning and indefatigable industry of the German scholars.

Neander's Ecclesiastical History.

The author says in his preface that the chief aim of his life, from an early period, had been to represent the history of the Church of Christ as a speaking proof of the Divine power of Christianity, as a school of Christian experience, and a voice sounding through all ages, of edification and warning for all who are willing to listen. His works prove indefatigable zeal and vast erudition.—*Enc. Am.*

Pearson on the Creed.

This admirable exposition of the Creed, originally preached to his parishioners in the form of sermons, has been long and deservedly considered among the best and most useful theological productions of our language.

8vo, $2 00, D. Appleton & Co., New-York.

Owen's Works.

3 vols. 12mo, $3 00.

Howe's Works.

The great men of the commonwealth coming between the courtly poets, and grave, imaginative writers of the age of Elizabeth, and the airy and graceful wits of Charles's days, have been too often passed over with silence, not to add contemptuous disdain. Yet they embrace names still held in veneration, and still cherished with love.—*Church Record.*

2 vols. 8vo, $4 00.

Burnet on the Thirty-nine Articles.

This work has always been regarded among the standard theological works in the English language; and though it may have peculiar attractions for an Episcopalian, as an exposition of his articles of faith, yet, as a treasury of Biblical and theological knowledge, it is alike valuable to Christians of every communion.—*Chr. Observer.*

1 vol. 8vo, $2 00, D. Appleton & Co., New-York.

Calvin's Institutions of the Christian Religion.

This work, whatever may be thought of its doctrinal merits, is, as a system of theology, entitled to much admiration. The peculiarities of the system may be condemned, but the learning, the Scriptural knowledge, and the philosophical ability with which they are at once developed and supported, must be acknowledged by all whose minds are not the victims of religious or political prejudice.—*Edinb. Enc.*

Translated by Allen, 2 vols. 8vo, $5 00, New-York.

Watson's Institutes.

An able expounder of the faith of the Wesleyan Methodists.

Tomline's Theology.

This work of Bishop Tomline sets forth the doctrinal views held in his time by a large part of the Established Church of England.

Dwight's Theology.

The author, from long and habitual attention to exactness of thought, of arrangement, and of language, was accustomed, in conversation, in the desk, and while dictating to an amanuensis, to present the conceptions of his mind in a form and manner so finished as to need, usually, few or no corrections to prepare them for the press. This was the case with these discourses.—*Preface.*

Gill's Body of Divinity.

In this work the peculiar tenets of the Baptists are explained and defended. It has long been a standard work.

Paxton's Illustrations.

The only object which the author proposed to himself in composing this work was to illustrate the Scriptures; he has therefore uniformly and studiously rejected every particular in Oriental geography, natural history, customs, and manners that was not subservient to his design.—*Preface.*

Leslie on Deism.

Since infidelity is constantly reviving, and, though repeatedly laid prostrate by the weapons of truth, still rises with unexhausted vigour, the champion of Christianity will do well neither to disdain nor neglect such arms as Leslie has prepared for him, of which time has not injured the temper nor taken off the edge.—*Christ. Obs.*

Leland's Deistical Writers.

This work contains a summary view of the most noted books that have been published against revealed religion for above a century past, together with proper observations upon them.—*Preface.*

Verplanck's Essays on the Evidences of Christianity.

An able and earnest protest against the exclusive preference assigned by many writers, twenty years since, to the external or historical evidences of Christianity as compared with the internal.

Erskine's Internal Evidences for Revealed Religion.

This small volume, the first production of Mr. Erskine's pen, secured him at once a high place among theological writers.

Newcome's Harmony of the Four Gospels.

Archbishop Newcome's Harmony, though no harmony is perfect, furnishes, perhaps, the best groundwork for any future publication on the subject.—*Christ. Obs.*

Leighton's Works.

"Archbishop Leighton was," says Bishop Burnet, "possessed with the highest and noblest sense of Divine things that ever I saw in any man. And he had laid together in his memory the greatest treasure of the best and wisest of all the ancient sayings of the heathens, as well as Christians; and he used them in the aptest manner possible."—*Ed. Enc.*

8vo, $3 00, Edinburgh, 1840.

Jeremy Taylor's Works.

A pious and devotional temper, copiousness of learning, fertility of illustration, opulence of matter, and oftentimes exquisite beauty, characterize the writings of this great master.

3 vols. 8vo, $17 00.

Baxter's Works.

Dr. Isaac Barrow said that "his practical writings were never mended, and his controversial ones seldom confuted." —*Penny Cyc.*

4 vols. 8vo, $2 00, London, 1838.

Barrow's Works.

Although his divinity is less read now than formerly, it is not unfrequently resorted to as a mine of excellent thoughts and arguments. Passages of sublime and simple eloquence frequently occur.—*Enc. Am.*

2 vols., $5 50.

Bates's Works.

We scruple not to recommend them to every person living

in retirement, who wishes to improve as well as enjoy a sequestered life in such a way as will produce happiness to himself, prove beneficial to society, and glorify the God who formed him and appointed him his station in the world.—*Christian Observer.*

XI. PERIODICALS.

"Pray you, use your freedom;
And so far, if you please, allow me mine,
To hear you only; not to be compelled
To take your moral potions."—MASSINGER.

Silliman's Journal of Science.

North American Review.

Edinburgh Review.

London Quarterly Review.

I would recommend these Reviews, voluminous as they are, to be thoroughly read and studied.—*Chancellor Kent.*

American Review and Metropolitan Magazine.

Conducted by an association of gentlemen in the city of New-York; recently commenced, but full of promise.

Democratic Review.

Miscellaneous and able, devoted especially to a vindication of the doctrines of the party whose name it bears.

Northern Light.

Miscellaneous, though intended principally for the discussion of questions in Political Economy, Industrial Science, and Education.

Southern Literary Messenger.

Miscellaneous.

Knickerbocker.

Miscellaneous.

American Journal of Education.

American Journal of the Medical Sciences.

(Edited by Isaac Hayes, M.D., quarterly.)

Boston Medical and Surgical Journal (monthly).

Both works of long standing and high authority.

American Jurist and Law Reporter.

I consider it one of our most useful and valuable law publications, at once accurate, comprehensive, and national, and comprising the double merit of adaptation to merchants as well as to professional men.—*Judge Story.*

Franklin Journal and Register of Inventions.

For mechanics, engineers, &c.

Niles's Register.

Made up, for the most part, of official documents, and extremely valuable as a register of statistics in various departments of trade and industry. Excellent.

American Almanac.

A rich repository of facts.

American Museum.

Made up of selections from the foreign reviews.

Westminster Review.

Foreign Quarterly Review.

Both conducted with great ability.

Blackwood's Magazine.

Under the editorial guidance of the celebrated Professor Wilson.

Penny Magazine.

Saturday Evening Magazine.

Both these Magazines are conducted with special reference to the wants of the young and uneducated. They are excellent.

London Athenæum.

London Spectator.

These are weekly papers, mainly occupied with reviews of current literature and with literary intelligence. They are very able and spirited.

Journals of Education.

Of these there are many. The most valuable are those published in Albany (by Francis Dwight), in Boston (by Horace Mann), and in Kentucky.

XII. ENCYCLOPÆDIAS, &c.

"There is a kind of physiognomy in the titles of books no less than in the faces of men, by which a skilful observer will as well know what to expect from the one as the other."—BUTLER'S *Remains.*

Encyclopædia Americana.

We consider this publication as creditable to the editors and their coadjutors, and to the enlightened and enterprising publishers who have undertaken to furnish a work of reference well worthy to occupy a place among the books of every man of intelligence, taste, and enlightened curiosity.—*Am. Quart. Rev.*

It is mainly a translation of the *German Conversations Lexicon*, with the addition, however, of much new matter, especially on the United States.

13 vols. 8vo, $22 50, Philadelphia, 1830.

Brande's Encyclopædia.

We recommend it as a most useful work, and equally so to all classes.—*London Athenæum.*

$3 00, New-York.

Edinburgh Encyclopædia.

In this work all the great questions of civil and religious liberty have been advocated, the inalienable rights of humanity pled, and the sound doctrines of our faith established and expounded.—*Dedication.*

Rees's Encyclopædia.

This is an enlargement and revision of Chambers's Cyclopædia. In many departments it is very full and able.

Penny Cyclopædia.

The plan of this work was to give pretty fully, under each separate head, as much information as can be conveyed within reasonable limits. It also attempts to give such general views of all great branches of knowledge as may help to the formation of just ideas on their extent and relative importance, and to point out the best sources of complete information.—*Preface.*

$2 00 a volume.

Encyclopædia of Religious Knowledge.

SYNCHRONISTIC TABLES.

Note.—The years given in these tables are those of the birth of the respective authors, as far as they could be obtained.

SYNCHRONISTIC TABLES,

EMBRACING THE LITERARY MEN NAMED IN THE FOREGOING PAGES DOWN TO 1800.

Literary History is naturally divided into Ancient, Middle, and Modern. The Ancient terminates with the retirement of science into the convents in the 6th century; the Middle begins with the downfall of the great Roman Empire, about 500 A.D., and the commencement of literary civilization in the various European nations, without the support of ancient classical civilization; and the last begins about 1450, when the study of the classics was renewed, and knowledge revived in Europe.

(A.) ANCIENT.

Years.	Sacred Writers.	Greeks.	Romans.
B.C.			
1869	Job.		
1491	Book of Genesis.		
1491	Book of Exodus.		
1490	Book of Leviticus.		
1451	Book of Deuteronomy.		
1451	Book of Numbers.		
1427	Joshua.		
1406	Judges.		
1312	Ruth		
1250		Orpheus.	
1055	1st Book of Samuel.		
1055	David.	Homer.	
1025	Solomon.		
1018	2d Book of Samuel.		
1015	1st Book of Chronicles.		
1013	Song of Solomon.		
1004	1st Book of Kings, i.-xi.		
1004	2d Book of Chronicles, i.-ix.		
1000	Proverbs.		
975	Ecclesiasticus.		
950		Hesiod.	
897	1st Book of Kings, xii., etc., etc.		
862	Jonah.		
800	Joel		

Years.	Sacred Writers.	Greeks.	Romans.
B.C.			
787	Amos.		
752			(Rome built.)
750	Micah.		
740	Hosea.		
713	Nahum.		
698	Isaiah.		
680		Archilochus.	
630	Zephaniah.		
626	Habakkuk.		
623	2d Book of Chronicles, x., etc., etc.		
612		Sappho.	
590	2d Book of Kings.		
588	Jeremiah.		
587	Obadiah		
584		Pythagoras.	
574	Ezekiel.		
550		Hecatæus.	
544		Theognis.	
536		Anacreon.	
534	Daniel.		
530		Pherecydes.	
520	Haggai.		
520	Zechariah.		
509	Esther.		
500		Stobæus.	
495		Sophocles.	
490		Pindar.	
490		Æschylus.	
484		Herodotus.	
480		Euripides.	
471		Thucydides.	
469		Socrates.	
469		Hippocrates.	
460		Hellanicus of Mytilene.	
458		Lysias.	
457	Ezra.		
456		Aristophanes.	
450		Xenophon.	
436		Isocrates.	
434	Nehemiah.		
430		Plato.	
404		Apollodorus of Athens.	
400		Ctesias.	
397	Malachi.		
387		Æschines.	
385		Demosthenes.	
385		Aristotle.	
382		Theophrastus.	
378		Zeuxis.	
360		Theopompus.	
300		Euclid.	
276		Eratosthenes.	
275		Theocritus.	

Years.	Sacred Writers.	Greeks.	Romans.
B.C.			
260		Callimachus.	
250		Archimedes.	
242			Livius Andronicus.
232			Ennius.
232			Cato the Censor.
203		Polybius.	
200			Plautus.
200			Terence.
125		Apollonius Rhodius.	
106			C. Lucilius.
105			Cicero.
100			Julius Cæsar.
90			Lucretius.
86			Sallust.
86			Catullus.
70		Dionysius.	
68			Virgil.
64			Horace.
59			Livy.
54		Strabo.	Pomponius Mela
49		Diodorus.	
43			Ovid.
41			Tibullus.
40			Propertius.
35			Cornelius Nepos.
19			Vell. Paterculus.
Christ.			
5			M. Seneca.
10			Quintus Curtius.
20			Manilius.
30			Valerius Maximus
37		Josephus.	
39	St. Matthew (wrote Gospel).		
40			Pliny the Elder.
40			Juvenal.
40			Clement of Rome
42			Quintilian.
43			Martial.
44	St. Mark.		
55	St. Paul (was writing).	Plutarch.	
60			Phædrus.
60	St. James wrote.		L. A. Seneca.
62			Pliny the Younger
63	St. Luke (wrote Gospel).		Valerius Flaccus.
64	St. Peter wrote.		
68	St. John wrote		Aulus Gellius
69			Tacitus.
80		Pausanias.	
97	Apocalypse written.		
110			Florus.
115			Justinus.
			Suetonius.

Years.	Sacred Writers.	Greeks.	Romans.
A.C.			
130		Galen.	Tertullian.
150			Irenæus.
154			Justin Martyr.
185		Origen.	
190		Sextus Empiricus.	
192		Clement of Alexandria.	
240		Herodian.	
250		Philostratus.	
260		Diogenes Laertius.	
264		Eusebius.	
296		Athanasius.	
310			Prudentius.
340			Ambrose.
340			Jerome.
344		Chrysostom.	
354			St. Augustine.
370			Amm. Marcellinus
370			Eutropius.
380			Aurelius Victor.
455			Boethius.

(B.) MEDIÆVAL.

Years.	English.	German.	French.	Ital. and Spanish.
A.C.				
593			Gregory of Tours.	
672	Bede.			
780		Eginhard.		
840	Erigena.	Ottfried.		
881		Earliest Ballad.		
1060				Roscellin.
1063				Cid.
1079			Abelard.	
1150	Gulielmus Tyrius.			
1157			Brantome.	
1160	Geoffrey of Monmouth.			
1173	William of Malmsbury.	Minnesingers.		
1180			The Norman Alexander.	
1207		Niebelungenlied.		
1213	Matthew of Westminster.			
1214	Roger Bacon.			
1221				Bonaventura.
1230				Giovanni Villani.
1240			Doëte de Troyes.	
1241				Matheo Villani.

Years.	English.	German.	French.	Ital. and Spanish.
A.C.				
1245				Marco Polo.
1265	Duns Scotus.			Dante.
1266				Cino da Pistoria.
1270	Occam.			
1304				Petrarca.
1313				Boccacio.
1328	Chaucer.			
1337			Jean Froissart.	
1340	Gower.			
1340	Langlande.			
1340	Mandeville.			
1370				Bruni.
1380				Bracciolini.
1380				Poggio.
1388		Thomas à Kempis.		
1400			Raimond de Sebonde.	Leonardo da Vinci.
1406				Leo Baptiste Alberti.
1406				Valla.
1410			Joan of Arc.	
1421				Platina.
1433				Ficinus.
1435				Columbus
1444				Bramante.
1445			Comines.	
1448				Lorenzo de Medici.

(C.) MODERN.

Years.	Engl. & Amer.	French.	German.	Ital., Span., & Port.	L. & N. Coun.
A.C.					
1454				Politianus.	
1460		Monstrelet.			
1463				Mirandola.	
1467					Erasmus
1469				Machiavel.	
1470	Walsingham.			Bembo.	
1473			Copernicus.		
1474				Las Cases. Michael Angelo.	
1474				Ariosto. Trissino.	
1477				Giorgione. Titian.	
1480	Sir T. More.			Gil Vincente. Raphael.	
1483		Rabelais.	Luther.	Guicciardini.	
1489	Cranmer.				
1492		Margar. of Valois.		Vida.	
1493				Firenzuola.	
1494		Francis I.	Hans Sachs.	Vega.	

Years.	Engl. & Amer.	French.	German.	Ital., Span., & Port.	L. and N. Coun
A.C.					
1494				Correggio.	
1497			Melancthon.		
1500	Barclay.	Montluc.		BenvenutoCellini.	
1500	Ridley.				
1500	Hooper.				
1503	Wyatt.			Mendoza.	
1505	Knox.	Marot.			
1506	Buchanan.				
1509		Calvin.			
1512				Vasari.	
1513		Du Bellay.		Lascaris.	
1517	Fox.		Gesner.		
1518				Palladio.	
1519		Beza.			
1520	Surrey.				
1522	Jewell.				
1524				Camoens.	
1527	Sackville.			Ferreira.	
1532		Jodelle.			
1533		Montaigne.			
1538				Baronius.	
1538				Guarini.	
1542		Mary Stuart.		Bellarmin.	
1544				Tasso.	
1546	Drake.				Tycho Brahe.
1547	Frobisher.			Cervantes.	
1549		Philip de Mornay.			
1550	Napier.				
1551	Camden.				
1551	Coke.				
1552	Sir W. Raleigh.			Sarpi (Paul or Pietro).	
1553	Spenser.			Chiabrera.	
1553	Hooker.	De Thou.			
1555		Malherbe.			
1556		Perron.			
1559		Sully.			
1560			Fischart.	An. Carracci.	Arminius.
1561	Fr. Bacon.				
1562				Lope Felix de Vega.	
1562	Daniel.			Gongora.	
1563	Sir Phil. Sidney.				
1563	Drayton.				
1564	Shakspeare.			Galileo.	
1566	Ben Jonson.				
1568	Chapman.				
1571			Kepler.	Campanella.	
1572	Bishop Hall.				
1573		Hippolyte.			
1573	Laud.	Regnier.			
1575			Boehm.		

Years.	Engl. and Amer.	French.	German.	It., Sp., & Port.	L. and N. Coun.
A.C.					
1579	Harvey.			Bentivoglio.	
1579				Davila.	
1580		Hardy.			
1580	Fairfax.				
1581	Herbert of Cherbury.				
1583					Episcopius.
1583					Grotius.
1584	Selden.	Duchesne.			
1584	Usher.				
1585	Drummond.				
1585	Beaumont and Fletcher.				
1588	Winthrop.*				
1592		Gassendi.			
1593	Geo. Herbert.				
1593	Walton.				
1594	Herrick.	Balzac.			
1596		Des Cartes.	Opitz.		
1600	Sir M. Hale.				
1601				Calderon.	
1602	Chillingworth.				
1606		Corneille (P.).		Borelli.	
1607	Fanshaw.	M'lle Scuderi.			
1608	Clarendon.				
1610	Fuller.	Dufresne.			
1612		Arnauld.			
1613	Taylor.	Rochefoucault.			
1613	Leighton.	Perrault.			
1613	Hammond.	St. Evremond.			
1614	More (Henry).				
1615	Baxter.				
1617	Ashmole.				
1618	Cowley.			Murillo.	
1620	Pepys.	Molière.			
1621	Evelyn.	La Fontaine.			
1623	Waller.	Pascal.			
1625	Burton.	Corneille (T.).			
1626	Boyle.	Mad. de Sevigne.			
1627		Bossuet.			
1628	Sir Wm. Temple.				
1629					Huygens.
1630	Barrow.				
1630	Tillotson.				
1631	Dryden.				
1632		Flechier.			
1632	Wood.	Bourdaloue.	Puffendorf.		
1633	South.				
1634	Hooke.	Mme. Deshoulières.			
1635	Willoughby.				
1635	Stillingfleet.				
1636	Bull.	Boileau.			
1638		Malebranche.			

Years.	Engl. and Amer.	French.	German.	It., Sp., & Por.	L. & N. Co.
A.C.					
1638		Simon.			
1639		Racine.			
1640	Wycherley.				
1643	Burnet.	La Bruyere.			
1643	Newton.	Chardin.			
1643	Strype.				
1644	Stanley.				
1647	Feltham.	Bayle.	Leibnitz.		
1651	Otway.	Fénélon.			
1651	Lee.				
1652		Dampier.			
1654	Evelyn.				
1655		Montfaucon.			
1655		Vertot.	James Bernou-illi.		
1656	Halley.	Tournefort.			
1657		Dupin.			
1657		Fontenelle.	Kaempfer.		
1660	Southern.	Beausobre.			
1661		Rapin.			
1661		Rollin.			
1661		L'Hôpital.			
1662	Henry.				
1663		Massillon.			
1664	Prior.				
1666	Wotton.				
1667	Swift.		John Bernouilli		
1667	Harris.				
1668	De Foe.		J. A. Fabricius.		
1670	Congreve.				Celsius
1671	Philips.				
1671	Shaftesbury.				
1672	Addison.			Muratori.	
1672	Bolingbroke.				
1673	Rowe.				
1674		Barbeyrac.			
1675	Calamy.				
1675	Samuel Clarke.				
1677		Saurin.			
1678	Neal.				
1678	Parnell.				
1680	Steele.				
1681	Young.				
1682		Charlevoix.		Facciolati.	
1688	Pope.				
1688	Gay.				
1689	Richardson.	Montesquieu.			
1690	Lady Montagu.				
1692	Bradley.	Count de Cay-lus.			
1694	Chesterfield.	Voltaire.	Mosheim.		
1695	Simpson.				
1698	Warburton.	Bernard de Jussieu.		Metastasio	
1698	Anson.				
1700	Thomson.	Pothier.			

Years.	Engl. and Amer.	French.	German.	It., Sp., & P.	L. & N. C.
A.C.					
1703	Edwards.				
1703	Wesley.				
1705	Hartley.	Duclos.			
1706	Franklin (B.).*				
1707	Fielding.	Crebillon.	Euler.	Goldoni.	
1708	Wm. Pitt, earl of Chatham.		Hagedorn.		
1708	Lyttleton.		Haller.		
1709	Johnson				
1709	Armstrong.	Mably.			
1710	Reid.				
1710	Ferguson (J.).				
1710	Watson.				
1710	Simpson.				
1711	Hume.				
1712	Cullen.	Rousseau (J. J.).			
1712	Fothergill.	Madame d'Epinay.			
1713		Diderot.			
1714	Shenstone.				
1715		Helvetius.	Gellert.		
1715		Condillac.	Kleist.		
1716	Garrick.	Goguet.		Ulloa.	
1716	Gray.	Barthelemy.			
1717		D'Alembert.			
1718	Blair.				
1718	Henry.				
1718	Walpole.	Raynal.			
1719	Kennicott.		Gleim.		
1720	Collins.	Bridaine.			
1720	Hurd.				
1720	Smollett.				
1721	Akenside.		A. W. Sch egel.		
1721	Sheridan.				
1723	Adam Smith.	Marmontel.	Mayer.		
1724	Home.		Klopstock.		
1724	Ferguson (A.).		Kant.		
1725	Mason.	Montucla.			
1726	Black.	Millot.	Pfeffel.		
1728	Hunter.				
1729	Goldsmith.	Le Brun.	Lessing.		
1729	Cook.		Mendelsohn.	Parini.	
1730	Burke.	Florian.			
1731	Cowper.				
1731	Churchill.				
1731	Cavendish (H.).				
1732	Goldsmith (O.).	Thomas.			
1732		Beaumarchais.	Adelung.		
1732		Lalande.			
1733	Priestley.		Wieland.		
1733	Robertson		Niebuhr (Carstens).		
1734	Mitford.				
1734	Warton.				
1735	Beattie.				
1736	Tooke.	Lagrange.	Rosenmueller.		

Years.	Engl. and Amer.	French.	German.	It., Sp., & P.	L. & N. C.
A.C.					
1736	Patr'k Henry.*				
1737	Gibbon.			Galvani.	
1738		De Lile.			
1739		La Harpe.	Fuseli.		
1740		La Perouse.			
1741		Lavater.			
1743	Paley.	Lavoisier.	Jacobi.		Ewald.
1744	Holcroft.		Herder.		
1745		Bonstetten.		Volta.	
1746		Mad. de Genlis.			
1746	Sir Wm. Jones.	Maury.			
1746	Shaw.	Dupaty.			
1746	Russell.				
1746	Cox.				
1746	Northcote.				
1747	Parr (Samuel).	Rochefoucault.			
1748	Fox (C. J.).		Hoeltz.		
1748		Ginguené.	Buerger.		
1748			Tenneman.		
1749	Bentham.	La Place.	Goethe.	Alfieri.	
1750	Trumbull.*		Werner.	Fabroni.	
1751	Sheridan.				
1752	Roscoe.	Mad. Campan.	Eichhorn.	Yriarte.	
1752	Belsham.				
1752	Rumford.				
1752	Freneau.*		Dohm.		
1752	Dwight.*	Legendre.	Mueller (John von).	Filangieri.	
1753	Stewart.			Monte Vincenzo.	
1753	Humphrey.*				
1754	Crabbe.	Mad. Roland.			
1755	Barlow.*				
1755	Flaxman.				
1756				Chladni.	
1757				Canova.	
1758	Pinkerton.		Gall.		
1758	Fisher Ames.				
1758	Hannah More.				
1759	Burns.	Andrieux.	Schiller.		
1759	Pitt.	Ducis.			
1759	Wilberforce.				
1760	Wraxall.		Heeren.		
1760	Hazlitt.				
1760	Godwin.				
1761			Kotzebue.		
1762	Rogers.		Fichte.		
1763			Jean Paul F. Richter.		
1764	Pinkney.*	Chenier.			
1765	Sir J. Mackintosh.				
1766	Capt. Beaver.	Mad. de Staël.			
1766		Arnault.	Bouterweck.	Botta.	
1766	Leslie.				

Years.	Engl. and Amer.	French.	German.	It., Sp.,& P.	L. and N. Coun.
A.C.					
1766	Wollaston.				
1767		Daru	Wachler.		
1767	Astley Cooper.	Benj. de Constant.			
1768	Bruce.				
1769		Picard.	Humboldt.		
1769		Chateaubriand.			
1770		De Gerando.	Krug.		
1770	Canning.	Le Mercier.			
1770	Wordsworth.				
1771	Scott.		Fellenberg.		
1771	Montgomery.				
1772	Coleridge.				
1773			Tieck.	Sismondi.	
1773	Paine.*		Frier.		
1774	Southey.		Mohs.		
1774	Hall.				
1775	Lamb.	Michaud.	Rotteck.		
1775			Schelling.		
1775			Feuerbach.		
1776	Wakefield.		Schlosser.		
1777	Campbell.		Gauss.		
1778	Brown.	De Candolle.			
1778	Godwin.				
1779	Wash. Alston.*		Niebuhr (B. G.).		
1779	Sir H. Davy.				Berzelius.
1779	Brougham.	Champollion (J. J.).			
1780	Moore.	De Béranger.			Krusenstiern.
1780	Lingard.			Cicognara.	Oersted.
1781			Reaumer.		
1784	Cunningham.		Menzel.		
1785	H. K. White.				
1785	Pierpont.*				
1787	Dana.*	Guizot.	Uhland.		
1788	Byron.				
1789	Wilson.		Neander.		
1789	Hillhouse.*				
1789	Mackenzie.				
1790		Champollion (Y. F.).			
1790	Parry.	Mad. La Roche Jacquelin.			
1790		Lacretelle.			
1791	Milman.				
1791	Sprague.*	Villemain.	Koerner.		
1791		Victor Cousin.			
1792	Shelley.				
1792	Sands.*				
1793	Mrs. Hemans.				
1793	Clare.				
1794	Wilcox.*				
1794	Bryant.*				

Years.	Engl. and Amer.	French.	German.	It., Span., & Por.	L. & N. Coun
A.C.					
1795	Drake.*				
1796	Keats.				
1796	Halleck.*				
1797	Godman (J. D.)		Heine.		
1797			Müller (Charles Ottfried).		
1798	Hood.				
1799	Pollok.				

Those marked * are American.

INDEX

OF THE WORKS MENTIONED IN THE HANDBOOK

INDEX.

A.

Page

Abelard 102
Abercrombie's Inquiry concerning the Intellectual Powers. 257
Abercrombie's do. do. Moral Feelings 258
Adams's, Mrs. John, Letters .. 237
Adams's, John, Letters 237
Adams's Defence of the American Constitution........... 251
Adams's Roman Antiquities .. 208
Addison...................... 76
Adelung...................... 136
Advancement of Learning.... 260
Æschylus.................... 66
Æschylus translated 274
Æschines.................... 160
Agricultural Society, series of publications of.............. 288
Aikin, Miss, Court of Queen Elizabeth 214
Aikin, British Poets 279
Akenside.................... 78
Alberti, Leo Baptista 162
Albertus Magnus 102
Alexander, Manufacture of Iron 290
Alexander the Norman....... 70
Alexandro Magno, El Poema de......................... 72
Alexander on Canons of Scripture 291
Alfieri 95
Alighieri, Dante.............. 71
Alison's History of Europe 213
Allston, Washington.......... 84
Ambrose.................... 183
American Almanac........... 297
American Journal of Education........................ 297
American Jurist.............. 297
American Museum........... 297
American Review or Metropolitan 296
Ames, Fisher................ 178
Amherst's Embassy to China.. 240
Anacreon 66
Andrieux 90
Andronicus Livius 67

Page

Anselm, St.................. 101
Anson's Voyage............. 241
Afer, P. Terentius............ 67
Appianus 122
Aquinas 102
Arago, Eloge of Watt........ 230
Arc, Joan, Life of........... 144
Archilochus 65
Archimedes.................. 111
Ariosto 94
Ariosto, Orlando Furioso, translation of.................... 280
Aristarchus.................. 111
Aristophanes................. 66
Aristophanes translated....... 275
Aristotle, Ethics and Politics.. 259
Aristotle 97
Armstrong on Agriculture 287
Armstrong................... 77
Arminius.................... 187
Arnauld 108
Arnault...................... 90
Arnold's Lectures............ 209
Arnott's Physics 281
Ashmole, Hist. of the Order of the Garter.................. 145
Athanasius 100, 182
Athenæum, London 296
Audubon's American Birds... 285
Augustin, Saint 100, 183
Averroes.................... 183

B.

Bacon, Francis........... 103, 126
Bacon, Roger 112
Bacon's and Locke's Essays .. 260
Baillie, Joanna............... 82
Balzac 165
Bancroft's History of the U. S.. 222
Barclay, Alexander........... 72
Barlow, Joel 84
Baronius..................... 135
Barrow's Travels in China.... 240
Barrow's Austria............. 245
Barrow's Works 295
Barrow's Life of Peter the Great....................... 229
Barthelemie, Travels of Anacharsis 242

Page
Basnage 190
Bates's Works 295
Baxter's Life and Times 232
Baxter 170, 295
Bayle 170
Baylies' Hist. Memoir of New-Plymouth 224
Bayly 83
Beattie 79
Beaumarchais 99
Beaumont and Fletcher 74
Beausobre 190
Beaver, Captain, Life of 148
Beche, de la, Compend on Geology 283
Beck, Chemistry 284
Beck, Medical Jurisprudence .. 286
Bede 124
Belknap's New-Hampshire ... 223
Belknap's Am. Biography 234
Bell 118
Bellarmin 186
Bellay, du 140
Belsham 129
Belzoni's Tour to Egypt 154
Bembo, Cardinal 163
Bentham 105
Bentivoglio's Letters 165
Bentivoglio, Hist. of the Wars of Flanders 135
Béranger 91
Berkeley 103
Berzelius 119
Berverley's Hist. of Virginia... 224
Beza 186
Bigelow, Elements of Technology 289
Bigelow's Travels 157
Biographie Universelle 149
Black 117
Black Hawk, Life of 146
Blackwood's Magazine 297
Blair 175
Blair's Lectures 267
Blake's Biographical Dictionary 149, 233
Blunt's Hist. of the Reformation 212
Blunt's Amer. Coast Pilot 290
Boccacio 71, 94, 161
Boëckh 203
Boëckh, Public Economy of Athens 203
Boethius 101
Boileau 89
Bolingbroke's Letters on History 172
Bonaventura 102
Bonstetten 110

Page
Bonnycastle's Canada 245
Bonnycastle's Newfoundland . 245
Boscan 95
Bossuet, Universal History 197
Bossuet 167, 189
Boston Medical and Surgical Journal 297
Boswell's Life of Johnson 230
Botta, Hist. of the Am. Revolution 222
Bougainville's Voyages 152
Bourdaloue 167
Bourrienne 143
Bouterweck 138
Bowditch, Practical Navigator. 290
Boyle 113
Bracciolini 161
Bradford's American Antiquities 220
Bradley 115
Brahe, Tycho 112
Brainard, John 86
Brainard, Life of 235
Brande's Encyclopædia 298
Brant, Joseph, Life of 237
Brantome 140
Brewster's Martyrs of Science. 230
Brewster s Life of Newton ... 230
Bridaine 173
Bridgewater Treatises 286
Brookes's Travels to the North Cape 155
Brougham's Speeches 273
Brougham, Lord, Brit. Statesman 234
Brown 106
Brown's Mental Philosophy ... 257
Brown's Julia of Baiæ 250
Browne's, Sir Thomas, Religio Medici 276
Bruce's Travels in Egypt 242
Bruni, Leonardo 161
Bryant, Selections 279
Bryant's Poems 85, 279
Brydge's Imaginative Biography 149
Buchanan 126
Buchanan's Journey 155
Buckingham's America 249
Buel's Farmer's Instructer 287
Buerger 93
Buffon, Natural History 285
Bull 189
Bulwer's England and the English 249
Bulwer's France 250
Burckhardt 153
Burke, Prior's Life of 147

Page
Burke 176
Burke's Works 273
Burnet's History of the Reformation 212
Burnet's History of his own Times 141
Burnet's Lives 226
Burnet on the Thirty-nine Articles 293
Burns 80, 277
Burton's Anatomy of Melancholy 166, 263
Busch 139
Butler's Classical Geography .. 239
Butler's Kentucky 225
Butler's Analogy 104, 191, 260
Byron 81

C.

Cæsar 120, 206
Cæsar, translation of 206
Cæsar's Commentaries 139
Calamy 141
Calcottt, Mrs., History of Spain 214
Caldcleugh, Travels of 155
Calderon 96, 166
Callimachus 66
Calvin 185
Calvin's Institutions 293
Camden 126
Camoens 95
Campan, Madame de 142
Campbell 80, 278
Campbell's Annals of Tryon County 223
Campbell's Four Gospels 292
Campbell's Lectures on Theology 292
Campbell's Philosophy of Rhetoric 267
Canning's Speeches 180, 273
Canova, Life of 148
Capefigue 133
Carpin, Lope Felix de Vega ... 96
Carus, T. Lucretius 68
Carey's Political Economy 253
Cary's Dante 280
Casas, Las 140
Cassius, Dion 123
Castelneau 142
Catlin's Indians 245
Catullus 68
Cave's Primitive Christianity .. 207
Cave's Lives of the Apostles . 226
Caylus, Count de 131
Cecil, Life of 145
Cecil's Remains 266
Celsius 115

Page
Centuriæ Magdeburgenses 136
Cervantes 96, 166
Chalmers's Moral and Intellectual Constitution 261
Champollion 154
Channing's Prose Works .. 179, 272
Chapman, George 73
Chaptal's Chemistry 284
Charlevoix 151
Chateaubriand 91
Chateaubriand's Travels . 154, 242
Chatham 174
Chaucer 72, 275
Chaucer, Life of 144
Chemistry 45
Chenier 89
Cherbourg, Lord 126, 141
Chesterfield 174
Chiabrera 95
Chillingworth 188
Christ, Life of 225
Chronicles of the Pilgrims 220
Chrysostom 101, 182
Churchill 79
Churton, History of the Early English Church 210
Cicero 99
Cicero, Life of 143
Cicero's Offices, translated 263
Cicero's Orations, do. 269
Cicero's Epistles, do. 269
Cicero on Old Age, do. 263
Cicero on Friendship, do. 264
Cicero on Oratory, do. 269
Cicognara's Sculpture 148
Cid, el Poema de 72
Clare 82
Clarendon 127
Clarendon's Rebellion 213
Clarke, E. D., Life and Remains of 233
Clarke, Samuel 103, 191
Clarke, Willis G. 86
Clement of Alexandria ... 100, 181
Clement of Rome 182
Cleaveland's Mineralogy 284
Cleveland, Voyages of 247
Clinton, De Witt, Life of 236
Cocceius 189
Cochrane, Travels of 156
Coinsi 70
Coleridge 80, 180
Coleridge's Aid to Reflection .. 285
Coleridge's Friend 258
Coleridge's Table-Talk 258
Collard, Royer 110
Collections of Hist. Society of New-York 221

Page

Collections of Hist. Society of Massachusetts 221
Collins 78
Columbus 151
Combe's Constitution of Man .. 261
Combe's Travels in the United States 249
Combe's Elements of Phrenology 262
Combe's do. of Physiology 286
Comines 129
Condillac 109
Congreve 76, 170
Constant 110
Constitution of the U. S. 251
Cook's Voyages 239
Copernicus 112
Corneille, Pierre 88, 171
Cornwall, Barry, Life and Works of Johnson 146
Correspondence of Schiller and Goethe 179
Course of Legal Study 256
Cousin 110
Cousin's Psychology 256
Cowley 74, 169
Cowper 79
Cox's History of Austria 128
Coxe's Travels 158
Crabbe 79
Crabb's Synonymes 267
Cranmer 185
Crebillon 89
Cressy's Bridge-building 290
Crichton's Arabia 217
Croly 81
Ctesias 120
Cudworth 103
Cullen 116
Cunningham's Lives of Painters and Sculptors 228
Cunningham 80
Curtius 121
Cuvier, Life of 232
Cuvier's Animal Kingdom 285

D.

Daille 188
D'Alembert 116
Damascus, John of 101
Dampier's Voyages 240
Dana, Richard H. 84
Dana's Poems and Prose Works 273
Daniel, Samuel 73
Daniell's Physics 282
D'Anquetil, History of France 215
Dante, translation of 280
Daru 132

Page

D'Aubigny's History of the Reformation 212
Davidson, Miss, Remains of ... 279
Davidson, the sisters, Misses .. 87
Davila 135
Davis, History of China 218
Davy, Sir H., his Life 149
Davy, Sir H., Consolation in Travel 261
Davy, Sir H., Salmonia 261
Davy, Elements of Philosophy 284
Dean's Philosophy of Life 287
Debates in the Convention of New-York 252
Debates in the Convention of Massachusetts 252
Debates in the Convention of Virginia 252
De Candolle 119
De Foe's Robinson Crusoe 174
De Gerando 110
De Gerando on Self-education . 262
Delile 90
Delolme on British Constitution 255
Democratic Review 296
Demosthenes 160
Demosthenes, Orations of, translation 269
Denmark, Sweden, and Norway 215
Dennie's Works 273
Des Cartes 108, 114
Deshoulières, Madame 89
Dick, Celestial Scenery 286
Dick, Sidereal Heavens 286
Diderot 90, 109
Diodorus 122, 150
Diogenes Laertius 144
Dionysius 121
Distinguished Females 234
Dobson's Life of Petrarch 227
Dobrezhoffer 151
Dohm's Memoirs 152
Donatus ....
Downing's Landscape Gardening 288
Downing's Cottage Residences 288
Drake 151
Drake, Joseph R. 85
Drake's Indians 220
Drayton 73
Drew, Samuel, Life of 231
Drummond 74
Dryden 75, 168, 276
Dryden's translation of Virgil. 275
Duchesne 130
Ducis 90

Page
Duclos 142
Duer's Lectures on the Constitution of the United States . . . 251
Dufresny 88, 139
Dumas, Progress of Democracy 215
Duncan's Seasons 266
Dunlap's Hist. of New-York . . 223
Dupaty 152
Dupin, Voyages in Great Britain 154
Dupin's Ecclesiastical History . 190
Dwight's Theology 83, 294
Dwight, H. C., Travels in Germany 157
Dwight, Travels in New-England 156

E.

Ecclesiastical History 48
Edgeworth, Miss, Moral and Popular Tales 264
Edinburgh Encyclopædia 298
Education, Journal of 298
Edwards 104
Eginhardt 124
Eichhorn 137
Elementary Course for Candidates for the Ministry 48
Elementary Authors for the Student and young Practitioner in Medicine 50
Elementary Course for the study of Law 53
Ellis, Mrs. 265
Empiricus, Sextus 98
Encyclopædia Americana 298
Encyclopædia of Religious Knowledge 299
Ennius, Quintius 67
Epinay, Madame d' 142
Episcopius 187
Erasmus 162, 185
Erasmus, Life of 228
Eratosthenes 150
Erigena 101
Erskine 295
Eschenburg's Manual of Classical Literature 267
Euclid 111
Euler 115
Euler's Letters 282
Euripides 66
Euripides, translated 274
Eusebius, Ecclesiastical History 207
Eusebius 100, 181
Eustace 154
Eutropius 124

Page
Evans, Millwright's Guide 290
Evangelists and Acts of the Apostles 206
Evelyn 168
Everett's Works 273
Evremond, St. 170
Ewbank's Hydraulics 298

F.

Fairfax 74
Fanshaw 74
Federalist, the 251
Feltham's Resolves 271
Fénélon's Telemaque 89, 171
Fénélon's Ancient Philosophers 262
Ferguson's Rom. Republic 127, 204
Ferguson on Civil Society 254
Ferguson's Lectures 282
Fessenden's Agriculture 287
Fichte 107
Ficinus 184
Fielding 77, 179
Fischart 91
Fisher's Physics 281
Fisk's Travels in Europe 243
Flaccus, Quintius Horatius 68
Flaxman's Lectures on Sculpture 270
Flechier 167
Fletcher, History of Poland . . . 216
Florian, History of the Moors . 213
Florus 123
Fontenelle 89, 175
Foreign Quarterly Review 297
Forrey's, de, Climate of the United States 247
Forster's Statesmen of the Commonwealth 229
Forsyth's Italy 243
Fox's History of James II. 214
Fox's Book of Martyrs 145, 229
Fox's Speeches 273
Francis I. 87
Franklin 115
Franklin Journal 297
Franklin's Life and Writings 238, 253
Franklin's Expedition 157
Frazer's Persia 217
Freneau, Philip 83
Frier 107
Frobisher 151
Froissart 70, 129
Fuller, Thomas, Worthies of England 127
Fulton, Robert, Life of 238
Fuseli's Lectures 270
Fuseli, Life of 147

G.

Page
Galen........................ 112
Galileo 113
Galileo's Letters 165
Gangora 96
Garrick 78
Gasparin of Barziza 161
Gassendi 108
Gauss 118
Gay 76, 172
Gellert 92
Genlis, Madame de 177
Gibbon's Decline and Fall of the Roman Empire 128, 205
Gill's Body of Divinity 294
Gillie's Ancient Greece 201
Gleim 92
Gliddon's Ancient Egypt 200
Godwin's Caleb Williams 178
Goethe 93, 178
Goguet 131
Goldsmith's Prose Works 273
Goldsmith 78, 128, 276
Goldsmith's Animated Nature. 285
Goldsmith's Greece 200
Goldsmith's Rome 203
Good's Book of Nature 281
Gordon's History of New-Jersey 224
Gorton's Biographical Dictionary 149, 233
Gower 72
Graham's History of North America 222
Grant's, Mrs., Memoirs 237
Grant's Nestorians 248
Gray's Letters 175
Gray's Botanical Text-Book .. 285
Greenleaf's Course of Legal Study 56
Greenleaf's Survey of Maine.. 223
Greppo on Hieroglyphics 209
Griscom's Animal Mechanism. 286
Griswold's American Poets ... 279
Grotius 187
Guicciardini 134
Guizot's History of Civilization 209

H.

Hagedorn 92
Hagi Baba of Ispahan 157
Hale, Sir Matthew 188
Hale's History of the United States 220
Hale's Contemplations 259
Hall 191
Hall, Voyage to the Eastern Seas 155
Hall's Satires 73
Page
Hallam's History of the Middle Ages 210
Hallam's History of Literature 219
Hallam's Constitutional History of England 129
Halleck 85
Halleck, Fitz-Greene, Selections 279
Haller 116
Halley 115
Hamilton, Life of 236
Hammond 189
Hammond's Political History of New-York 222
Hardy 88
Harrington's Oceana 255
Harris 151
Hartley 104
Harvey 113
Hawkins's Voyages. 240
Haynes, Lemuel, Life of 237
Hayward's Physiology 286
Haywood's Tennessee 225
Hazlitt's Essays 177, 268
Head's Travels 157
Heber, Bishop, Life of 231
Heber's India 248
Hecatæus 119
Heeren's Ancient History 199
Heeren's Researches 203
Heeren's Greece 203
Heeren's Political System of Europe 211
Heldenbuch 71
Heliodorus 161
Helvetius 109
Hemans, Mrs., Life and Writings 233
Hemans, Mrs., Poems 82, 278
Henderson's Tour to Iceland .. 154
Hengstenberg's Christology ... 292
Henry's History of England ... 127
Henry 190
Henry, Patrick 177
Herbert's Country Parson. 164, 266
Herder 92, 136
Herodianus 123
Herodotus 120, 201
Herodotus, translation of 201
Herrick 74
Herschel's, Sir J., Discourses.. 282
Herschel's Astronomy 282
Hesiod 65
Heyne 94
Hillhouse's Works 84, 273
Hippocrates 112
Hippolyte 88
History of Rome (Lardner's Cabinet Cyclopædia) 204

Page
Hitchcock's Geology 283
Hobbes........................ 103
Hoelty........................ 93
Holcroft...................... 79
Holmes, Oliver 86
Home.......................... 78
Home Education 263
Homer......................... 65
Hood.......................... 82
Hooke 114
Hooker's Ecclesiastical Polity. 186
Hooper 186
Horace, translated............ 275
Horne's Introduction.......... 291
Horsley....................... 191
Howe's Works 293
Howitt, Mary.............. 82, 265
Howitt, Rural Life in England 247
Howitt, Rural Life in Germany 247
Huber, on Bees................ 282
Hugo.......................... 91
Humboldt's Narrative 243
Humboldt on New Spain 154
Hume 104
Hume, History of England 127, 211
Humphrey, David 84
Hunter........................ 116
Hunter's Sacred Biography.... 233
Hurd 173
Hutchinson 105
Hutchinson's Massachusetts... 221
Huygens 114

I.

Iamblichus.................... 98
Idler, the 271
Ignatius...................... 181
Insect Architecture.......... 285
Irenæus................... 99, 182
Irving's Astoria 249
Irving's Life of Goldsmith 233
Irving's Life of Columbus 221
Irving's Conquest of Grenada. 214
Isocrates..................... 160
Israeli, Amenities of Literature 272
Israeli, Curiosities of Literature 272

J.

Jacobi........................ 107
James II., Life of............ 146
James's History of Chivalry .. 210
James's Naval History of England 212
Jameson's and Leslie's Travels 157
Jameson's, Mrs., Female Sovereigns 232
Jameson's, Mrs., Female Characters of Shakspeare 268

Page
Jay, John, Life of............ 235
Jefferson's Life and Writings 236, 254
Jerome 183
Jewell 186
Jodelle 37
Jonson, Ben, his Works....... 73
Johnson, Samuel 77
Johnson, Lives of Britsh Poets 147, 230
Johnson, Dr., Excursions...... 158
Jones, Sir William, Life of.... 147
Josephus...................... 199
Jouffroy...................... 111
Jussieu 115
Justin the Martyr 183
Justinus...................... 123
Juvenal....................... 70

K.

Kæmpfer 151
Kalm's Travels 152
Kames's, Lord, Criticism...... 266
Kane's Chemistry 284
Kant.......................... 106
Keats..................... 82, 278
Kempis, Thomas à 184
Kennicott..................... 191
Kent's Commentaries......... 252
Kepler........................ 113
Kirby, Entomology of North America 284
Klaproth, Historical Tables of Asia 156
Kleist........................ 92
Klopstock..................... 92
Knapp's Theology 292
Knickerbocker 296
Knox, M'Crie's Life of.... 144, 228
Körner 94
Kotzebue 93
Kotzebue's Narrative of a Voyage 156
King.......................... 197
Krusenstern.................. 153
Kuzzilbach, the 158

L.

Laborde's Journey to Mount Sinai 248
La Bruyère 168
Lacretelle.................... 132
Lactantius.................... 100
La Fontaine's Fables .. 88, 167, 280
La Fontaine, a German novelist 178
Lagrange...................... 117
La Harpe...................... 177

Page
Laing's Tour in Sweden 244
Laing's Residence in Norway . 244
Laing's Visit to Holland 244
Lalande 117
Lamartine 91
Lamb's Works 80, 272
Landers, Journal of the....... 242
Landon, Miss L. E. 82, 278
Landor's Imaginary Conversations 149
Langland, Robert 72
La Perouse, Voyages 153, 241
La Perouse 87
Laplace 117
Lardner's Mechanics 283
Latrobe's Mexico............. 244
Laud 187
Lavater 110
Lavoisier 117
Lawyer, the 265
Le Bas, Life of Wickliffe 226
Le Bas, Life of Cranmer...... 226
Le Bas, Life of Laud......... 226
Le Brun 90
Lee 75
Lee, Mrs., Old Painters 228
Lee's Elements of Geology 283
Lee's Memoirs of the Southern War 225
Leland's Deistical Writers.... 294
Le Mercier 91
Legendre..................... 119
Leibnitz 106, 114
Leighton's Works 295
Leslie 118
Leslie on Deism 294
Lessing 92, 176
Letters from Abroad 243
Letters from Palmyra and Zenobia 250
Lewis and Clarke's Travels... 243
L'Hôpital 115
Lieber's Political Ethics 255
Lieber's Hermeneutics 255
Lieber's Labour and Property. 255
Liebig's Organic Chemistry ... 284
Liebig's Agricultural Chemistry 288
Life in Mexico 244
Lindley's Theory of Horticulture 288
Lingard, History of England.. 211
Listener, the 265
Lives of Early Navigators 232
Lives of Eminent Men........ 233
Livingston, William, Life of... 237
Livingston, Rev. John, Life of. 237
Livy 131
Livy, translation of 205

Page
Lobeyra, Vasco de............ 163
Locke 103, 256
Lockhart, Life of Burns 231
Lockhart, Life of Scott....... 231
Lockhart, Life of Napoleon... 232
Lockhart, Life of Valerius.... 250
Lombard, Peter 102
London Spectator 298
Longinus, translation of 270
Loudon's Encyclopædia of Agriculture 287
Loudon's Encyclopædia of Gardening 288
Lowe's Elements of Agriculture 288
Lowell Offering 264
Lucilius 67
Luther 91, 185
Luther and his Times......... 228
Lyell, Elements of Geology... 283
Lyell, Principles of Geology... 283
Lyman's Diplomacy of the United States.................. 222
Lysias 159
Lyttleton 127

M.

Mably 131
Macartney's Embassy to China 240
Macauley's Miscellany........ 272
Machiavel 94, 134, 164
Mackintosh 106
Madden's United Irishmen.... 229
Madison Papers 251
Mahan's Civil Engineering.... 289
Mohammed, Life of 234
Mackenzie's Voyage 153
Malcolm's Memoirs of Central India 157, 248
Malcolm's Memoirs of British India 217
Malebranche 108
Malherbe.................... 87
Malmesbury, William of...... 125
Malte Brun, Universal Geography 239
Mandeville's Voyages 150
Manier's Journey through Persia........................ 148
Manilius, Marcus 69
Manilius, Paulus............. 163
Mantell's Wonders of Geology 283
Marbois, History of Louisiana. 225
Marcellinus, Ammianus....... 123
Margaret of Valois 87, 140
Marlborough, Duke of, his Life 146
Marmontel 142
Maro, Publius Virgilius 68

Page
Marot........................ 87
Marsh's Lectures............. 292
Marshall's Life of Washington 235
Martialis, M. Valerius......... 69
Martyn, Henry, Life of........ 230
Marytr, Justin................ 99
Mason.................... 78, 180
Massillon..................... 171
Mathematical and Physical Sciences.................... 44
Mather's Magnalia............ 221
Matheson and Reed's Travels. 158
Maury, Principles of Eloquence 268
Maury...................... 177
Maximus, Valerius........... 122
Mayer...................... 116
M'Call's Georgia............. 224
Mackintosh, Sir James, Life of 231
Mackintosh, History of England 211
Mackintosh, Progress of Ethical Philosophy................ 260
M'Culloch's Dictionary....... 290
M'Culloch's Universal Gazetteer....................... 239
M'Culloch's Statistics of British Empire.................... 211
Mediæval History............. 35
Medici, Lorenzo di............ 94
Medicine, Authors on......... 50
Melancthon.............. 163, 185
Mellen, Grenville............ 86
Memoirs of Duchess d'Abrantes 234
Memoirs of American Missionaries....................... 238
Mendelsohn................. 107
Mendoza................. 95, 135
Menzel..................... 139
Messages of the Presidents of the United States........... 252
Metastasio.................. 95
Michaud.................... 132
Michelet.................... 210
Mignet..................... 133
Millington, Civil Engineering.. 290
Millot...................... 132
Milman..................... 81
Milman, History of Christianity 207
Milner's Ecclesiastical History. 208
Milton's Prose Writings....... 260
Milton's Poems........... 74, 276
Mineralogy and Geology...... 45
Minnesingers................ 71
Mirandola.................. 134
Mirror for Magistrates........ 145
Mitford's Greece......... 128, 200
Mitylene, Hellanicus of....... 120
Moffat's Missionary Tour in Southern Africa........... 246
Page
Mohr....................... 118
Molière.................. 88, 173
Monstrelet.................. 130
Montagu, Lady............... 172
Montagu's Selections......... 271
Montaigne............... 108, 164
Montesquieu, Spirit of the Law 109, 254
Montfaucon.................. 130
Montgomery.................. 80
Montgomery's Lectures....... 268
Montluc.................... 140
Moore.................. 80, 278
Moore's View of Society in France in 1771............ 242
More's, Mrs. H., Works....... 264
Morrell's Voyages............ 241
Morris, Gouverneur, Life of.... 236
Morrison, Horæ Sinicæ........ 154
Morton's New-England's Memorial................... 220
Mosheim, Ecclesiastical History 207
Müller, Johannes von, Universal History........... 137, 198
Muratori.................... 135
Murray, Hist. of British America....................... 218
Murray, Encyclopædia of Geography..................... 239
Mutiny of the Bounty........ 249

N.

Napier..................... 113
Napoleon's Court and Camp.. 234
Napoleon, History of......... 232
Naso, P. Ovidius............. 69
Natural Hist. of North America....................... 46
Neal's History of the Puritans. 214
Neander's Ecclesiastical History...................... 292
Nepos, Cornelius............. 121
Newcome, Harmony of the Gospels....................... 295
Newman's Rhetoric.......... 268
Newton..................... 114
Nichols, Literary Anecdotes... 147
Niebelungenlied.............. 71
Niebuhr, History of Rome.... 204
Niebuhr, Description of Arabia 153
Niles's Register............. 297
Norman's Yucatan........... 247
Northern Light.............. 296
Nott's Counsels to Young Men 260

O.

Occam...................... 184
Old Humphrey's Addresses... 266

Page
Old Humphrey's Thoughts.... 266
Olin, Dr., Travels 245
Olmstead's Astronomy........ 283
Opitz 91
Oriental Translation Fund 159
Origen 100, 181
Orleans, Charles, Duke of..... 87
Orpheus 65
Otis, James, Life of........... 235
Ottfried, Harmony of the Gospels 70
Otway........................ 75
Owen, Works of 260, 293

P.

Paine, Robert Treat 84
Paley........................ 105
Paley's Horæ Paulinæ 291
Paley's Evidences of Christianity 291
Paley's Natural Theology..... 291
Paley's Moral Philosophy 258
Pambour on Locomotion 289
Pambour on Steam-Engine 289
Parry's Voyages.............. 240
Pascal 113
Pascal's Thoughts............ 259
Pascal's Letters 168
Paterculus, Velleius 121
Pausanias.................... 150
Paxton's Illustrations 294
Payne's Elements of Mental and Moral Philosophy 257
Pearson on the Creed......... 293
Pellico, Sylvio, Memoirs of.... 233
Penny Cyclopædia............ 299
Penny Magazine.............. 297
Pepys's Memoirs.............. 141
Percival, James G. 85
Perrault 169
Perron 187
Perry, Commodore, Life of.... 238
Petavius..................... 188
Petrarch, Life of.............. 144
Petrarch 71
Petrarch, translation of........ 280
Pfeffel 136
Phædrus 69
Pherecydes 119
Philips's Recollections of Curran 230
Philips, the Poet.............. 76
Philips's Political Economy.... 253
Philosophical Miscellanies..... 263
Philostratus 143
Picard 90
Pierpont, John................ 84
Pilgrim's Progress............. 259
Pindar....................... [illegible]
Pindar, translated 275
Pinkerton, Collection of Voyages 152
Pinkney 179
Pistoria, Cino da.............. 71
Pitkin's History of the United States 221
Pitkin's Statistics 255
Pitt, William, Speeches... 178, 273
Pitt, his Life 147
Platina....................... 134
Plato......................... 97
Plautus, M. Accius............ 67
Playfair's Preliminary Discourses 281
Pliny 160
Pliny, Letters of, translated.... 269
Plotinus...................... 98
Plutarch...................... 88
Plutarch's Lives........ . 122, 226
Poetischer Hausschatz 94
Poggio's History of Florence .. 133
Politian.................. 34, 162
Pollok's Course of Time ... 82, 278
Polo, Marco 150
Polybius..................... 120
Polybius, translation of........ 202
Pope..................... 76, 276
Pope's Letters................ 172
Pope's translation of Homer... 274
Porphyry..................... 98
Porter, Ker, Travels of........ 155
Porteus 191
Portraits of Illustrious Persons of Great Britain 149
Potter, A., Application of Science to the Arts 289
Potter, Grecian Antiquities.... 203
Potter, A., Political Economy.. 253
Prescott's Conquest of Mexico. 244
Prescott's History of Ferdinand and Isabella 214
Prideaux's Connections 199
Priestley...................... 105
Priestley, Lectures on History. 209
Principles of Morals and Legislation....................... 254
Prior 75
Pritchard's Physical History... 286
Proclus 99
Procter....................... 82
Propertius, Sextus Aurelius ... 68
Prudentius, Aurelius 70
Proud, History of Pennsylvania 224
Ptolemy 112
Public Works in the United States...................... 245

Page
Publications of the British Society for the Diffusion of Useful Knowledge ... 287
Puffendorf ... 136
Pythagoras ... 97, 111

Q.

Quill, American Mechanic ... 290
Quincy, Josiah, Life of ... 235
Quintilian ... 160
Quintilian's Institutes, translated ... 269

R.

Rabelais ... 163
Racine ... 88, 171
Raimond de Sebonde ... 184
Raleigh, Sir Walter ... 126
Rambler, the ... 271
Ramsay's South Carolina ... 224
Rapin ... 131
Rauch's Psychology ... 257
Raumer ... 138
Recreations of Christopher North ... 272
Red Jacket, Life of ... 237
Rees's Encyclopædia ... 298
Regnard ... 132
Regnier ... 88
Reid ... 104, 256
Remusat ... 153
Renwick's Mechanics ... 283
Retz, de, Memoirs of ... 227
Reviews, Edinburgh and London Quarterly, North American ... 296
Reynard ... 89
Reynolds's, Sir Joshua, Discourses ... 268
Reynolds, Exploring Expedition 249
Rhodius, Apollonius ... 72
Richardson, Samuel ... 172
Richter, Jean Paul ... 93, 179
Ridley ... 186
Ridley, Life of ... 145
Ritter, Geography ... 159
Roberts, Manufacture of Iron . 290
Roberts, Emma, Memoirs of the Rival Houses of York and Lancaster ... 149
Roberts's Life of Hannah More 232
Robertson's History of Scotland and India ... 200, 212
Robertson's History of Charles V. ... 212
Robertson's History of America 212
Robinson's Researches in Palestine ... 248
Rochefoucault ... 141, 168

Page
Roche Jacqueline, Madame ... 143
Rockwell, Life at Sea ... 159, 248
Rogers ... 80, 277
Roland, Madame, Memoirs ... 143
Rollin's Ancient History ... 198
Rollin's Belles-Lettres ... 269
Roman History ... 34
Romilly's Memoirs ... 231
Roscellin ... 102
Roscoe, Lorenzo de Medici ... 227
Roscoe, Leo X., Life of ... 227
Rosenmüller ... 191
Ross's Voyages ... 240
Rotteck ... 138
Rousseau ... 89, 109, 176
Rowe ... 76
Ruinart, Lives of Martyrs ... 145
Rumford ... 118
Russel's History of Aleppo ... 152
Russell's Life of Cromwell ... 228
Russell's Barbary States ... 216
Russell's Egypt ... 216
Russell's America ... 128
Russell's Palestine ... 216
Russell's Principles of Statistical Inquiry ... 254
Russell's Modern Europe .. 128, 209
Russia and the Russians ... 247

S.

Sachs, Hans ... 91
Sackville ... 73
Sacred History of the Old Testament ... 198
Sacred Scriptures ... 291
Salisbury, John of ... 102
Sallust ... 121
Sallust, translation of ... 206
Salt, Voyage to Abyssinia ... 154
Sands ... 86
Sappho ... 65
Sarpi ... 135
Saturday Evening or Penny Magazine ... 297
Saturday Evening ... 263
Saurin ... 173
Schelling ... 108
Schiller ... 93, 137
Schlegel's Lectures on Philosophy of History ... 219
Schlegel's Lectures on History of Literature ... 219
Schlegel, A. W. ... 92
Schlösser ... 138
Schmidtmayer, Travels ... 155
Schmucker's Psychology ... 257
School and Schoolmaster ... 262
Schoolcraft's Expedition .. 156, 246

Page
Schwartz, Life of............. 239
Science of Government....... 256
Scoresby's Journal........ ... 156
Scotland and Ireland, History of 36
Scott's Life of Luther......... 228
Scott's Lives of the Novelists. 148
Scott, Sir Walter..... 80, 180, 277
Scotus, Duns................. 184
Scriptores Historiæ Augustæ... 123
Scuderi, Mademoiselle 165
Sedgwick, Miss, Means and Ends....................... 265
Sedgwick, Miss, Home........ 264
Sedgwick, Miss, Live and Let Live....................... 264
Sedgwick, Miss, Poor Rich Man, &c., &c............... 265
Sedgwick, Miss, Letters from Abroad..................... 243
Sedgwick, Mr. T., Public and Private Economy........... 253
Ségur, Count, Russian Expedition......................... 242
Selby's Illustrations of British Ornithology................ 286
Selden's Table-Talk.. ... 164, 270
Selections from Edinburgh Review...................... 274
Selections from Foreign Literature.................... ... 274
Seneca, Marcus..... 160
Seneca, Lucius Annæus ... 69, 99
Sepulchres of Etruria......... 246
Sevigné, Madame de.......... 167
Sforzozi, History of Italy...... 218
Shaftesbury.................. 103
Shakspeare 73, 277
Shaw 152
Shelley, Travels........... ... 81
Shenstone..................... 78
Sheppard's Mineralogy 284
Sheridan.............. ... 79 176
Sidney, Sir Philip, Arcadia 164, 270
Sidney, Discourses on Government...................... 255
Sigourney, Mrs.. 86
Silliman's Journal 296
Simon 190
Simpson, F.................. 116
Simpson, R.................. 115
Sinclair, Miss, Scotland and the Scotch 249
Sinclair, Miss, Shetland and the Shetlanders............ ... 249
Sismondi, History of Literature in South of Europe 218
Sismondi, History of the Italian Republics.............. 216
Sismondi, History of the Roman Empire................. 204
Smedley, History of Venice... 215
Smedley, Reformation in France 213
Smellie's Philosophy......... 282
Smith, Adam, Wealth of Nations 105, 252
Smith and Dwight's Researches 248
Smith, Dictionary of Antiquities 208
Smith, History of Education... 262
Smith, History of New-York.. 222
Smollett..................... 175
Smyth's Lectures on Modern History..................... 208
Socinus...................... 186
Socrates 97
Sophocles.................... 67
Sophocles, translated........ 275
South 189
Southern 75
Southern Literary Messenger.. 296
Southey, Robert...... 80, 181, 277
Southey, British Poets........ 279
Southey's History of Brazil ... 217
Southey's Life of Wesley 146
Southgate's Tour in Persia.... 248
Spain, Portugal, and Low Countries, History of........... 36
Sparks's Life and Writings of Washington............ ... 235
Sparks's American Biography . 235
Spectator, the........ 271
Speculative and Political Philosophy.................... 29, 40
Spenser.................. 73, 276
Sprague, Charles 85
Spurzheim on Education 262
Staël, Madame de 180, 246
Stanley, History of Philosophy. 146
Steele........................ 171
Stephens's Egypt............. 245
Stephens's Greece 245
Stephens's Central America... 244
Stephens's Travels in Yucatan 244
Sterne 175
Stewart, Dugald...... .. 105, 256
Stewart's Visit to the South Sea 241
Stewart's translation of Romans 292
Stewart's translation of Hebrews............ 292
Stewart's Voyages........... 241
Stillingfleet............... ... 190
Stobæus 99
Stoddard's Louisiana.... 225
Story, Commentaries on American Law................. 252
Strabo 150

Page
Strickland, Canals and Railroads 290
Strickland, Agnes, Queens of England ... 229
Strype ... 196
Stuart ... 128
Stuart, Mary ... 37
Suetonius ... 121
Suggestive Works ... 30
Sully, Memoirs of ... 227
Surrey, Earl of ... 72
Swift ... 75, 172

T.

Tacitus ... 122, 206
Tacitus, translated ... 206
Tanner's Canals and Railroads in the United States ... 245
Tasso ... 94
Tasso, Jerusalem Delivered ... 280
Tasso, Life of ... 145
Taylor, Jeremy, Works of ... 295
Taylor, Theory of Another Life 263
Taylor, Natural History of Society ... 219
Taylor, Natural History of Enthusiasm ... 263
Taylor, Natural History of Fanaticism ... 263
Taylor, Natural History of Spiritual Despotism ... 263
Temple, Sir William ... 146, 169
Tenneman ... 137
Tennyson ... 83
Tertullian ... 182
Thales ... 111
Thatcher's Indian Biography .. 238
Theocritus ... 66
Theology, General ... 46
Theology, Biblical ... 47
Theophrastus ... 98
Theopompus ... 120
Thiebault's Memoirs of Frederic the Great ... 229
Thierry, Augustin ... 133
Thierry, Amadée ... 133
Thiers, History of the French Revolution ... 133
Thirlwall's History of Greece. 202
Thomas ... 176
Thomson's Seasons ... 77
Thomson's History of Chemical Philosophy ... 281
Thorwaldsen ...
Thou, de ... 130
Thucydides ... 120, 201
Tibullus, Albius ... 68
Tieck ... 92
Tillotson ... 172

Page
Tocqueville, Democracy in America ... 252
Todd's Student's Manual ... 252
Tomlin's Theology ... 294
Tooke, Diversions of Purley ... 167, 267
Tournefort ... 114
Tours, Gregory of ... 124
Travels and Voyages ... 27
Troyes, Doëte de ... 70
Trumbull ... 83
Trumbull's Autobiography ... 236
Trumbull's History of Connecticut ... 224
Turgot, Life of ... 147
Turner, Sacred History ... 199
Turner's Edition of Planck's Introduction ... 292
Turner's Anglo-Saxons ... 210
Two Years before the Mast ... 241
Tyrius, Gulielmus ... 125
Tytler's Universal History ... 197

U.

Ulkland ... 94
Ulloa ... 152
United States, History of .. 38
Upham's Elements of Mental Philosophy ... 257
Ure's Dictionary of Arts, &c... 289
Ure's Philosophy of Manufactures ... 289
Usher ... 188
Utopia, Sir Thomas Moore's .. 163

V.

Valla, Laurentius ... 134, 162
Vancouver's Voyages ... 241
Van Schaack, Peter, Life of... 236
Vasari, Lives of Painters ... 145
Vega ... 95
Verplanck's Discourses ... 272
Verplanck's Essays ... 294
Vertot's Roman Revolution ... 204
Victor, Aurelius ... 124
Villani, Giovanni ... 125
Villani, Matteo ... 125
Villemain ... 132
Vincente ... 95
Vinci, Leonardo da ... 112
Volta ... 117
Voltaire ... 89, 109, 131, 174

W.

Wachler ... 138
Wachsmuth ... 139
Waddel's Voyages ... 241
Wakefield, Memoirs ... 143

Page
Waller 74
Walpole 142, 175
Walsingham 126
Walton's Lives 145, 226
Walton's Angler.............. 261
Warburton 173
Ware's Zenobia.............. 250
Ware's Probus 950
Ware's Julian 250
Washington Papers 253
Watson................. 127, 293
Watson's Anecdotes 142
Wayland's Political Economy. 253
Wayland's Elements of Moral Science..................... 259
Webster's Speeches 274
Werner 117
Westminster, Matthew of..... 125
Westminster Review 297
Whately's Rhetoric 267
Whately's Logic 257
Wheaton's Law of Nations... 252
White, Henry Kirke.......... 81
White, Natural History of Selborne 282
Whittier 86
Wickliffe................... 184
Wieland................. 92, 176
Wilberforce, Life of...... 148, 231
Wilbraham's Travels......... 158
Wilcox, Charles 85
Wilde's Tasso 228
Wilkes's Exploring Expedition 159
Wilkinson's Ancient Egypt 158, 200
Williams's Alexander the Great 233
Williams's History of Vermont 233
Williams's Missionary Enterprises 246

Page
Williams's History of North Carolina 224
Willis........................ 86
Willoughby 114
Wilson 81
Winthrop's Journal.......... 220
Wirt's British Spy.......... 181
Wirt's Life of Patrick Henry.. 239
Wolff....................... 106
Wollaston 118
Wolsey, Life of 144
Wood, Athenæ Oxonienses 146
Wordsworth, William 80, 277
Wordsworth's Ecclesiastical Biography.................... 148
Wordsworth's Greece......... 202
Wotton...................... 169
Wrangel's Expedition......... 240
Wraxall's Memoirs of his Own Times...................... 143
Wyatt's Conchology 285
Wyatt, Sir Thomas........... 72
Wycherly 75

X.

Xenophon, translation of...... 202
Xenophon................. 97, 120
Xenophon's Anabasis......... 139
Xenophon's Memorabilia...... 266

Y.

Yarrell's Fishes 285
Yates and Moulton's History of New-York.................. 223
Young, Alexander......... 76, 276
Yriarte...................... 96

Z.

Zimmerman's Solitude........ 358

THE END.

www.ingramcontent.com/pod-product-compliance
Lightning Source LLC
LaVergne TN
LVHW020218110826
845151LV00003B/753